I0819302
FRANKLIN
EXPERT'S CHOICE
BURNS HOT
B&B

Grill Time!

ALSO BY NOAH GALUTEN

The Don't Panic Pantry Cookbook: Mostly Vegetarian Comfort Food That Happens to Be Pretty Good for You

DEVIL
XL LUMP CHARCOAL

NOAH GALUTEN

Grill Time!

Why You Should Be Grilling for Better, Healthier, Easier, and More Delicious Meals

ALFRED A. KNOPF NEW YORK 2026

A BORZOI BOOK

FIRST HARDCOVER EDITION PUBLISHED BY
ALFRED A. KNOPF 2026

Text copyright © 2026 by Noah Galuten
Photographs copyright © 2026 by
Kristin Teig Photography LLC

Penguin Random House values and supports copyright. Copyright fuels creativity, encourages diverse voices, promotes free speech, and creates a vibrant culture. Thank you for buying an authorized edition of this book and for complying with copyright laws by not reproducing, scanning, or distributing any part of it in any form without permission. You are supporting writers and allowing Penguin Random House to continue to publish books for every reader. Please note that no part of this book may be used or reproduced in any manner for the purpose of training artificial intelligence technologies or systems.

Published by Alfred A. Knopf, a division of
Penguin Random House LLC, 1745 Broadway,
New York, NY 10019.

Knopf, Borzoi Books, and the colophon are registered trademarks of Penguin Random House LLC.

Book design by Sebit Min

Library of Congress Cataloging-in-Publication Data
Names: Galuten, Noah author | Teig, Kristin photographer.
Title: Grill time! : Why you should be grilling for better, healthier, easier, and more delicious meals / Noah Galuten; photographs by Kristen Teig.
Description: New York : Alfred A. Knopf, 2026. | Includes index. |
Identifiers: LCCN 2025019977 | ISBN 9780593804278 (hardcover) | ISBN 9780593804285 (ebook)
Subjects: LCSH: Barbecuing | LCGFT: Cookbooks
Classification: LCC TX840.B3 G356 2026 |
DDC 641.7/6—dc23/eng/20250702
LC record available at https://lccn.loc.gov/2025019977

penguinrandomhouse.com |
aaknopf.com

Some of the recipes in this book may include raw eggs, meat, or fish. When these foods are consumed raw, there is always the risk that bacteria, which is killed by proper cooking, may be present. For this reason, when serving these foods raw, always buy certified salmonella-free eggs and the freshest meat and fish available from a reliable grocer, storing them in the refrigerator until they are served. Because of the health risks associated with the consumption of bacteria that can be present in raw eggs, meat, and fish, these foods should not be consumed by infants, small children, pregnant women, the elderly, or any persons who may be immunocompromised. The author and publisher expressly disclaim responsibility for any adverse effects that may result from the use or application of the recipes and information contained in this book.

Printed in China
1 2 3 4 5 6 7 8 9 10

The authorized representative in the EU for product safety and compliance is Penguin Random House Ireland, Morrison Chambers, 32 Nassau Street, Dublin D02 YH68, Ireland, https://eu-contact.penguin.ie.

To Tianfu, our small anxious dog, who dutifully helps clean up any food that falls on the ground.

Also to Iliza, Sierra, and Ethan. I love our family so much.

CONTENTS

Introduction *xi*

Cooking for Different People Who Eat Different Things . . xii
Treating Your Grill as an Extension of Your Kitchen xii
Leftovers Are Your Friend xii
Good Grill Hunting xiv
Fuel xvi
Tools xx
Bonus Items xxii
How to Clean a Grill xxiv
How to Light a Grill xxiv
How to Build a Two-Zone Fire and How to Smoke-Grill . . xxv
Grill Temperatures xxvii

About the Recipes in This Book *xxviii*

What Does It Mean to Feed Your Family? xxviii

Burgers, Sandwiches, Pita, Sausage, and . . . a Hot Dog 4

Backyard Bacon Cheeseburgers . . . 8
Nostalgia Steak Sandwich 2.0 . . . 11
Chicago-Style Char Dogs . . . 12
Chicken Teriyaki Sandwiches with Jalapeño-Cabbage Slaw . . . 16
The Juiciest Turkey Burgers . . . 19
Cumin Lamb Burgers . . . 21
Tofu Bánh Mì with Lemongrass BBQ Sauce . . . 22
Smoky Grilled Caprese Sandwich . . . 24
Better Grilled Veggie Wraps . . . 26
Za'atar-Blackened Mahi-Mahi Pitas . . . 29
Pork Souvlaki Pitas . . . 30
Pork Chop Sandwiches with Grilled Pineapple and Chili Crisp Mayo . . . 32
Beer Brats . . . 35
How to Smoke-Grill a Sausage . . . 36

Veggie Sides 38

Broccolini with Preserved Lemon . . . 42
Zucchini Spears with Balsamic, Mint, and Garlic . . . 44
Grilled Asparagus and Wilted White Cheddar . . . 47
Grilled Artichokes alla Garlic Knots . . . 49
Charred Brussels Sprouts . . . 50
Grilled and Glazed Baby Bok Choy . . . 52
Citrus and Fennel Salad . . . 55
Charred Cauliflower with Tahini-Yogurt Sauce . . . 57
Perfect Grilled Potatoes . . . 58
Jimmy Nardellos with Red Yuzu Vinaigrette . . . 60
Kabocha Macha . . . 63
Miso-Butter Corn . . . 65
Buttered Soy Sauce Mushrooms . . . 66
Baba Ghanoush . . . 68
Grilled Avocado Tostadas with Chipotle-Lime Crema . . . 70
Fettunta . . . 73
Mezcal Charro Beans . . . 75
"Kebab Plate" Rice . . . 76

Big Salads 78

Southwest Veggie Chop 82
Spicy Grilled Chicken Caesar with Garlic Bread Croutons 85
Grilled Chicken Tricolore with Charred Pepperoncini Vinaigrette 88
Peanut-Miso Steak and Soba Salad 91
Grilled Shrimp Niçoise 92
Sausage and Peppers Pasta Salad 95

Vegetarian Mains 96

Mediterranean Quinoa with Grilled Halloumi and Charred Fennel 100
Mabo-Stuffed Mushrooms with Yaki-Onigiri 102
Stuffed Poblanos with Cilantro-Lime Tahini 105
Grilled Veggie Burritos 107
Huevos Divorciados 109
Salsa Ranchera and Salsa Verde 110
Grilled Spaghetti Squash with Charred Cherry Tomato Sauce 112
Blackened Broccoli-Cheddar Split Pea Soup 115
Smoked Potato Tacos 117

Chicken (and a Turkey Breast) 120

Quick and Simple Grilled Chicken Breast 124
Achiote-Lime Chicken Breast 126
Shish Tawook 129
Ode to a Benihana Birthday Party 131
Chicken "Gyoza" Eggplant 132
Ginger-Buffalo Wings 134
Pickle-Brined Drumsticks with Spicy Honey 137
Shallot-Dijon Chicken Thighs 139
Smoke-Grilled Turkey Breast (for Cold Cuts) 140
Smoke-Grilled Pollo a la Brasa with Ají Verde 142

Beef
146

Taverna Steak 150
California Tri-Tip Two Ways 152
Hermosillo-Style Carne Asada 154
Punchy, Funky Beef and Broccoli 166
Soy and Citrus Skirt Steak 169
Nước Chấm Brisket Noodle Bowl 170
Smoke-Grilled Bone-In Rib Eye with Mansion Butter 172

Pork
174

Buttermilk-Brined Pork Chop with Grilled Lemon 178
Pork Secret 180
Sausage and Lentils with Grilled Leeks 183
"Pretend It's the '90s" Honey-Balsamic Pork Tenderloin 185
Coconut-Crusted Tiki Pork Ribs 186
Smoke-Grilled Baby Backs 188
BBQ Pork Belly Bossam 190

Seafood
192

Grilled Clams with Cocktail Butter 196
Grilled Oysters with Miso-Ginger Calabrian Chili Butter 198
Grilldas (or Grilled Squid Gildas) 201
Charred Garlic-Butter Sriracha Shrimp 203
Quick-Grilled Fish Steak 204
Crispy-Skinned Fish Fillet 206
Grilled Fish Tacos with Chile Crunch 208
Whole Grilled Fish Tacos with Maggi Onions 211
Smoke-Grilled Miso Black Cod 212

Acknowledgments *216*
Index *217*

OSHKOSH

INTRODUCTION

I am a grill dad.

But while I have been a frequent griller for over twenty years, I grill *so much more* since becoming a dad. During the summer and spring months, the vast majority of our lunches and dinners at home incorporate the grill in some way. I've also been known to wear a jacket on a cold winter night (albeit a *California* winter night) to quickly char some protein and vegetables over a hot flame. Basically: it is *always* Grill Time.

But since becoming a dad, *what* I grill and *how* I grill has also changed. Now pretty much everything I grill falls under one of two categories:

1. CONVENIENCE GRILLING: Better, Faster, Easier, Cleaner

This is all about getting a balanced dinner on the table as quickly and easily as possible. Gas grills are a *huge* convenience here, where I can cook a meal that is faster, more nutritious, and *way* easier to clean up than I would ever be able to do with pans, ovens, and oil splatter. (This absolutely applies to charcoal, too, even though it takes a few extra minutes to heat the coals than it does to flick on a gas burner.) To get char and texture like this indoors, whether on a pork chop or some spears of asparagus, is frankly a pain in the ass to clean up and requires a lot more skill. That doesn't even get into the lingering (and often complained about) smells that come from cooking a piece of fish on the stove. But it's not just fish either. High-heat searing can set off smoke alarms while *also* adding the lingering smell of aerosolized fat that clings to the walls of your kitchen.

2. WEEKEND PROJECT GRILLING: Smoke-Grilling for Maximum Flavor

When you have a little more time and forethought on your side, you can devote your energy to Weekend Project Grilling. This kind of grilling uses the powers of charcoal and wood smoke to imbue your food with that unmistakable, un-fake-able primal flavor that human beings have found addictive since they started lighting a fire and putting meat near it. The best steak I have ever cooked in my life (Smoke-Grilled Bone-In Rib Eye with Mansion Butter, page 172) is reverse-seared to a perfect internal temperature using a two-zone fire with wood-tinged smoke, before being finished over white-hot coals. But it is not just about meat either—infusing smoke flavor into potatoes and tomatillos on a grill creates my favorite vegetarian tacos in the world (see page 117). This hybrid of indirect grilling and smoking, taught to me by BBQ legend Kevin Bludso, is an amazing technique that will be used several times in this book, all without requiring a ton of fancy equipment.

Cooking for Different People Who Eat Different Things

Another important factor in *Grill Time!* is the reality that when you are cooking for a lot of people, there are usually a lot of different tastes and needs. I am trying to teach my children to have healthy relationships with food (we have a "you don't have to like it but you have to try it" rule in our house), but the reality is that tastes evolve and change; and sometimes certain people who are eating at your house are just going to have different dietary desires or restrictions.

But with a decent-sized grill, it is *so much easier* to cook multiple foods at the same time, or one after the other. Vegetarians, carnivores, pescatarians, and "boneless, skinless chicken breast only" people can all be accommodated on a single grill with minimal extra work and cleanup. Can you imagine trying to cook zucchini, chicken, shrimp, steak, and broccolini at the same time with pots and pans, let alone clean up? You might as well just order takeout. But on the grill, all it takes is a few strokes of a good brush and your "kitchen" is clean.

Treating Your Grill as an Extension of Your Kitchen

Grilled proteins and vegetables don't have to be at the center of your plate to make a dish *better, faster, cleaner, and easier.* Sometimes they just add some accent to improve a dish, while also making your culinary life more convenient. I really encourage people to think about the grill as a way to improve *any* of their meals. I believe that a little bit of intentional char is free flavor.

For example, my wife and I, like so many other people, often find ourselves working from home. On days like that a Big Salad is the perfect lunch, and nothing adds heft and flavor to a huge salad like grilled vegetables, or protein, or both. I have never in my life sautéed a chicken breast for a salad, but I have grilled one probably a hundred times.

One way or another, I use the grill almost every day, even if it is just to char some aromatics like shallots, onions, peppers, and tomatoes to bring flavor and life to things like Salsa Ranchera and Salsa Verde (page 110), a pot of Mezcal Charro Beans (page 75), "Kebab Plate" Rice (page 76), or a Sausage and Peppers Pasta Salad (page 95). There is no faking a little bit of char, and there is no easier way to achieve it than on the grill.

Meanwhile, a grill can also be your closer. Brining or marinating things like chicken, skirt steak, or flanken short ribs is like a down payment on flavor and convenience. Once you've done that, it means you can get food on the table with *tons* of flavor in just a few minutes.

Leftovers Are Your Friend

Another great thing about smoke and char is that they survive *really well* in a Tupperware in the fridge, and in many cases taste great cold. Whether I'm grilling over charcoal or gas, I always try to grill more than I need, knowing that leftovers are a perfect add-in to those Big Salads we were just mentioning, or stuffed into a quesadilla for a quick lunch for the kids. Or if you're my wife, you can just eat half of a cold leftover steak while standing in front of the refrigerator with the door open. It all works.

You can also get ahead on the week by grilling vegetables and aromatics that you know will end up in things like tomorrow's Blackened Broccoli-Cheddar Split Pea Soup (page 115). Leftovers and make-ahead grilling will set you up for future meals.

Good Grill Hunting

There are a *lot* of grills on the market. For the purposes of this book, we are really focusing on two kinds of grills: gas and charcoal. There are a lot of variables within those categories, so here are some of the main ones to think about:

GAS GRILL

Some hardcore grillers out there like to turn their noses up at gas grills because nothing beats the flavor and heat of charcoal and wood. I totally get that perspective, but I also *love* my gas grill. I would say that about two-thirds of the grilling I do at home is on the gas grill because, frankly, it is incredibly convenient. The key when looking for a gas grill is to find one that has at least two burners, so that you can have different control points and the ability to create a two-zone fire (see page xxv) when necessary. Gas grills come in a wide array of prices, but try to look for a gas grill that can get as hot as possible—if it can't get up to 500°F on the hottest part of the grill, you will just never get the char you want on certain items without overcooking the inside.

DAD HACK

If you are using a propane grill, always try to keep a second tank on hand so you don't find yourself running out of gas partway through a cookout.

KETTLE-STYLE CHARCOAL GRILL

There are a lot of brands out there, but I love the classic Weber grill that has been keeping dads—and all the enthusiasts—grilling for decades. I prefer a larger-size 22-inch grill, to have more space to be able to create a good two-zone fire with all of the wood and charcoal pushed to one side. I also highly recommend buying a charcoal basket, which helps to keep the heat to one side, as well as a hinged grate, which means you can add more charcoal and wood to the grill without having to remove the entire grill top.

These are a very affordable option for charcoal grilling that works really well.

KAMADO OR BIG GREEN EGG

These have become increasingly popular in recent years. They can get incredibly hot and retain heat quite well, too. I think of them as almost a cross between an oven and a grill. While they are incredible for certain things like chicken and steaks, they are not ideal for the kind of two-zone grilling I like to do for the hybrid smoke-grill method that gets used in this book (you can still do it, it's just a little more difficult). However, the kamado-style grills will be great for all of the direct grilling that encompasses the vast majority of recipes in this book.

THE PK GRILL

If you're willing to upgrade from a kettle-style grill, this is my top recommendation. I got turned on to this grill by my friend Jordan Mackay, the coauthor of three beloved cookbooks with the great Aaron Franklin: *Franklin Barbecue, Franklin Smoke,* and *Franklin Steak.* He and Aaron Franklin use these grills as their lifelong everyday grills, and when I started cooking on them, I understood why. (Aaron Franklin also has a signature version of these grills, designed in collaboration with PK. That is the charcoal grill you see being used in photos throughout this book.)

The Original PK Grill (depending on sale pricing) is usually between $500 and $600, with upgrades to larger ones with more surface area. I want to point out that they are *not* a sponsor of this book; I just think they make the best grill. Made of solid, rust-proof aluminum, they are both portable and essentially indestructible, with a simple, intuitive design. The oblong shape makes it much easier to cook over two zones at once, creating better airflow than a circular kettle grill. With top *and* bottom vents, you have the ability to really control your fire and airflow. It also preheats really quickly (aluminum conducts heat more efficiently than steel), making it great for hot-and-fast grilling, too. It is the preferred grill of lots of professionals, including pretty much all of the top competitors in the Steak Cookoff Association.

One of my favorite things about this grill is its durability and longevity. This is a grill that I could pass down to my kids one day. Or maybe grandkids, since hopefully I'll still be alive and using mine when my kids are old enough to have their own grill. Anyway, if you plan to grill a lot, this thing kind of pays for itself in the long run.

SANTA MARIA–STYLE

If you've got one of these, you probably already know what you're doing. This type of grill, with its adjustable rack height, will work well with all of the recipes in this book. While it will be a *little* bit tougher to get that smoke flavor without a cover, you can just use more wood to compensate. (See the Fuel section, page xvi, for more info on wood and charcoal.)

HIBACHI/BINCHO GRILL

These are great for cooking small quantities of food. They use long- and clean-burning binchotan charcoal . . . but if you're cooking for your whole family, it is just not quite big enough.

TRAEGER

These pellet smokers with simple, adjustable knobs are super popular due to their incredible convenience. But they are more smokers than grills. For me, I would rather use a charcoal grill or a proper offset smoker (which are designed for classic smoked BBQ). The Traeger is a middle-ground item that certainly can get the job done, but is not something I use at home.

Fuel

NATURAL GAS AND PROPANE

For gas grills, you will either be using natural gas, which is piped in from a gas line, or propane. As I mentioned before, if you're going with propane, I highly recommend keeping a backup tank at the ready for when that first one runs out. Natural gas means never running out and is certainly more convenient but is a higher-cost setup. Also, keep in mind that not all gas grills are built for natural gas hookups.

CHARCOAL

With apologies to binchotan and coconut charcoal, I am going to focus on the two most ubiquitous (and my favorite) types of charcoal: briquettes and lump. While the *type* of charcoal can impart flavor, I mostly think of charcoal as the heat source and use wood smoke (explained later) for flavor.

Briquettes

These are composite charcoals made of a mix of mostly wood, with some binders and minerals to help them burn more consistently and evenly. If I'm buying briquettes, I look for "natural" briquettes, which are made from wood and a binder, such as vegetable ash, with less additives. Briquettes tend to be a more consistent product than lump, but also typically don't get as hot. Just make sure to avoid any "match light" or "self-starting" charcoal, as they are soaked in lighter fluid, which creates a nasty smell and flavor.

Lump Charcoal

Lump charcoal is made from pure hardwood and nothing else. It typically burns hotter and faster than briquettes, giving a more primal feeling to your grilling, with a level of live-fire imperfection that makes it all a little bit more fun to me. But if you're not planning to actively grill for more than 45 minutes to an hour, the shorter burn time won't really matter at all. You also get the benefit of a "pure" fuel source with no additives whatsoever. The size of the charcoal can vary greatly here as well. There are lots of different types of lump charcoal, coming from different types of wood. The only time I will call for a specific type of lump charcoal is for Hermosillo-Style Carne Asada (page 154), which calls for mesquite, as is the tradition in Hermosillo, Mexico.

USING LUMP AND BRIQUETTES TOGETHER

Sometimes the best of both worlds is a mixture of, well, both worlds. This way you get the high-heat chaos of lump, mixed with the longer burning, lower-heat control elements of briquettes.

At the end of the day, the most important thing is to try a bunch of brands, find one that you like, and then keep on using it. The more you can reproduce your grilling conditions, the better you'll get with it, and the more consistently you'll be able to reproduce your preferred results.

A LITTLE GOES A LONG WAY.
Texas Style
WARNING
CARBON MONOXIDE HAZARD
Burning charcoal inside can kill you. It gives off carbon monoxide, which has no odor.
NEVER burn charcoal inside homes, vehicles or tents.
B&B
BETTER BURNING
CHARCOAL
BURNS LONG • BURNS HOT
USA
COMPETITION
CHARCOAL BRIQUET
OAK & HICKOR
XL LUMP
weber
PECAN
FIRESPICE
Wood Chunks
Trozos de madera
Fragments de bois
Pedaços de madeira
OAK CHUNKS

Contains / Contient / Cont. Net. 6 L (350 cu in)
weber

WOOD CHUNKS

For me, wood is not about heat—it's about flavor. Gas cooking is for convenience, but when I want to really impress people, I cook with charcoal and wood together. Everything I learned about cooking with wood, I learned from my friend and mentor, the one and only Kevin Bludso.

Once we get into this kind of cooking, it's important to remember that charcoal is for temperature control and wood is there to create flavorful smoke. Bigger pieces of wood generally create more flavor than smaller ones, so while I use split logs for large offset smokers, I use wood chunks for grills and smaller smokers. I am not a fan of chips or pellets, as I sort of consider them to be another one of those half measures that can never quite produce the deeper flavor that I get from larger pieces of hardwood.

What I love about wood chunks is that you can really control the amount of smoke and flavor as well. Each recipe that calls for wood chunks in this book will detail the amount of wood and my preferred flavors, but here's a good guide when shopping for seasoned wood chunks (seasoned as opposed to fresh wood, which is often too moist to cook with consistently—though any wood you buy from a traditional retailer will certainly be seasoned).

Oak
Post oak is the gold standard in central Texas and my personal favorite for everyday smoking. It burns well and tastes great on everything, with an almost sweet flavor that highlights without overpowering. Red oak is my preferred substitute if I can't find post oak. I almost always cook with some oak, and flavor it with another accent wood, like fruitwoods, nut woods, or hickory.

Pecan
This is a wonderful and slightly more delicate, nuanced smoke flavor. I use this when I don't want to overpower the flavor of more subtle items, like a fillet of black cod or a piece of salmon. It is also a great accent wood and tastes great on beef when mixed with post or red oak.

Fruitwoods
Apple is one of the most popular woods to smoke with, and tends to create a darker smoke color on your food (especially on longer smokes). I tend to mix fruitwoods with oak, a pairing that tastes excellent on pork. I avoid fruitwoods with beef. Cherry wood is far less commonly used, and has its own unique fruity characteristics.

Hickory
This is a classic BBQ wood for a reason. It burns really well, and has some sweet-and-savory notes that just work wonderfully on pork and chicken. This one can be used all on its own with great results, or mixed with an oak, fruit, or pecan wood.

Mesquite
This has a very strong, powerful smoke flavor. Use mesquite wood with caution, as it can overpower a meat, and the flavor is not for everyone. Some people definitely adore this flavor. See what you think. Mesquite charcoal, however, is very popular and the standard charcoal in much of Mexico.

Tools

You can really go down a grilling-tool rabbit hole if you want to. But I only care about a few core items to arm me for good outdoor cooking.

CHIMNEY FIRE STARTER

Chimney fire starters are the most efficient ways to start a fire. They help to stack the charcoal in a cylinder, allowing you to heat them from underneath using either paper or natural fire starters. I have two of these, in case I want to cook hotter or over a larger bed of coals and can light twice as much charcoal at once.

A LONG-NECKED LIGHTER

This is the number one thing I am constantly looking for, though it is somehow always missing from its usual spot. (My wife likes to light candles.) As a result, I now always have a couple on hand, including an electric one I keep charged so that I don't have to worry about it running out of fuel.

TONGS AND A SPATULA

A pair of good, heavy-duty grill tongs and a spatula will pretty much be all you'll ever need to handle your food on a grill. Sometimes for more delicate pieces I might use a fish spatula—which is the best indoor cooking spatula, so you should probably have one of those anyway. I own a grilling fork, too, but have literally never used it.

GRILL BRUSH

Keeping a clean grill is the best way to prevent your food from sticking. Look for a strong brush that you can use to really scrub the grill when need be. Try to avoid a grill brush with small wire bristles, which can break off and be a bit dangerous. Look for a brush with long brush extensions that come from the handle so you can really put some elbow grease into it.

NEUTRAL OIL

In almost all cases, you will want to oil your grates before putting the food on. Some people use spray cans of oil, but the truth is that you'll be wasting a lot of oil that way and spraying your fire more than your grill grates. A squeeze bottle of neutral oil (I like vegetable or avocado) is great to keep on hand, and you can use it for drizzling onto a piece of meat, or onto a paper towel to oil the grates.

MAYONNAISE

Mayo is hands down one of the best ingredients when you're grilling. It's not even about flavor either—in most cases, people won't even be aware that it was used at all. Mayo is an emulsified fat with a high smoke point, so even a thin veil of mayo brushed onto an ingredient will give it nonstick properties while aiding in caramelization. Mayo is also an amazing way to allow seasonings to adhere to an ingredient. It is an essential trick I learned from my friend, the great chef and seafood expert Ari Kolender, when grilling fish. But mayo can also be used to make delicious sauces, like chimichurri mayo, which can be slathered onto grilled bread for a Nostalgia Steak Sandwich 2.0 (page 11).

SHEET PANS

The hardest thing about grilling is carrying stuff to the grill from the kitchen and vice versa. Get some sheet pans to make your life easier. I always have half-sheet pans (the standard size to fit in home ovens) as well as some quarter-sheet pans with wire rack inserts for smaller things. The half-sheet pans become my workhorse carrying tray, and the quarters are great for salting pieces of meat overnight and keeping them in the fridge. In a pinch, you can also throw a quarter-sheet pan (or a sizzle plate) on the grill to keep things warm or to roast something that might fall through the grates.

INSTANT-READ THERMOMETER

You need a food thermometer. Unless you're cooking the same piece of meat over and over from the same meat vendor on the line in the same restaurant every day . . . use a good instant-read thermometer. It's not just for big hunks of meat either—it is my favorite discovery for cooking potatoes perfectly every time, too; see Perfect Grilled Potatoes (page 58).

SKEWERS

Whether they are metal skewers or wooden/bamboo skewers (which need to be soaked prior to using), they are wonderful tools for smaller pieces of meat or vegetables. I use them for Shish Tawook (page 129): my favorite way to grill chicken breast.

PAINTBRUSH, GARDENING TROWEL, AND METAL BUCKET

These are just basic tools to easily clean out ash from the bottom of your charcoal grill. The bottom of a charcoal grill can have lots of nooks and crannies filled with ash, and a paintbrush is the perfect tool to brush it all into your trowel. Then use your trowel to dump the ash into your bucket.

Bonus Items

GRILL PAN

This is absolutely not essential—but a perforated grill pan (think of it like a sheet pan with holes) is really convenient if you want to cook things like cherry tomatoes, garlic cloves, or smaller-cut vegetables right on the grill. I don't use this often, but it can be superconvenient from time to time.

INFRARED THERMOMETER

If you want to test the temperatures and hot spots of your grill, you can use an infrared thermometer to gauge temperatures; see Grill Temperatures (page xxvii). I typically don't do this and will just feel the heat with my hand, but it *is* convenient to get to know your grill. A good gauge otherwise is to hold your hand over the grill or coals. If you can only keep it there for a second or two, that is high heat.

DAD HACK

The Toast Test

If you want to learn the hot and cold spots of your gas grill and don't want a fancy infrared thermometer or a bunch of oven thermometers, buy a loaf of cheap white bread. Let the grill preheat for a good 20 minutes over high heat, then oil the grates and slowly cover the grill with slices of bread. After a minute or two, flip them over (in the same order you laid them down), and look at the color of the bread to see your hot spots and cold spots.

How to Clean a Grill

There are really only two key things to do to keep your grill clean.

1. KEEP THE GRATES CLEAN.

This is the first step to ensuring that your food doesn't stick to the grill or leave behind any gnarly flavors. I typically let the grill go for a few minutes after I'm done cooking on it, then give it a quick scrape. Then the next time I cook, I'll preheat the grill for several minutes and then give it a heavier scrape once everything has burned off and is much easier to remove.

2. CLEAN OUT THE BOTTOM AND WATCH OUT FOR GREASE.

Whether you're cooking with charcoal or gas, meats release fat and grease. Grease can catch fire. Gas grills will have some kind of pan or grease catch that can be taken out and dumped or scraped into the garbage—so always keep an eye on that. If you *do* find yourself having a grease fire, keep it contained, let it burn off, and don't mess with the grill until it's out (though you should remove any food that's on the grill and set it aside if you can do it safely).

Make sure to clean out your charcoal and wood ash, too, as it could hold grease and will eventually mess up your flow of oxygen. I like to clean out fully cooled ash with a garden trowel and an old paintbrush, simply by brushing the ash into the trowel and dumping it into an ash pail.

How to Light a Grill

GAS GRILLS

If you're lighting a gas grill, I've got great news for you. You just . . . turn it on. The only important thing here is to make sure that the grill is fully lit once the gas is on so you're not just blasting gas into the air without igniting it. If you can't get it to light right away, turn off the gas and start over. Most gas grills will have a little electric, battery-powered igniter. If it's not working, try to replace the battery or just use a long-necked lighter to ignite it.

CHARCOAL GRILLS

When you're working with charcoal, it's all about getting your coals to the right level of burn before grilling. Stack the charcoal in the large top chamber of a chimney starter (or two chimneys if you need a lot of coals), then lay either some newspaper, brown paper, or natural fire starters in the smaller chamber on the bottom. Place it in a safe area (like on the grill grates, or the bottom grates of your grill) and light the bottom. Once it is burning, it will ignite the charcoal. Let it burn until the charcoal is turning from black to white, then dump the coals into the bottom part of your grill. Use tongs or a garden trowel to move the coals if necessary.

How to Build a Two-Zone Fire and How to Smoke-Grill

The premise of a two-zone fire is the ability to cook with some heat on the grill without having *direct* heat, giving your grill an oven-like property.

SETTING UP TWO ZONES ON A GAS GRILL

On a gas grill, having two zones is useful for cooking items slower-and-lower without burning them, like the Mabo-Stuffed Mushrooms with Yaki-Onigiri (page 102) or Chicken "Gyoza" Eggplant (page 132). To achieve a two-zone fire on a gas grill, you simply put one burner on high, while leaving the other one off or turning it down to low. Then you can place food on the cooler side and close the grill, allowing it to roast.

SETTING UP A TWO-ZONE CHARCOAL FIRE

Fill a chimney starter with charcoal. Light it and allow the coals to heat until they are just beginning to turn gray. Pour them onto one side of the grill. If you are working with a round kettle grill, add the coals to a grill basket on one side to keep them contained.

That's it. You've made a two-zone fire. For best results use a grill grate with a hinge, which allows you to add more charcoal to the fire without needing to remove the whole grill grate. Let the top grill grate preheat for at least 5 minutes before cooking on it, and as always, make sure your grates are cleaned and oiled.

SMOKE-GRILLING

My favorite use of a two-zone fire is to "smoke-grill," which mixes the best characteristics of indirect low-and-slow BBQ and direct-heat charcoal grilling. This is a two-zone fire in which all of the hot coals are pushed to one side of the grill. Then you lay wood chunks on the coals, giving that amazing smoke flavor to your food. This is my favorite way to cook ribs, a split whole chicken, potatoes, tomatillos, thick steaks, and so much more.

Smoke-Grilling with Charcoal

Set up a two-zone charcoal fire, then lay one or more wood chunks on top of the hot coals. Allow them to burn for about 5 minutes before adding any meat or vegetables to the cooler zone (fresh smoke has a slightly harsher flavor, and you want to let that burn off before applying it to raw meat or vegetables, which are at their most vulnerable state of the cook).

For best results, close the vent over the fire and open it over the cooler side, to create airflow to pass the smoke through the food. If you have a grill with vents on the bottom as well (like a PK Grill), open the vent underneath the fire, and close the one under the cooler side. This will create optimal smoke airflow.

Maintain your fire by adding more charcoal for heat, and more wood for smoke flavor, as needed to keep the fire going. If the fire goes out, start another chimney of charcoal and keep cooking.

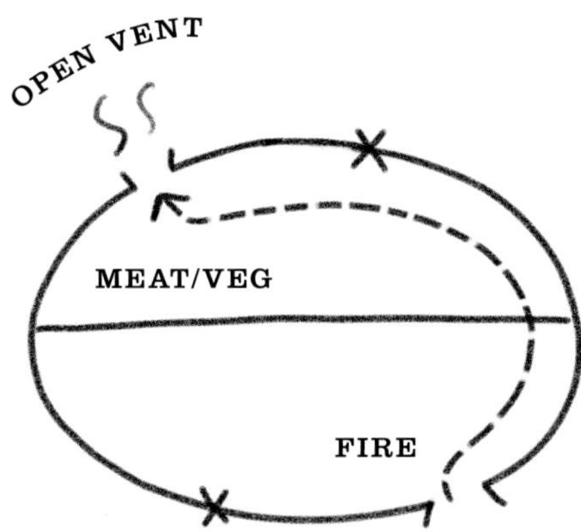

Optimal Setup for
Two-Zone Smoke Grill

Grill Temperatures

The recipes in this book will use the standard nomenclature of "high," "medium-high," "medium," etc. But this is why, if you're using a gas grill, you want one with some power, where "high" is actually hot. For reference, here are the common temperatures for each heat:

High: 500°F and above
Medium-high: 400° to 500°F
Medium: 350° to 400°F
Medium-low: 300° to 350°F
Low: 250°F

INTERNAL TEMPERATURE GUIDE

While these temperatures are a great guide for cooking, they are not a catchall guarantee. For example, depending on the thickness of the cut and the cooking method, there will often be some carryover cooking, meaning the temperature will rise a bit from the residual heat.

BEEF
STEAK, TRI-TIP, AND BURGERS

Rare: 120°F
Medium-rare: 130°F
Medium: 140°F
Medium-well: 150°F
Well: 155°F+

PORK
TENDERLOINS AND THICK PORK CHOPS

Ideal Temperature: Medium-rare/medium: 140° to 145°F
Well-done: 155°F+

PORK RIBS
AND PORK BELLY

Tender at 190° to 195°F

CHICKEN

Breast: Fully cooked at 150°F
Dark meat: Fully cooked at 165°F, but stays moist and tenderizes up to about 190°F

FISH FILLETS

Ideal Temperature: Very tender and juicy: 125° to 130°F
Somewhat firm: 130° to 140°F
Firm: 145°F
Dry and firm: 150°F

POTATOES

Fluffy and perfect at 208° to 211°F.
(This works for baked potatoes, too.)

ABOUT THE RECIPES IN THIS BOOK

This food is a true representation of what I cook for my family. As a Los Angeles native, these recipes are heavily influenced by the varied and incredibly delicious cuisines and ingredients I've been surrounded with for most of my life, as well as some discoveries I've made while eating and traveling both in America and abroad.

But this food is also enriched with ideas, ingredients, and techniques that I've learned while working side by side with some of the best chefs in the world. I owe so much of my knowledge to masters of their craft who I have gotten to collaborate with, and in many cases coauthor cookbooks with. People like Kevin Bludso, Jeremy Fox, Sarah Minnick, Ari Kolender, Nyesha Arrington, Eloy Aluri, Frank Pinello, and Josh Scherer have all, in their own ways, changed the way I think about food and cooking for the better.

DAD HACK

Buy a rice cooker. Being able to throw some rice in a good electric cooker that you can set-and-forget means you can be outside grilling and come back to hot steamed rice to fill out your meal while the rest of the meal is still hot-off-the-grill.

In the end, I'm a chef, dad, and passionate home cook who has invented precisely nothing. My food has been shaped by countless line cooks, prep cooks, dishwashers, family members, food photographers, bartenders, writers, and friends. I like to think of myself as an academic first and foremost, turning my passion and curiosity into this collection of recipes, written and honed while cooking probably nineteen of the twenty-one meals per week for my family. (My wife . . . does not enjoy cooking.)

As you flip through the recipes, be on the lookout for little signifiers pointing out which recipes are Wood and Charcoal Only or Charcoal Only. But if a recipe doesn't specifically call for wood or charcoal, it means you can absolutely cook it on a gas grill.

What Does It Mean to Feed Your Family?

The idea of feeding my family is something I think about a lot. I cook dinner most nights. I make oatmeal in the morning. I pack lunches and snacks. I cut up fruit at the end of the night or make popcorn so we can watch a movie. There are a lot of different ways to feed our families. At its core, it's a very simple concept: They need to eat something to stay alive, and eating something nutritious is certainly a whole lot better than eating something that isn't good for you.

I want my kids to have a healthful diet but also a healthy relationship with eating. I don't "sneak" greens into a smoothie, but instead I show them the big handful of hearty greens being chucked into a blender, and then I explain what they are and why they're good for us. I continue to insist that fiber is more important than protein (increased fiber in our diets significantly reduces "all cause" mortality, cardiovascular disease, and cancer). I think that the quality of our "base" ingredients might matter more than the few things we sprinkle on top; that the quality of the pasta, rice, bread, flour, lentils, and beans that make up the majority of the meal matter more than whether the few bites of broccoli or chicken are organic. But I also try to shop at farmers markets and teach my kids about seasonality and sustainability, trying to help make healthier people on a healthier planet, if I can. As a dad who cares about food and has built a career around it, I also want them to try lots of things, to experience different cultures, to receive pleasure, and to have curiosity.

But feeding my family is about more than the food we put in front of them. They also feed off of our emotions. I've come to realize that we feed them so much more with how we feel and how we act than we do with what we say. My wife is a part of our family. I have to remind myself that I am, too, and that "doing everything you're supposed to do" is not just a matter of accomplishing a list of tasks. Getting the kids dressed and filled with breakfast, packing their lunch and dropping them at school, and cooking dinner and reading them a book at night are all part of it, but it's not all of it. I frequently forget that *how* I am doing matters just as much as *what* I am doing.

I believe things like stress, anxiety, and depression feed our families, too. Anger is worse for us than Doritos ever could be. We think maybe it's not so bad if we're directing our negative emotions at *ourselves* instead of the ones we love. But it turns out that's not true. Destructive emotions grow like mold when you leave them in the dark.

For a long time, we were taught that masculinity is about having a job and "putting food on the table." We were told that men are strong and silent; they eat steak and drink brown spirits and cry in private (maybe after drinking a lot of brown spirits) or not at all. But I think that being a good father and a good husband and a good man is about putting food on the table, yes, in one way or another. But also it's about how we do it. It means taking care of everybody, which includes us, too. It's admitting our mistakes and failures to our kids and our partners, and actively, constantly, trying to improve, no matter how many times we fail or step backward and need to try again. It's important to remember that trying matters and better is better. I used to think that feeding my family was about food. But it is so much more than that. We also feed them with our actions and our emotions, and with how we treat ourselves—it is all of it, all at once.

This book is my love letter to this sentiment, and to my family. It is about nutrition, sustenance, pleasure, and getting food on the table. But perhaps more than anything it's about forming a small community—a place to converge, and to bring other people in. There's a primal symbolism in gathering around a fire, and using it to feed ourselves and each other.

Grill
Time!

Burgers, Sandwiches, Pita, Sausage, and . . . a Hot Dog

Backyard Bacon Cheeseburgers 8
Nostalgia Steak Sandwich 2.0 11
Chicago-Style Char Dogs 12
Chicken Teriyaki Sandwiches with
Jalapeño-Cabbage Slaw 16
The Juiciest Turkey Burgers 19
Cumin Lamb Burgers 21
Tofu Bánh Mì with Lemongrass BBQ Sauce 22
Smoky Grilled Caprese Sandwich 24
Better Grilled Veggie Wraps 26
Za'atar-Blackened Mahi Mahi Pitas 29
Pork Souvlaki Pitas 30
Pork Chop Sandwiches with
Grilled Pineapple and Chili Crisp Mayo 32
Beer Brats 35
How to Smoke-Grill a Sausage 36

Marconi
HOT
"HOT DOG" PEPPER

Burgers and hot dogs are probably the most "classic Americana" cookout activity: a middle-aged father squeezing lighter fluid into a Weber kettle grill before unwrapping pre-formed hamburger patties, charring the crap out of them, and then putting them on a bun with American cheese and ketchup.

Fortunately, we can do a little better than that. This section teaches you how to make a way-better backyard burger (and turkey burger, and lamb burger), how to smoke a sausage on the grill, and how to make my favorite hot dog in the world. But I also want to open up your mind to the wider world of wonderful handheld backyard grill food. If you prep your spreads and sauces and toppings in advance, you can make so many more delicious things for your pool party or weekend family hang: pitas topped with pork souvlaki or za'atar-blackened mahi-mahi, smoky grilled Caprese sandwiches, teriyaki chicken sandwiches, pork chop sandwiches, and so much more.

Backyard Bacon Cheeseburgers

MAKES 4

Smash burgers are very popular (or they were when I wrote this), and I get why. But this is the more substantial burger I actually want to eat in the backyard with my friends and family. High-quality beef, barely formed into a patty, charred, and rare on a screaming-hot grill, with a slice of wilted smoked cheddar, a smear of "special sauce" on a soft potato roll, with a whisper of thinly sliced raw onion, a slice of crispy bacon, and crunchy iceberg lettuce. The key is to buy the best ground beef you can find and mostly leave it alone (80/20 lean/fat ratio is ideal). Don't compact it or overwork it—just lightly shape it into patties and season it right before it goes on the grill.

On bacon: Bacon is optional, but to be honest, everyone is always happier when it's on their burger. I sort of hate grilling bacon, and prefer roasting it in a 400°F oven, in a single layer on a parchment-lined sheet pan until golden and mostly crisp with a little bit of chew left. Cook more than you need, because it is a law of the universe that people will try to eat it before you make the burgers.

INGREDIENTS

Special Sauce
¼ cup mayonnaise
1½ teaspoons ketchup
1½ teaspoons mustard
1 teaspoon dill relish (or sweet, if that's your preference)
2 dashes of hot sauce
A scant pinch of cayenne
A pinch of salt
A few twists of freshly ground black pepper

Backyard Burgers
1 pound 10 ounces ground beef (80/20)
4 soft potato rolls or the best hamburger buns you can find
Kosher salt and freshly ground black pepper
4 slices smoked orange cheddar
4 extremely thin slices white or yellow onion (for best results, use a mandoline slicer)
4 slices bacon, cooked and snapped in half
Iceberg lettuce, torn into 8 burger-size sheets

METHOD

Make the special sauce: In a bowl, whisk together the mayo, ketchup, mustard, relish, hot sauce, cayenne, salt, and pepper to combine. Set aside.

Make the backyard burgers: Preheat the grill to high heat, then clean and oil the grates well.

Divide the beef into 4 equal portions. If the beef is at all wet, pat it dry with a paper towel. As gently as possible, shape the meat into patties just slightly wider than your buns. Gently indent the center of the patties with your thumb to form an indent in the center of the patty—this will help them cook evenly without puffing up in the center. Keep them in the refrigerator until you are ready to grill. (If it will be longer than a few minutes, cover them with plastic or parchment.)

Grill the cut sides of the buns until just barely toasted, then take them off and slather both sides generously with special sauce and set them aside. Season the top sides of the burgers generously with salt and pepper, then lay them, seasoning-side down on the grill. Season the other side with salt and pepper. Cook them until they are just barely charred on the first side, about 2 minutes (or longer, if you want them more cooked). Flip the burgers and lay the smoked cheddar slices on top, followed by the onion slices, and halved bacon slices. Allow the burgers to cook for another 90 seconds, or until cooked to your desired temperature. I aim for a quite-rare burger of about 120°F.

Divide iceberg among the bottom buns and place the burger patties on top. Close the buns and serve immediately.

Nostalgia Steak Sandwich 2.0

(with Chimichurri Mayo and Tomato-Onion Salad)

MAKES 2

When I was a kid in Los Angeles, there was a small burger chain called All-American Burger. I used to love their steak sandwich—a long, thin, tender whole piece of steak on a greasy hoagie roll, drenched in way-too-much mayonnaise, dressed with onions and lettuce. This is the amped-up version. (Remember: When it comes to nostalgia, it has to be 50 percent better to taste just as good.) In the end, it all works thanks to a good hoagie roll; a lightly spicy, herbaceous chimichurri mayo; tomato and onions that marinate in salt; and, most important, thinly pounded sirloin steak that is incredibly tender and can be bitten through without completely destroying the sandwich in the process. It brings me great joy to know that my kids now get to eat the better version of my childhood favorite.

INGREDIENTS

Chimichurri Mayo

- 1 cup mayonnaise
- ¼ cup tightly packed fresh Italian parsley
- ¼ cup tightly packed fresh cilantro leaves and tender stems
- 4 garlic cloves, peeled but whole
- 2 tablespoons sliced shallot
- 1 tablespoon red wine vinegar
- 1 Fresno or jalapeño pepper, stemmed and seeded (or leave the seeds in for more heat)

Steak Sandwiches

- 12 thin half-moon slices of tomato (about 5 ounces)
- 12 thin half-moon slices of white onion
- Salt and freshly ground black pepper
- 2 teaspoons extra-virgin olive oil
- 8 ounces sirloin steak, about ½ inch thick
- 2 (6-inch) hoagie rolls or the best sandwich rolls you can find

METHOD

Make the chimichurri mayo: In a blender, combine the mayo, parsley, cilantro, garlic, shallot, vinegar, and chile and blend until smooth. Transfer to a bowl and set aside.

Make the steak sandwiches: Preheat the grill to high heat, then clean and oil the grates well.

Place the tomato and onions in a medium bowl. Season them with a pinch of salt and a few twists of pepper. Add 1 teaspoon of the olive oil and toss to combine. Let marinate while you get ready to pound out the steak.

Lay a long sheet of plastic wrap on the counter or a large cutting board and lay the steak on one side of it, with some extra space around it on all sides. Fold the other side of the plastic over it (the goal is to pound the steak out in a protected area, while giving it room to expand).

Using a flat meat mallet or the bottom of a heavy skillet, pound the steak until it is about ⅛ inch thick. Transfer the steak to a cutting board and cut it into 4 long rectangle-like pieces. Drizzle the steak with the remaining 1 teaspoon olive oil and toss it until just barely coated. Season the steak well with salt and pepper.

Cut the hoagie rolls through the side, but not all the way through to create hinged bread. Open the rolls, then spread a thin layer of the chimichurri mayo onto the insides of the roll.

Lay them cut-side down straight on the grill, just until the bread is golden and toasted with some blackened edges, 60 to 90 seconds. Take the rolls off the grill and set them aside. Add the pieces of steak to the grill and let them cook until there is some nice color and char on one side, about 2 minutes. Flip them over and cook just until the raw color is cooked off, about 45 more seconds.

While the steaks are grilling, spread more chimichurri mayo onto the rolls. Lay the steak into the sandwiches, slightly overlapping as necessary. Top them with the tomato-onion mixture, pouring on the juices as well. Cut the sandwiches in half and serve immediately—or wrap them up in foil or sandwich paper until they are ready to be consumed. They are best right away, but will keep well for an hour or so if need be.

Chicago-Style Char Dogs

MAKES
6 CHAR DOGS

After having eaten hot dogs all over the world, I am here to tell you that a Chicago-style char dog is the best on the planet. I enlisted my friend Tad Stacey, a Chicago native who cares more about hot dogs and sandwiches than anyone I know, to help me out with this recipe. It's a classic Chicago-style dog (albeit with way less of that nuclear green relish than most establishments would give you), tested over and over again. Here's what we learned: The best char-dog is butterflied before being grilled and the bun must a) have poppy seeds and b) be steamed. It is also crucial to really get some char on that hot dog, which creates a lovely contrast against all of the pickled bits, tomato, and vegetal crunch. It is an exercise in delicious extremes. Do all kids like a loaded Chicago dog? No. But one can hope they would enjoy the simple pleasures of a plain char dog on a steamed bun.

Notes: Since poppy seed hot dog buns can be hard to find, I've included a method for adding them to plain grocery store buns. However, if you don't feel like turning on the oven to bake the poppy seeds onto the bun, you can simply steam plain buns.

Vienna Beef frankfurter sourcing is difficult in certain parts of the country; Hebrew National quarter-pounder franks are the best substitute. All of the other condiments are readily available online.

(continued)

SALTY CREW

INGREDIENTS

1 large egg
3 tablespoons water
6 standard white hot dog buns
About 2 tablespoons poppy seeds
6 hot dogs, ideally Vienna Beef frankfurters (see Notes, page 12)
About ¼ cup yellow mustard, ideally Plochman's
6 rounded tablespoons diced white onion
About 1 tablespoon Chicago-style relish or sweet relish
1 beefsteak tomato, cut into ¼-inch-thick half-moons
Celery salt
A jar of hot pickled sport peppers, ideally Marconi
Kosher dill pickles, cut into ⅛th spears

METHOD

Preheat the grill to high heat, then clean and oil the grates well.

Meanwhile, preheat the oven to 350°F. Line a sheet pan with parchment paper.

Crack the egg into a medium bowl and whisk in the water until you have a unified egg wash. Brush the tops and bottoms of the buns with the egg wash and then dust them generously on both sides with the poppy seeds. Lay the buns closed and cut side down on the baking sheet (so that the maximum possible surface area is exposed to the oven). Place the sheet pan in the oven and cook until the buns are barely browned and the poppy seeds are set, about 3 minutes. Remove them and let them cool.

Meanwhile, set up a steamer basket for the buns. You can use a standard metal or bamboo steamer basket over a pot of simmering water on the stove. Personally, I like to run an extension cord and plug in a rice cooker outside by the grill so I can steam and grill all in the same place. Either way works, as long as you are steaming the buns.

Butterfly a hot dog by slicing it in the middle, lengthwise, all the way down (but not all the way through). As you cut, try to peel the hot dog open, like you're opening a book. Once you can peel it open, flip it over and gently press it down flat. Repeat this with the other hot dogs.

When you're ready to eat, lay the hot dogs cut-side down on the grill and allow them to cook until they are sizzling and taking on good color with some charring around the edges, about 3 minutes. Flip them over and repeat with the other side.

Meanwhile, place the hot dog buns in the steamer. Allow the buns to steam until they are warmed through and soft, 2 to 3 minutes.

When the dogs are charred and the buns are steamed, close the butterflied hot dogs as best you can and lay them in the buns, with the buns opened fairly wide to make room for the condiments. Working assembly line–style, add about 2 teaspoons mustard in a thick squiggle across a dog, followed by 1 rounded tablespoon of onions. Lay about ½ teaspoon of green relish on top, spreading it across the whole dog. Tuck 2 half-moon slices of tomato on one side of each bun, between the bun and the hot dog with the round part facing up. Season the tomato with a small sprinkle of celery salt. On the opposite side, lay sport peppers along the length of each hot dog (usually 2 or 3 per). Lay a pickle spear, skin-side up, on top of each dog. Close the buns and serve immediately.

Chicken Teriyaki Sandwiches with Jalapeño-Cabbage Slaw

MAKES 4 SANDWICHES

I've always had an affinity for the turn-and-burn mashup that is a chicken teriyaki sandwich. Though they are frequently served on a roll with mayo, lettuce, and tomato, I wanted to make a new version filled with vegetal crunch and heat and fun. A mayo-vinegar hybrid slaw with cabbage, jalapeño, and fresh ginger is the perfect accompaniment for this sweet, spicy, and tangy sandwich. This makes enough slaw to serve some extra on the side as well. For best results, mix the slaw right before serving.

INGREDIENTS

Teriyaki-Marinated Chicken

¾ cup sake
¾ cup soy sauce
¾ cup mirin
1 tablespoon honey or granulated sugar
1½ pounds boneless, skinless chicken breast

Slaw Dressing

½ cup mayonnaise
2 tablespoons red wine vinegar
2 tablespoons honey
1 tablespoon soy sauce
2 teaspoons toasted sesame oil
1 teaspoon Dijon mustard
1 teaspoon grated fresh ginger

To Finish

4 sturdy hamburger buns or other sturdy sandwich rolls
Mayonnaise
6 loosely packed cups finely shredded cabbage, green, red, or ideally a mix
2 medium carrots, grated
½ cup loosely packed finely chopped fresh Italian parsley
3 scallions, thinly sliced
1 jalapeño pepper, diced (seeded for less heat)
Salt

METHOD

Marinate the chicken: In a small saucepan, combine the sake, soy sauce, mirin, and honey and bring to a bubble over high heat. Once the mixture is bubbling, reduce it to a simmer. Allow to simmer for 1 minute, then set it aside and let it cool to room temperature.

Meanwhile, lay a chicken breast flat on a cutting board. Press your nondominant hand, palm down, on the top of the chicken breast. Starting on the thicker side, use a sharp knife to slice the chicken breast in half horizontally to make 2 cutlets. Repeat this with the remaining chicken breasts. Once the marinade is cool, transfer it to an airtight container or ziplock bag, along with the chicken. Toss slightly to make sure that all of the chicken is coated in marinade. Place in the refrigerator for at least 1 hour and up to 6.

Make the slaw dressing: In a large bowl, whisk together the mayo, vinegar, honey, soy sauce, sesame oil, mustard, and ginger. Set the bowl of dressing aside.

To cook and finish: Preheat the grill to medium-high heat, then clean and oil the grates very well.

Meanwhile, reserving the marinade, lift the chicken from the marinade and let all of the marinade drip off of it. Pat the chicken breasts dry and set them aside.

Return the teriyaki marinade to a small saucepan and bring to a bubble over high heat. Once it is bubbling, reduce it to a gentle simmer for 5 minutes, then turn off the heat.

Toast the inside of the buns briefly on the grill, just until they have some light blackening on the edges, about 90 seconds, then set them aside. Brush the chicken cutlets on both sides with a thin veil of mayo, then lay them on the grill. Grill until the first side is browned with bits of blackening around the edges, about 5 minutes. Flip them over and grill until they are just cooked through, with an internal temperature of 150°F, 3 to 6 minutes, depending on thickness.

Remove the chicken cutlets from the grill and lay them on a plate. Pour the reheated teriyaki sauce over them and toss to coat. Transfer them to a cutting board and cut them as needed to fit onto the 4 buns, with some overhang.

To the bowl with the dressing, add the cabbage, carrots, parsley, scallions, and jalapeño and toss until well combined. Season to taste with salt.

Place the chicken on the buns, then top with a generous handful of the slaw. Serve immediately, with more slaw on the side.

The Juiciest Turkey Burgers

(with Goat Cheese, Pickled Peppers, and Sprouts)

MAKES 4 BURGERS

This turkey patty, filled with fresh shallots and rosemary, stays super juicy and gets a great char thanks to the mayonnaise (don't tell people who think they don't like mayo—they won't notice it). The trick is to keep the patties somewhat wetter than you might be comfortable with. Form them on parchment and then cut the parchment into squares around the patties, allowing you to pick them up and lay them straight onto the grill, before peeling back the paper. Otherwise I recommend just shaping them and laying them straight from your hand onto the grill.

For pickier kids, you can obviously simplify the condiments, as the patties themselves are the star here.

INGREDIENTS

Dijonnaise

¼ cup mayonnaise
1½ tablespoons Dijon mustard

Goat Cheese Spread

4 ounces soft goat cheese
2 tablespoons extra-virgin olive oil
1 tablespoon whole-milk yogurt
1 tablespoon finely chopped shallot
1 teaspoon finely chopped fresh thyme
Salt
Several twists of freshly ground black pepper

Turkey Burgers

2 tablespoons finely chopped shallot
2 tablespoons mayonnaise
1 tablespoon panko bread crumbs
1 tablespoon finely chopped fresh rosemary
1 garlic clove, grated or finely chopped
1 teaspoon soy sauce
¾ teaspoon kosher salt
¾ teaspoon Worcestershire sauce
¼ teaspoon crushed red pepper (optional)
A few twists of freshly ground black pepper
1 pound ground turkey (93/7)
Extra-virgin olive oil
4 whole wheat burger buns, split
About 12 rings hot pickled peppers
2 ounces sprouts, such as clover

METHOD

Make the Dijonnaise: In a small bowl, combine the mayo and mustard and whisk to combine. Set aside.

Make the goat cheese spread: In another small bowl, stir together the goat cheese, olive oil, yogurt, shallot, thyme, salt to taste, and pepper. Set aside.

Make the turkey burgers: Preheat the grill to high heat, then clean and oil the grates well. For best results, form the patties right before grilling.

Lay a sheet of parchment paper down on a baking sheet or portable cutting board.

In a large bowl, combine the shallot, mayo, panko, rosemary, garlic, soy sauce, salt, Worcestershire sauce, crushed red pepper (if using), and black pepper. Stir it thoroughly, then fold in the ground turkey until well combined, being careful not to overmix. Lightly oil your hands with olive oil, then, trying your best to divide the mix evenly, shape the turkey mixture into 4 patties that are slightly wider than the burger buns, laying each patty down on the parchment paper. Cut the parchment paper into squares around the burger patties.

Spread a thin layer of Dijonnaise onto the cut sides of each bun and grill them until just toasted, about 30 seconds, then take them off the grill. Lay the patties on the grill, then carefully peel off the parchment. Allow them to cook until they have a good amount of color and char on the bottom side, 3 to 4 minutes. Then flip them over and continue grilling until the thickest part of the patties are cooked through (165°F on an instant-read thermometer).

While the patties are cooking slather the bottom buns with the remaining Dijonnaise.

Top the buns with the cooked burger patties. Divide the pickled peppers among them, followed by the sprouts. Slather the top buns with the goat cheese spread, then close the burgers and serve immediately.

A BOAT BEER
BLONDE ALE

Cumin Lamb Burgers

(with Gruyère, Curry Ketchup, and Dill Yogurt)

MAKES 4 BURGERS

This flavor-packed lamb burger is inspired by the one from a restaurant in Los Angeles called The Golden State, where I used to wait tables a long time ago. This is a slightly more streamlined version, featuring "dump-and-stir" curry ketchup and dill yogurt, and a patty seasoned simply with salt, black pepper, and ground cumin. A hefty wad of peppery arugula and nutty, sweet Gruyère cheese brings all of these strong, addictive flavors together in perfect harmony. This is an excellent "gateway" dish for kids (or adults) who aren't sure if they like lamb.

INGREDIENTS

Curry Ketchup

½ cup ketchup
1 tablespoon curry powder
1 teaspoon Worcestershire sauce
½ teaspoon granulated garlic
Salt

Dill Yogurt

½ cup whole-milk Greek yogurt
1 garlic clove, grated or finely chopped
2 tablespoons finely chopped dill fronds
1½ teaspoons extra-virgin olive oil
Salt and freshly ground black pepper

Lamb Burgers

1½ pounds ground lamb
4 hamburger buns (I prefer brioche buns, if you can find them), split
About 2 cups loosely packed arugula
Kosher salt and freshly ground black pepper
About 2 teaspoons ground cumin
4 slices Gruyère cheese (Swiss cheese or white cheddar will also work well)

METHOD

Make the curry ketchup: In a medium bowl, whisk together the ketchup, curry powder, Worcestershire sauce, and granulated garlic. Season to taste with salt, then set aside. It is servable right away, but at its best when the spices have had a chance to bloom for an hour or so.

Make the dill yogurt: In a medium bowl, stir together the yogurt, garlic, dill, and olive oil. Season aggressively with salt and pepper.

Make the lamb burgers: Preheat the grill to high heat, then clean and oil the grates well.

Divide the lamb into 4 portions, then gently shape each into a patty that is slightly wider than the buns, being careful not to overwork the meat. Gently indent the center of the patties with your thumb to form an indent in the center of the patty—this will help them cook evenly without puffing up in the center.

When you are ready to grill, lay the cut side of the buns down on the grill and toast them until just blackened at the edges, about 60 seconds, then take them off the grill. Set them down, cut-side up, and dress the bottom buns with curry ketchup and the top buns with dill yogurt. Divide the arugula among the top buns, pressing it into the dill yogurt to hold in place.

Season the top side of each burger patty aggressively with salt and pepper. Apply a dusting of cumin, then lay them seasoning-side down on the grill. Season the other side with more salt, pepper, and cumin. Grill until they have a nice char on the bottom side, about 2 minutes, then flip them over. Lay the Gruyère on top and cook to your preferred doneness. I prefer medium-rare, about 130°F internal temperature.

Once cooked, lay the patties on the curry ketchup, close the buns, and serve immediately.

Tofu Bánh Mì with Lemongrass BBQ Sauce

MAKES
4 SANDWICHES

Much of the great food in the world exists due to awful things happening to a lot of people. Bánh mì is no different: It came about when baguettes, along with French Imperialism, arrived in Vietnam in the 1860s. This version is very much a personal riff on the classic version, using grilled tofu, đồ chua (pickled daikon and carrot), and a blended lemongrass BBQ sauce to create a crunchy, spicy, sweet, and aromatic vegetarian sandwich. If you're having a backyard BBQ, this will make both vegetarians and carnivores very happy. (Tofu can be grilled a few hours or even a couple days in advance, then refreshed right before eating.) The BBQ sauce can be made up to a week in advance and kept in the refrigerator—just warm through before serving. The đồ chua can be made up to 2 weeks in advance.

The key to this recipe is drying the tofu quite well and grilling it low-and-slow.

DAD HACK

If you can't find great, fresh baguette, a "take-and-bake" from the grocery store is a good second option. Just try to bake it pretty close to when you plan on eating.

INGREDIENTS

Lemongrass BBQ Sauce
¾ cup sliced fresh lemongrass stalks
¼ cup firmly packed brown sugar, light or dark
¼ cup apple cider vinegar
¼ cup rice wine vinegar
2 tablespoons fresh lime juice
1 tablespoon soy sauce
¼ cup ketchup
1 teaspoon toasted sesame oil
½ teaspoon Worcestershire sauce
1 medium shallot, roughly chopped
4 garlic cloves, smashed with the side of a knife
1-inch knob fresh ginger
20 twists of freshly ground black pepper
Salt

Grilled Tofu Bánh Mì
1-pound block extra-firm tofu (not silken)
1 large baguette, cut into quarters, or 4 individual sandwich-size baguettes (about 5 to 6 inches long each)
About ½ cup mayonnaise
1 Persian (mini) cucumber, cut into long matchsticks
Đồ Chua/pickled daikon and carrot (recipe follows)
1 jalapeño pepper, sliced into rings (seeded if you want it less spicy)
1 bunch of cilantro, leaves and tender stems

METHOD

Make the lemongrass BBQ sauce: In a blender, combine the lemongrass, brown sugar, both vinegars, the lime juice, soy sauce, ketchup, sesame oil, Worcestershire sauce, shallot, garlic, ginger, pepper, and salt to taste and blend until smooth. Transfer the mixture to a medium saucepan and bring to a bubble over medium-high heat. Reduce to a gentle simmer and cook for 5 minutes, stirring occasionally. Turn off the heat and leave the saucepan covered until the mixture comes to room temperature.

Make the grilled tofu bánh mì: Drain the tofu and lay it on a cutting board. Slice it in half horizontally, to create two wide rectangles. Then quarter each of those rectangles lengthwise, creating 8 tofu long rectangles total. Pat them dry with paper towels, using multiple sheets until they are mostly dry.

Brush them on all sides with the lemongrass BBQ sauce, making sure to leave extra sauce behind to finish the sandwiches, and allow them to marinate for at least 30 minutes and up to 12 hours (if it is longer than 2 hours, cover them and place them in the refrigerator).

When you are ready to cook, set up a two-zone fire. If grilling with gas, set one side to medium-high heat and the other to low heat. Clean the grates especially well and grease them thoroughly.

Lay the tofu on the cooler side of the grill in a single layer. Cover the grill and cook until the tofu is golden-brown with some blackening on the first side, about 10 minutes. Flip it over and repeat with the other side, another 10 minutes. Set aside and brush with more BBQ sauce.

Meanwhile, in either a 350°F oven or on the cooler side of the grill, refresh the baguettes whole until the outside is warm and crisp, about 5 minutes. Slice the baguettes through horizontally and spread mayonnaise on both sides. Spoon the remaining BBQ sauce on both sides, dividing it evenly. Divide the tofu among the bottoms, then garnish to taste with large quantities of cucumber, pickled vegetables, jalapeño slices, and cilantro. Close the baguettes, then serve.

ĐỒ CHUA
PICKLED DAIKON AND CARROT

Makes 1 pint

1 small or ½ medium daikon (about 8 ounces), peeled
1 large or 2 small carrots (about 4 ounces), peeled
1½ teaspoons fine sea salt
½ cup hot water
1½ teaspoons sugar
½ cup rice wine vinegar

Cut the daikon and carrot into matchsticks. (If you have a mandoline with a julienne setting, this saves a lot of time.) Place them in a medium bowl with the salt and toss them until well combined. Allow them to sit for about 2 hours, to release their excess liquid.

Meanwhile, in a mason jar or other nonreactive container, combine the hot water and sugar and stir until the sugar is dissolved. Add the vinegar and allow to cool to room temperature.

Once the carrots and daikon have sat for 2 hours, squeeze out the liquid and add them to the brining liquid. They are ready to eat right away, but will keep very well for up to 2 weeks.

Smoky Grilled Caprese Sandwich

SERVES 2 TO 4

Behold, an *actually* grilled cheese sandwich. There's something I really adore about this rustic, charred Caprese sandwich: olive oil–brushed focaccia charred and crisped on a hot grill with fresh and smoked mozzarella wilted into tomatoes, basil, red wine vinegar, and paper-thin onions. This is a great lunch sandwich for 2, or served quartered for a fun little appetizer. You can also easily scale this up: Prep as many as you want, grilling 2 (or however many fit on your grill) at a time and making it the perfect thing to feed a family or two. The key is finding a high-quality focaccia, but a good East Coast–style hoagie roll will work, too.

INGREDIENTS

A roughly 6-inch square piece focaccia or similar-size round about 6¾ inches across
3 tablespoons extra-virgin olive oil
1½ tablespoons red wine vinegar
About 8 paper-thin slices yellow onion
Salt and freshly ground black pepper
4 ounces fresh mozzarella cheese
1 medium-to-large tomato, cut into ½-inch slices
½ teaspoon granulated garlic
About 10 fresh basil leaves
4 ounces smoked mozzarella, grated

METHOD

Set up a two-zone fire. If grilling with gas, set one side to high heat and leave the other one completely off. Clean and oil the grates well.

Slice the focaccia in half horizontally through the center. Take about 1 tablespoon of the olive oil and use it to brush the outside crust of both pieces of focaccia, then set them down cut-side up. Drizzle another 1 tablespoon of olive oil on the inside of each piece and then drizzle with the red wine vinegar. Lay the onion slices on the bottom and season them with salt and pepper. Tear the fresh mozzarella and lay it in an even layer over the onions, seasoning with more salt and pepper and then drizzling with the remaining 1 tablespoon olive oil. Lay the tomato on top, seasoning this, too, with salt and pepper, but also adding the granulated garlic. Top with an even layer of basil, followed by the smoked mozzarella.

Close the sandwich. When you are ready to grill, lay it on the cooler side of the grill and close the grill lid. Allow it to cook, covered, until the bread is warm and the cheese is wilted, 8 to 10 minutes. Lift the lid and lay the sandwich on the hot side of the grill until the bottom has blackened grill marks, about 1 minute. Flip the sandwich over carefully, using a spatula and tongs, and repeat with the other side, about 1 minute.

Flip it back over and place it on a cutting board. Allow it to rest for about 1 minute, then cut in half or quarters, depending on your desires. Serve immediately.

Better Grilled Veggie Wraps

(with Avocado Hummus, Sprouts, and Feta)

MAKES 4 WRAPS

I love the *idea* of a grilled veggie wrap, and have frequently ordered them at places like grocery store sandwich counters as a "car lunch" amid a day of family grocery shopping and errands. Sadly, they are almost always quite bad, and usually drip vegetable juice onto your pants. So this is the version I actually want to eat—and the one that holds up well for a dad errand in the car, or even a family road trip. Avocado gets mashed in with store-bought hummus to create a flavorful glue that keeps the wrap together. Meanwhile, resting the vegetables and then draining off the liquid keeps out excess moisture—and sprouts are the perfect vehicle to soak up any that remains.

Note: If you are averse to "wraps," you can definitely use a good crusty hoagie roll instead.

INGREDIENTS

- 1 small-to-medium Italian eggplant (about 12 ounces)
- 2 medium zucchini (about 12 ounces total)
- 1 medium red onion
- 2 red or orange bell peppers, cut lengthwise into sixths
- 2 tablespoons extra-virgin olive oil, plus more for drizzling
- 1 tablespoon dried oregano or dried basil
- Salt and freshly ground black pepper
- A handful of fresh basil leaves (optional)
- 1 teaspoon red wine vinegar
- ¾ cup hummus
- 1 large avocado
- 2 tablespoons fresh lemon juice
- 4 large tortillas, ideally spinach tortillas
- 1 (3-ounce) package sprouts, such as alfalfa, broccoli, or sunflower
- 4 ounces drained water-brined feta (goat cheese also works really well)

METHOD

Preheat the grill to medium-high heat, then clean and oil the grates well.

Cut the eggplant and zucchini into 1-inch-thick rounds. Cut off the top of the onion, leaving the root intact (slicing off any dirt from the root end). Peel the onion and then cut into eighths through the root (this will keep the slices intact for grilling).

In a large bowl, combine the eggplant, zucchini, onion, and peppers and toss them with 1 tablespoon of the olive oil, the oregano, and salt and pepper to taste. Lay them on the grill in a single layer, working in batches if necessary. As the vegetables brown, 6 to 8 minutes, flip them over and repeat with the other side, another 6 minutes or so. Be aware that not all the vegetables will brown at the same time, so watch them carefully. Once browned on both sides, return them to the bowl.

Once all the vegetables are in the bowl, add the fresh basil (if using), vinegar, and a drizzle of olive oil. Toss to combine, then cover the vegetables and allow them to rest until they are room temperature.

When you are ready to make the wraps, drain the liquid from the vegetables, then taste them for seasoning and adjust with more salt and pepper.

Place the hummus in a medium bowl. Scoop out the flesh from the avocado and place it in the bowl, then mash it with a fork until it is combined with the hummus. Fold in the lemon juice and remaining 1 tablespoon olive oil.

Heat the tortillas in a skillet or on the grill. Spread them generously with the hummus mixture, then lay down the vegetables, getting a good mix on each wrap, plucking off the pieces of onion like flower petals, while leaving the roots behind. Divide the sprouts among the wraps and top them with the feta. Roll the wraps up like a burrito to seal them. Serve immediately or pack them up for a drive.

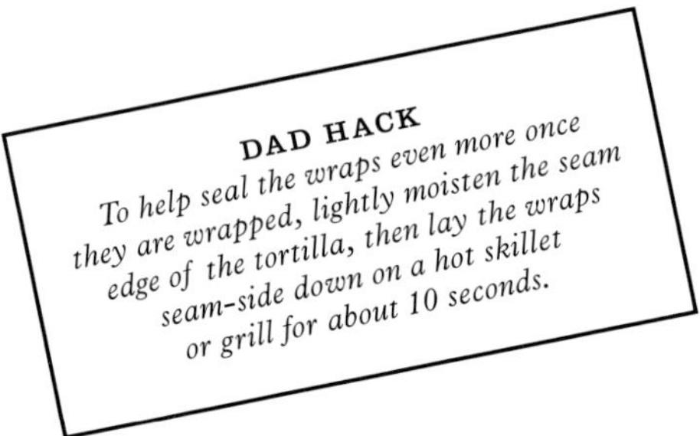

Za'atar-Blackened Mahi-Mahi Pitas

MAKES 4 PITAS

This has become my absolute favorite way to eat grilled fish. Za'atar—a Levantine seasoning mix that is one of the best spice blends ever created—here mimics a Southern blackening spice, to create a beautifully flavorful piece of fish. Served on a yogurt-slathered grilled pita loaded with herbs, vegetables, and olives, this is one of those dishes that everyone will assume is *way* more complicated than it is.

Note: If you can only find za'atar with salt already added, simply adjust the salt you are otherwise adding.

INGREDIENTS

1 small red onion, cut into ¼-inch-thick half-moons
3 tablespoons extra-virgin olive oil, plus more for drizzling
1 tablespoon red wine vinegar
Kosher salt
4 pitas or flatbreads
4 (1-inch-thick) mahi-mahi or similar steaky fillets (see Headnote, page 204), like swordfish (about 4 ounces each)
About 2 tablespoons mayonnaise
About 3 tablespoons salt-free za'atar, plus more for sprinkling
About ¼ cup whole-milk yogurt
Flaky salt
2 Persian (mini) cucumbers, cut into thin rounds
12 pitted dry-cured black olives or kalamata olives
About 1 cup soft herbs and tender stems (I like a mix of cilantro and dill)
1 lemon, quartered
Hot sauce (optional)

METHOD

Preheat the grill to high heat, then clean and oil the grates well.

In a bowl, combine the onion, 1 tablespoon of the olive oil, the vinegar, and a pinch of salt. Toss to coat and let the onions wilt while you prepare the rest of the meal.

Use the remaining 2 tablespoons olive oil to brush the pita on both sides.

Cut the fish into planks that are roughly 1 inch wide and 3 inches long (this does not need to be precise). Pat them dry with paper towels and then brush them with a thin veil of mayonnaise. Season them all over with salt and then coat them thoroughly with the za'atar.

Lay the pitas on the grill and allow them to cook until heated through and browning a bit at the edges, about 90 seconds per side. Simultaneously (if you have the space on your grill) or just after, lay down the fish. Cook until the herbs are blackened, about 3 minutes—then flip the pieces of fish and grill the other side until just cooked through and the fish has an internal temperature of 130°F, about 2 more minutes.

Slather some yogurt on the bottom of each pita and then season it with some za'atar and a pinch of flaky salt. Lay the fish on top, then top it with the cucumbers, olives, and wilted onions (leaving the juice from the onions behind). Top with the herbs and a drizzle of olive oil, a squeeze of lemon, and a pinch of flaky salt. Serve immediately, with hot sauce if you desire.

Pork Souvlaki Pitas

MAKES
4 PITAS

Souvlaki pitas belong in backyard cookouts right next to hamburgers and hot dogs. Basically: Feed your kids more souvlaki. Served everywhere across Greece in small restaurants, street stands, and tavernas, it is most commonly some form of seasoned, grilled meat (frequently pork), served in a toasted pita with tzatziki (cucumber-yogurt sauce), onions, tomatoes, and olive oil. My version is highlighted by a marinade made with fresh oregano, garlic, and lemon. If you don't want to use pork, this marinade would also work really well with boneless chicken breasts or thighs, or even sirloin steak.

Note: Some people prefer fresh dill in their tzatziki, but I like the cleaner, purer flavor of this version with no herbs, to complement the meat and its marinade.

INGREDIENTS

Marinated Pork Chops

4 garlic cloves, roughly chopped
Grated zest of 1 lemon
1½ teaspoons kosher salt, or to your desired salt level
1 cup loosely packed fresh oregano
2 tablespoons fresh lemon juice
1 tablespoon extra-virgin olive oil
¼ teaspoon crushed red pepper
10 twists freshly ground black pepper
1½ pounds boneless pork chops, 1 inch thick, butterflied or sliced into ½-inch-thick chops

Tzatziki

1 English cucumber
1 cup whole-milk Greek yogurt
3 tablespoons extra-virgin olive oil
2 garlic cloves, finely chopped
¼ teaspoon granulated garlic
Salt and freshly ground black pepper

To Finish

4 pitas or flatbreads
About 1 tablespoon extra-virgin olive oil, plus more for drizzling
About 1 teaspoon dried oregano
Salt and freshly ground black pepper
About 12 ounces tomato, sliced into half-moons
½ small red onion, sliced into thin half-moons

METHOD

Make the pork marinade: For best results, use a mortar and pestle, though it can also be made in a blender or food processor.

With a mortar and pestle: Combine the garlic, lemon zest, and salt in a mortar and pound it with the pestle until it forms a rustic paste. Add the oregano leaves and pound until you have a fairly consistent paste with no big chunks. Transfer it to a resealable container big enough to fit the pork. Add the lemon juice, olive oil, crushed red pepper, and black pepper. Mix it until thoroughly combined and then add the pork, tossing it until fully coated. Transfer to the refrigerator to marinate for at least 30 minutes and up to 8 hours.

In a blender or food processor, combine the garlic, lemon zest, salt, oregano, lemon juice, olive oil, crushed red pepper, and black pepper. Blend until a rustic sauce is formed. Add it to a large resealable container along with the pork, tossing until the pork is fully coated. Transfer to the refrigerator to marinate for at least 30 minutes and up to 8 hours.

Make the tzatziki: Slice off the ends of the cucumber and grate it on the medium holes of a box grater. Squeeze as much of the water out as you can (you don't need to be obsessive about it). You should end up with about ½ cup of grated cucumber. In a medium bowl, combine the squeezed cucumber, yogurt, olive oil, fresh garlic, and granulated garlic. Stir them together until fully combined, then season to taste with salt and pepper.

Keep at room temperature if serving within a couple of hours, or store for up to 3 days in the refrigerator for best results.

To finish: Preheat the grill to high heat, then clean and oil the grates well.

Lay the pork down and grill it until it is golden brown with little bits of blackening around the edges, about 4 minutes. Flip it over and repeat with the other side, another 3 to 4 minutes. Remove the pork from the heat and set it on a cutting board.

Brush the pitas on both sides with the 1 tablespoon olive oil, then season with the dried oregano, salt, and pepper. Grill the pitas until they are golden brown and starting to sizzle, about 1 minute, then flip them over and repeat with the other side, about 1 more minute.

Chop the pork into a rustic ½-inch dice. Spoon some tzatziki on each pita, then top it with pork, followed by tomato and red onion. Season the tomato and onion with salt and pepper and drizzle it with a little more olive oil. Serve immediately (you can even wrap it in some sandwich paper for easier eating).

Pork Chop Sandwiches with Grilled Pineapple and Chili Crisp Mayo

MAKES 4 SANDWICHES

In an era of big, thick pork chops (like the one on page 178), I have come to really enjoy a thin, quick-cooking one on a sandwich. It's also a great way to stretch some meat—a mere 8 ounces feeds four people. Once you've thrown your pork chops into a simple marinade and preheated your grill, this sweet, spicy, juicy, fruity, char-flecked sandwich comes together in just a few minutes. If the kids are ready to handle a little heat, this will become Pool Party Food 2.0. As an added bonus, the two-ingredient chili crisp mayo is a reminder of how easy it is to supercharge any sandwich. Extra chili crisp mayo is a nice condiment for some potato chips or French fries, too.

Look for bone-in pork chops, which have more flavor. In the words of my BBQ mentor Kevin Bludso: "Here's a pork chop sandwich—watch the bone."

INGREDIENTS

¼ cup orange juice
3 tablespoons soy sauce
2 garlic cloves, grated
½ teaspoon grated fresh ginger
4 thin bone-in pork chops (about 2 ounces each)
½ cup mayonnaise
2 tablespoons chili crisp (I prefer Fly By Jing Sichuan Chili Crisp)
1 small red onion, cut into four ½-inch-thick rings
4 (½-inch-thick) slices fresh pineapple
1 teaspoon neutral oil
Salt
4 potato rolls or hamburger buns, split
Potato chips (optional), for serving

METHOD

In a container that will fit all 4 pork chops, combine the orange juice, soy sauce, garlic, and ginger. Stir to combine, then add the pork chops, making sure each chop gets coated. Cover and marinate in the refrigerator for at least 30 minutes and up to 6 hours.

When you are ready to grill, preheat the grill to high heat, then clean and oil the grates well.

In a small bowl, stir together the mayo and chili crisp and set aside. In a medium bowl, combine the onions, pineapple, and neutral oil and gently toss just to coat. Season with a pinch of salt.

Once the grill is hot, lay the buns, cut-side down, and grill until they are just lightly charred and toasted, about 40 seconds. Flip them over and toast the other side for about 5 seconds, then lay them on a plate. Slather both cut sides generously with chili crisp mayo.

Lay the onions down on the grill first, allowing the first side to char nicely before flipping, about 3 minutes per side. Once cooked, roughly chop the onion and season it with more salt. Lay the pineapple slices and pork chops on the grill. Grill the pineapple for 1 minute per side, just to get some light color. As for the pork chops, make sure to get a good amount of color on the first side, about 2 minutes, before flipping. Then grill until just cooked, about 1 more minute.

Divide the onions among the bottom buns, followed by the pork chops and then the pineapple. Cover with the top buns and serve immediately, possibly alongside potato chips and more chili crisp mayo.

Beer Brats

(with Grilled Onions, Sauerkraut, and Spicy Brown Mustard)

MAKES 4 BRATS

Poaching sausages before grilling them is the best way to ensure that they don't burst on a hot grill, spilling out all of the fat and flavor that the sausage-maker carefully combined in the casing. The humble beer brat is the perfect way to embrace this poaching technique while adding tons of flavor in the process (the alcohol is long cooked off before it's eaten, so it's safe for kids). I also add onions to the poaching liquid, then grill them alongside the sausage. Spicy brown mustard and cold, crunchy sauerkraut creates the perfect balance . . . along with perhaps a cold beer. If you're not in the mood for a bun, this is also great on a plate with a fork and knife.

INGREDIENTS

1 medium yellow onion
4 uncooked bratwurst sausages
2 bay leaves, fresh or dried
24 ounces beer, such as a light German pilsner
Salt
4 hot dog buns or pretzel rolls
Spicy brown mustard
About ½ cup drained sauerkraut

METHOD

Cut off the top of the onion, leaving the root intact (slicing off any dirt from the root end). Peel the onion and cut into quarters through the root (this will keep the slices intact for grilling).

Place the bratwurst in a medium pot that will fit them snugly. Lay the bay leaves on top, followed by the onion quarters. Add beer just to cover, plus a generous pinch of salt, then place the pot over medium-high heat. Once it is bubbling from heat rather than just carbonation, reduce the heat to a bare simmer and poach the sausages until they reach an internal temperature of 145°F. You can start checking the temperature after 5 minutes. Once they are ready, remove the sausages and onions and allow them to rest for at least 5 minutes—but room temperature is best. The beer poaching liquid can now be discarded, or used to poach more brats if you desire.

Preheat the grill to medium-high heat, then clean and oil the grates well.

Toast the buns on the outside for just 1 minute per side, then set them aside. Lay the sausages and onions on the grill, turning as needed until the sausages are nicely browned on all sides and the onions take on some color, 3 to 4 minutes. Once the onions are finished, simply slice off and discard the root end. Season the onions with a pinch of salt.

Lay some mustard on the bottom half of each bun, then add the sausages, followed by more mustard. Top with onions and then the sauerkraut. Eat immediately.

How to Smoke-Grill a Sausage

MAKES 4 SAUSAGES

People will tell you that you need an offset smoker to smoke a sausage—but I disagree. Smoking on a grill gives you tons of flavor in a lot less time, while also bringing the sausage up to temperature nice and slowly without bursting the casing. Then it gets finished a little bit closer to the fire, crisping the skin to get the best of grilling and smoking at once. This is my absolute favorite way to cook a sausage, ideally served sliced, with some spicy mustard and freshly grated horseradish, just like I order it at Bitzinger Sausage Stand in Vienna, Austria. (Side note: Some people think Vienna is great because of its world-famous classical music. I, however, know that it's great because of things called Würstelstands: sausage stands built into its street corners, selling outstanding freshly cooked sausages and beer.)

This works with any type of sausage, which is a great way to buy whatever particular raw sausage each person in your family likes (chicken, pork, hot, mild, etc.) and add delicious smoke and a crispy casing to it.

INGREDIENTS

- Charcoal
- 2 chunks of your wood of choice (I like post oak, or a mix of hickory and pecan)
- 4 uncooked sausages of your choice (I love a simple salt-and-pepper pork sausage)
- German mustard, or your preference
- Grated fresh horseradish (optional)

METHOD

Set up a two-zone fire by lighting a chimney two-thirds full of charcoal. Once they have turned gray, set them on one side of the grill. Place the wood chunks on top of the charcoal and then close the lid and allow them to burn off for about 5 minutes. Open the vent over the cooler side and leave it closed over the hot side.

Lay the sausages on the cooler side of the grill. Allow them to cook until just cooked through (145° to 150°F internal temperature), about 20 minutes. If the casings are crispy, you can take them off and rest them for a moment before cutting. But if they are still a little soft to the touch, move them closer to the hot side of the grill and allow them to cook until the skins crisp up, 30 to 60 more seconds.

Slice and serve with mustard and grated fresh horseradish, if desired.

Veggie Sides

Broccolini with Preserved Lemon 42
Zucchini Spears with Balsamic, Mint, and Garlic 44
Grilled Asparagus and Wilted White Cheddar. 47
Grilled Artichokes alla Garlic Knots 49
Charred Brussels Sprouts. 50
Grilled and Glazed Baby Bok Choy 52
Citrus and Fennel Salad 55
Charred Cauliflower with Tahini-Yogurt Sauce. 57
Perfect Grilled Potatoes 58
Jimmy Nardellos with Red Yuzu Vinaigrette 60
Kabocha Macha 63
Miso-Butter Corn 65
Buttered Soy Sauce Mushrooms 66
Baba Ghanoush. 68
Grilled Avocado Tostadas with Chipotle-Lime Crema 70
Fettunta. 73
Mezcal Charro Beans. 75
"Kebab Plate" Rice. 76

I pretty much *never* fire up the grill without throwing a couple of vegetables on there. Grilled veggies are one of the fastest, simplest, and most delicious ways to add some nutrition to your family table, and to complement the rest of your meal. Some of these call for little more than a quick grill, a drizzle of olive oil, and a squeeze of lemon—that's all it takes to have a beautiful side dish. Two or three of them can be a meal unto themselves.

But this chapter will also show you how to make showstopper veggie sides; how to fold charred aromatics into rice and beans; how to add flavor complexity to a citrus salad; how to prepare baba ghanoush with way less mess; and even how to make perhaps the best garlic bread in the world.

As for shopping, I will always advocate for finding your nearest farmers market and supporting smaller farms. But no matter what, try your best to shop locally and seasonally. Just because you *can* buy asparagus in December, doesn't mean that you should.

Broccolini with Preserved Lemon

SERVES 4 TO 6

There is something about the combination of salt and time that intensifies flavor and adds an addictive quality to any ingredient, in this case, lemon. The classic pairing of broccolini and lemon is ramped up in flavor here, including every part of the preserved lemon (except for the seeds). As a result, you get a wonderfully delicious and simple side dish in just a few minutes. Leftovers are great, too, chopped up into a whole wheat quesadilla with a mild melting cheese like mozzarella or Monterey Jack for a quick kid (or fully grown adult) lunch.

Preserved lemon can very easily be found online and in many grocery stores these days. I prefer salt-only preservation, rather than those preserved with sugar as well.

INGREDIENTS

1 pound broccolini (as long-stemmed as you can find)
4 tablespoons extra-virgin olive oil
Salt
¼ cup finely chopped preserved lemon, seeds discarded (about 1 whole preserved lemon)
A pinch of crushed red pepper

METHOD

Preheat the grill to high heat, then clean and oil the grates well.

In a large bowl, toss the broccolini with 2 tablespoons of the olive oil and a nice pinch of salt. Grill the broccolini, allowing the first side to get a nice bit of charring and blackening on the edges before flipping, 2 to 3 minutes.

Meanwhile, in that same bowl, combine the remaining 2 tablespoons olive oil, the preserved lemon and crushed red pepper, and stir to combine.

Flip the broccolini and continue cooking until just tender, 1 to 3 more minutes, depending on the thickness. Once each piece is cooked, add it to the bowl with the preserved lemon mixture. Once they are all finished, toss them well, then arrange them on a serving platter, topping the broccolini with any remaining bits of lemon clinging to the bottom of the bowl.

Serve hot, warm, or at room temperature.

Zucchini Spears with Balsamic, Mint, and Garlic

SERVES 4 TO 6

The key to grilling zucchini is to get some char on it before it turns too wet and mushy. Quartering them into spears makes for a quick cook, while a brief marinade of olive oil and balsamic vinegar doubles as a dressing to pour over when they come off the grill. These are best at room temperature, after having some time to rest, and as a result are a great "make-ahead" dish or first item to cook on the grill.

Bonus: If you can find Costata Romanesco—a gorgeous, ridged heirloom zucchini—at your farmers market, I highly recommend it.

INGREDIENTS

5 medium zucchini or Costata Romanesco (see Bonus)
2 garlic cloves, very thinly sliced
3 tablespoons balsamic vinegar
1 tablespoon extra-virgin olive oil
Kosher or fine sea salt
Freshly ground black pepper
Flaky salt
About ¼ cup loosely packed fresh mint leaves

METHOD

Preheat the grill to high heat, then clean and oil the grates well.

Slice off and discard the stem and root end of the zucchini, then quarter them lengthwise into spears. (If you have quite small zucchini, they can be halved or left whole instead.) Lay the zucchini in a wide shallow container like a storage vessel or roasting pan (you can also use a resealable bag). Scatter in the sliced garlic, then pour in the balsamic vinegar and olive oil, and season well with salt and pepper. Toss with your hands and allow the zucchini to marinate for at least 10 minutes and up to 1 hour or so.

When you are ready to grill, lift the spears, allowing the marinade and garlic cloves to fall off and stay behind. Lay the spears on the grill, perpendicular to the grates, in a single layer. Cook until there is some light char on the first side, about 1 minute. "Roll" or flip each one forward to grill the second side and repeat for another minute. Roll/flip one more time to get the final side, then lay the zucchini on a serving platter.

Pour the remaining marinade over the top, along with the garlic, and allow the zucchini to rest, covered, until they come to room temperature (or for up to 2 hours or so). When it is time to serve, garnish with flaky salt and mint leaves.

Grilled Asparagus and Wilted White Cheddar

SERVES
4

Grilled asparagus is so good on its own that it requires very little to elevate it, so this preparation is embarrassingly simple: sharp, crumbly English white Cheddar, barely wilted over the warm asparagus. A squeeze of lemon and a drizzle of olive oil makes this a delightful celebration of spring. Or to put it even more simply: People eat more green things when you put cheese on top.

INGREDIENTS

1 bunch asparagus (about ¾ pound)
Extra-virgin olive oil
Kosher or fine sea salt
About 2 ounces aged English white Cheddar cheese
Flaky salt
Freshly ground black pepper
½ lemon

METHOD

Preheat the grill to high heat, then clean and oil the grates well.

Meanwhile, prepare the asparagus by snapping off the hard woody ends at the very bottom. If you feel where the tension is, the asparagus will naturally snap off where it wants to break.

On a plate or in a bowl, toss the asparagus with 1 teaspoon olive oil and sprinkle it with salt.

Lay the asparagus on the hot spot of the grill (obviously . . . turned so that they will not fall through the grates). Allow them to grill undisturbed until well charred on one side, 3 to 4 minutes (though it can vary depending on the thickness of the asparagus). Roll them forward or back a half turn, just to barely finish cooking the other side, about 1 more minute.

Transfer them to a serving plate in a single layer. Immediately shave or grate the Cheddar (on the large holes of a grater) directly over the asparagus. Drizzle another tablespoon or so of olive oil over the top, then sprinkle with a pinch of flaky salt and a few twists of pepper. Squeeze the lemon over the top and serve immediately, or at room temperature.

Grilled Artichokes alla Garlic Knots

SERVES 4 TO 6

Unpopular opinion alert: I really don't like aioli with grilled artichoke, no matter how many times *every restaurant in America* tries to serve them together. I always prefer a lighter, brighter option, the memories flooding back from my childhood, dipping steamed leaves into lemony, garlic-studded olive oil, scraping the flesh from my teeth, the grease smearing my face and hands. This method is a riff on the way that I learned to make garlic knots in a pizzeria by tossing them in oil, garlic, parsley, and Parmesan. (The garlic and oil often getting warmed up by sitting on top of the hot pizza oven.) But instead of a side of tomato sauce, this recipe uses finely chopped fresh tomatoes, highlighting that time of year in late spring when artichokes and tomatoes are both coming into their own in California. These are the get-your-hands-dirty grilled artichokes that I will serve my wife and kids for years to come.

INGREDIENTS

Salt
4 large artichokes
¼ cup extra-virgin olive oil, plus more for drizzling
8 garlic cloves, finely chopped
Freshly ground black pepper
¼ cup finely chopped fresh Italian parsley
1 medium-to-large tomato, finely chopped (whatever is best and ripe)
Freshly grated Parmesan cheese

METHOD

Set up a large, wide pot—like a Dutch oven—filled about halfway with water and place it over high heat. Season it well with a hefty pinch of salt.

To trim the artichokes, first, slice off the tip, about ½ inch from the top of the artichoke. Then cut off and remove most of the stem, leaving just about 1 inch attached. Pull off and discard the tough outer leaves. Quarter the artichoke lengthwise, through the stem. Use a spoon to scoop out the tough choke in the center, leaving behind the heart and leaves, and doing your best to keep the rest of the artichoke intact. Repeat with the remaining artichokes.

Once the water comes to a boil, reduce it to a simmer and add the artichokes, cut-side down. Keep the water at a gentle simmer and cover the pot. Allow the artichokes to poach until the insides are just tender but not mushy, 8 to 10 minutes. Lift them from the water and set them aside to cool.

Meanwhile, preheat the grill to high heat, then clean and oil the grates well.

In a large metal bowl, combine the olive oil and garlic (make sure the bowl does not have a rubber gripper, or anything that should not go on a grill), as well as a nice pinch of salt and several twists of pepper. If you don't have a bowl like this, you can use a wide pot. Place the bowl on the grill and allow the garlic to wilt in the oil—if it starts to brown at all, use a kitchen towel to remove the bowl from the grill and set it aside, about 3 minutes.

Drizzle the artichokes with enough oil just to barely coat, then lay them on the grill, cut-side down. Grill them until they are tender and have some blackening at the edges on all three sides, about 2-3 minutes per.

Meanwhile, to the bowl of garlic and oil, add the parsley, tomato, and a hefty grating of Parmesan cheese, about a cup or so grated on a Microplane, or ½ cup on a traditional grater. (You don't need to be precious about this.) Stir together until well mixed. Season to taste with more salt and pepper—it should taste quite well seasoned.

As the artichokes are ready, transfer them to the bowl with the garlic mixture. Once they are all finished, toss everything together, mixing with a large spoon if necessary, until everything is well combined.

Arrange the artichokes on a platter, making sure to top with any remaining bits of the garlic mixture left at the bottom of the bowl. Serve immediately.

Charred Brussels Sprouts

(with Soy and Balsamic)

SERVES 4 TO 6

I love when Brussels sprouts are left whole, to get charred on the outside but stay very tender on the inside. These are simply dressed with olive oil and salt before being cooked in a closed grill over gentle heat. Then they are tossed in a way-too-simple mixture of balsamic vinegar and soy sauce that soaks into the charred leaves. This recipe makes 2 full pounds of Brussels sprouts, because whenever I make just 1 pound, my wife eats most of them before anyone else gets to have dinner. If the grates of your grill are too far apart for the Brussels sprouts to fit, a grill pan or basket must be used instead.

These are a great side dish for when you are doing other two-zone grilling, like the Shallot-Dijon Chicken Thighs (page 139).

INGREDIENTS

- 2 pounds Brussels sprouts, brown stem-ends trimmed
- 1 tablespoon extra-virgin olive oil, plus more to finish
- Salt and freshly ground black pepper
- 2 tablespoons balsamic vinegar
- 2 tablespoons soy sauce or tamari

METHOD

Set up a two-zone fire. If grilling with gas, set one side to high and the other to medium-low. Clean and oil the grates well on the cooler side.

Place the sprouts in a large bowl and toss them with the olive oil, a generous pinch of salt, and several twists of pepper.

Lay the Brussels sprouts on the cooler side of the grill and close the lid. Check them after 10 minutes, turning them to get more color on the other side. Lower the lid and continue cooking until the sprouts are tender all the way through, about 10 more minutes, depending on size, removing cooked ones as they are finished.

While they are cooking, add the balsamic vinegar and soy sauce to the bowl that the sprouts were in. As the sprouts are cooked, add them back to the bowl. Toss well and then season to taste with more salt, if needed. Pour them onto a serving plate and drizzle with some olive oil.

Grilled and Glazed Baby Bok Choy

(with Tamari Vinaigrette)

SERVES 4 TO 6

This is an incredibly easy side dish to add on when you already have the grill going. Bok choy chars really quickly, giving you beautiful contrast between the crispy, blackened leaves and the slightly crunchy, vegetal stalks. Once charred, it gets quickly glazed with the dressing and then drizzled with more to finish.

INGREDIENTS

2 tablespoons extra-virgin olive oil
1 tablespoon rice wine vinegar
1 tablespoon toasted sesame oil
1 tablespoon tamari or soy sauce
¼ teaspoon crushed red pepper
4 heads of baby bok choy, halved lengthwise
Flaky salt

METHOD

Preheat the grill to high heat, then clean and oil the grates well.

Meanwhile, in a medium bowl, combine the olive oil, vinegar, sesame oil, tamari, and crushed red pepper. Mix it well.

Lay the dry bok choy halves cut-side down directly on the grill until they start to get some color on the stem and the leaves start to blacken, 90 seconds to 2 minutes. Flip them over and brush the cut side with the vinaigrette. Let them grill for another minute—just until the bottom gets some color. Then flip them over one more time to cook the dressed side for about 5 seconds.

Transfer them to a serving plate, cut-side up, and pour the remaining dressing over the top. Season them with a sprinkle of flaky salt. This can be served immediately, or at room temperature.

Citrus and Fennel Salad

(Grilled and Raw, with Avocado)

SERVES 4

Citrus, avocado, and fennel are a beloved salad combination in Southern California, especially as a way to eat something bright and fresh in the winter months. This recipe highlights those complementary flavors, showing off their raw beauty as well as how they change with a kiss of fire. This is an awesome way to bring some sunshine to the cold season, but it also tastes great year-round.

For the best-*looking* salad, look for a variety of oranges or a combination of any sweet-and-tart citrus you enjoy. I love a mix of navel, Cara Cara, and blood orange. Tangelos are also wonderful if you can find them. This salad is an ode to Laura from JJ's Lone Daughter Ranch here in California, who grows the best avocados and citrus, probably in the world. Her stand at the Hollywood Farmers' Market is a highlight every Sunday for my daughter and me.

INGREDIENTS

- 2 medium grapefruits
- 4 medium oranges, ideally of varying types and colors
- 2 small fennel bulbs (or 1 large one, if that's all you can find)
- 3 tablespoons extra-virgin olive oil, plus more for grilling
- Fine sea salt or kosher salt
- Freshly ground black pepper
- 1 lemon or Meyer lemon, halved
- 1 large or 2 small avocados
- 2 bunches of watercress or upland cress (or about 2 cups loosely packed baby arugula, mâche, or similar tender-leafed salad green)
- Flaky salt

METHOD

Preheat a grill to medium-high heat, then clean and oil the grates well.

Meanwhile, slice *one of* the grapefruits in half and set it aside.

Place the second grapefruit down with the stem-side up. Using a very sharp chef knife or serrated knife, cut it horizontally about ½ inch down from the top—just enough to expose the flesh of the fruit. Flip the grapefruit upside down and repeat with the other side. Now that it can stand upright, cut down the side of the grapefruit, following the curvature of the citrus to remove the peel, pith, and membrane to expose the flesh. Do this all the way around the entire fruit until there is no more outer pith. Turn the citrus on its side and cut it into rounds ½ inch or so thick, trying to release as little juice as possible. Use a fork to pick out any exposed seeds and set the slices aside. Repeat this with all four oranges.

Pick some of the small, tender fennel fronds from the fennel bulbs and set them aside. Slice off the stalks and discard them. Using a sharp knife or a mandoline, slice *one* of the fennel, starting from the stem end, into thin ribbons and place them in a medium bowl, discarding the root. Take the other fennel and slice it through the root into "steaks" ½ inch or so thick. Rub the fennel steaks with olive oil and season them with salt and pepper and set them aside.

Finally, brush the cut lemon and grapefruit halves with olive oil and take them out to the grill along with the fennel steaks.

Place the lemon and grapefruit halves cut-side down on the grill and allow them to grill until they are browned, about 4 minutes. Add the fennel steaks as well, grilling until they are golden brown with some blackened edges, about 4 minutes. Flip over and repeat with the other side.

Once cool enough to handle, squeeze the juice from the grilled grapefruit and lemon through a strainer into the bowl with the shaved fennel. Add the 3 tablespoons olive oil and toss to combine. Season to taste with salt and let marinate while you assemble the salads.

On a platter or individual plates, arrange the sliced grilled fennel, overlaid with the sliced oranges. Halve and pit the avocado, then cut it into slices and arrange it over the salad. Garnish with watercress. Lift the shaved fennel from the dressing and bunch it in the center of each plate or in the middle of the platter. Drizzle the remaining dressing over the salad, then garnish with flaky salt, pepper, and some reserved fennel fronds. Serve immediately.

Charred Cauliflower with Tahini-Yogurt Sauce

SERVES
4

In my previous cookbook I had a recipe that I just adored, in which charred vegetables got laid over chili powder–spiced drained yogurt, making a hot, creamy, acidic, beautifully balanced dish. This 2.0 version doesn't require any thickening thanks to the tahini, which eats up all of that excess liquid, while adding a delicious nutty undertone. You can *easily* substitute any vegetable here, but there is something especially wonderful about the balance of yogurt, sesame, and cauliflower. This is one of those recipes that accidentally turns into an appetizer, since everyone keeps walking by and swiping bite after bite with their hands (or asking Mom to do it for them).

INGREDIENTS

½ cup whole-milk yogurt
1 tablespoon tahini
1 tablespoon fresh lemon juice
1 tablespoon extra-virgin olive oil, plus more for coating and drizzling
1 garlic clove, grated or finely chopped
½ teaspoon smoked paprika
Salt
1 large head cauliflower
Flaky salt

METHOD

In a small bowl, whisk together the yogurt, tahini, lemon juice, olive oil, garlic, and smoked paprika, until well combined. Season to taste with salt. Leave the yogurt mixture out, covered, for up to an hour or two, or store for up to 4 days in the refrigerator. Allow it to come to room temperature before using.

Preheat the grill to medium-high heat, then clean and oil the grates well.

Meanwhile, cut the cauliflower head in half, straight through the core and the stem. Discard any leaves, then tear or cut the cauliflower into large florets. Cut the large bunches of florets down through their stems to keep them intact, into pieces that are roughly 2 inches wide (you don't want them so small that they will fall through the grates of the grill). Add the florets to a large bowl and toss them with a hefty pinch of salt and just enough olive oil to barely coat them.

Grill until the florets are starting to blacken at the edges, about 4 minutes. Turn them to blacken another side, continuing until they are just tender and have bits of blackening all over, 10 to 12 minutes total.

Once cooked, return the cauliflower to the bowl. Spread the tahini-yogurt across a serving plate, then lay the charred cauliflower on top in a single layer. Drizzle it with more olive oil and flaky salt and serve immediately.

Perfect Grilled Potatoes

SERVES
4

Want to know the secret to perfectly cooked potatoes? An instant-read thermometer. People will buy fancy thermometers to make sure that their smoked briskets and 2-inch-thick bone-in rib eyes are cooked perfectly, but when it comes to potatoes, they just stab them with a knife. But the truth is, potatoes have an ideal internal temperature for perfect fluffiness and tenderness (use this trick for baked potatoes, too!). To cook them on the grill, I like to find the smallest round potatoes I can that won't fall through the grates, so you can roll and turn them most easily.

These are just simple potatoes with olive oil and salt, and are great with all kinds of other things in this book. I adore them with many of the sauce accompaniments, like the Parsley Pesto (page 206), Ají Verde (page 144), or even just tossed with lemon juice, more olive oil, and Parmesan cheese. Grilled potatoes are also great for when different family members (or friends' kids) eat different things: Just set up a condiment bar and let them build their potatoes however they like them.

INGREDIENTS

1½ pounds small round creamy potatoes, like Magic Myrna, baby red, or Yukon Gold
About 1 tablespoon extra-virgin olive oil
Salt

METHOD

Set up a two-zone fire. If grilling with gas, set one side to high and the other to medium heat. Clean and oil the grates well.

Wash the potatoes and place them in a bowl. Toss them with the olive oil (just enough to coat them) and season them aggressively with salt. Lay the potatoes on the cooler side of the grill, being careful not pour any excess oil into the fire. Cover the grill, checking the potatoes occasionally for any flare-ups or burning, turning them as needed. Cook the potatoes until they reach an internal temperature in the range of 208° to 211°F—usually about 20 minutes, though it can really vary depending on size. As each potato finishes cooking, return it to the bowl. Once they're all off, you can also pause them as you do any other cooking, then briefly cook them on the hot side of the grill to refresh them and crisp the skin a touch, just about 1 minute.

Serve with desired condiments.

DAD HACK

It is easiest to grill these over a two-zone fire, but you can also just leave them on the coldest part of the grill while you are cooking other things. As long as you are turning your potatoes and keeping an eye on them to prevent burning, they are fairly durable. Just check for internal temperature to see when they're done.

Jimmy Nardellos with Red Yuzu Vinaigrette

SERVES 4 TO 6

Jimmy Nardello peppers have been the "ingredient of the summer" in Los Angeles for the past few years, to the point that they have found their way into farmers markets and even some grocery stores across the country. They are delicious both raw and cooked, with a crispy texture and lovely sweetness, but perhaps their greatest gift of all is their fully edible seeds. I prefer to grill them on just one side, to get char, but leave some of the raw vegetal crispness intact. The peppers are tossed in a simple-yet-luxurious vinaigrette, featuring red yuzu koshō (widely available online), a salty, fermented Japanese condiment made from yuzu citrus peels and red peppers. This recipe requires 5 minutes of active cooking and prep, all in, and kids and adults alike can eat with their bare hands, making it an absolute parenting win.

INGREDIENTS

- 2 tablespoons extra-virgin olive oil
- 2 tablespoons red yuzu koshō
- 1 tablespoon champagne vinegar
- 1 pound Jimmy Nardello peppers
- Flaky salt

METHOD

Preheat the grill to high heat and clean the grates well (no need to oil).

Meanwhile, in a large bowl, whisk together the olive oil, yuzu koshō, and champagne vinegar and set aside.

Lay the peppers (with no coating or seasoning) in a single layer over the grill. Allow them to char until lightly blackened on one side. As each pepper is finished charring, 2 to 3 minutes, flip it over and allow it to just barely kiss the heat, then add it to the bowl of yuzu vinaigrette. Once all of the peppers are finished, toss them together until well mixed. Season to taste with flaky salt and serve immediately.

Kabocha Macha

(Grilled Kabocha Squash with Salsa Macha and Lime)

SERVES 4 TO 6

Salsa macha—a nutty, spicy, and deliciously fragrant and toasty sauce that hails from Veracruz, Mexico—is made by gently frying nuts and/or seeds and dried chiles in oil, then blending them, often with a bit of vinegar. There are a lot of ways to make it, but since I often have sesame seeds, peanuts, and chiles de árbol on hand, this is the version I make. (You can substitute other nuts, or double the sesame seeds if you're peanut-averse.) Regardless, I love pairing it with grilled fall and winter squash, bringing cozy-weather flavors to a grilled vegetable side, along with some heat and acid. This side goes with anything, but is especially lovely with some Grilled Fish Tacos with Chile Crunch (page 208) or even just a simple grilled steak (Taverna Steak, page 150) or chicken (Achiote-Lime Chicken Breast, page 126).

If you can't find kabocha squash, any good roasting squash will work, but my favorite substitute is several delicata squash.

INGREDIENTS

Salsa Macha

½ cup extra-virgin olive oil
5 garlic cloves, peeled but whole
3 tablespoons raw or roasted peanuts
7 chiles de árbol (or less if you want it less spicy)
3 tablespoons raw or toasted sesame seeds
2 teaspoons red wine vinegar
Salt

Grilled Kabocha Squash

1 small-to-medium kabocha squash (3 to 3½ pounds)
Extra-virgin olive oil, for coating and drizzling
Salt and freshly ground black pepper
1 juicy lime, halved
Flaky salt

METHOD

Make the salsa macha: In a narrow (not wide) saucepan or pot, combine the olive oil and garlic cloves—if the cloves are especially large, you can slice them in half to ensure that they will be fully submerged under the oil. Set over medium heat and once the oil is gently bubbling, watch the garlic and allow it to cook until it takes on a golden-brown color and begins to blister slightly, about 3 minutes. If at any point you smell any burning or see any blackening, reduce the heat immediately. Remove the garlic with a slotted spoon and set it aside.

Add the peanuts next. If they are raw, allow them to cook for 2½ minutes. If they are already roasted, add the chiles de árbol as well and let them both cook for 90 seconds. Then, add the sesame seeds and let them cook for another 30 seconds. Transfer everything in the pan to a narrow, heat-resistant bowl. Add the vinegar, reserved garlic, and a pinch of salt.

Once it is cooled to room temperature, blend the mixture until it has a coarse texture with no big chunks. I prefer to do this with an immersion blender—just make sure that the head of the blender is fully submerged in the oil to prevent splatter. (Alternatively, blend it in a stand blender.)

Keep it at room temperature until serving, or store under refrigeration for up to 5 days.

Make the grilled kabocha squash: Preheat the grill to medium-high heat, then clean and oil the grates well.

Cut the squash in half through the stem (or just next to it, if it's too thick to cut through). Slice off the stem and the little knob on the other end and discard them. Scoop out and discard the seeds. Cut the squash into ½-inch-thick half-moons, place them in a bowl, and toss in just enough oil to barely coat. Season liberally with salt and pepper.

Lay the pieces of squash on the grill in a single layer. Once they have taken on color and are blackened in spots but not burned, about 7 minutes, flip them over. Repeat with the other side, another 6 to 7 minutes. Return them to the large bowl. Cover the bowl with a plate or metal tray and allow the squash to steam and keep warm for at least 3 minutes, or up to 2 hours (it is great at room temperature, too).

When you are ready to serve, arrange the squash on a serving platter. Squeeze the lime over them and then drizzle with more olive oil. Season with a pinch of flaky salt and then drizzle the salsa macha artfully and generously all over. Serve.

Miso-Butter Corn

SERVES 4 TO 6

This is my go-to summer BBQ side dish—grilled ears of corn slathered with a fatty, umami-laden butter that has a sky-high approval rating with kids and grown-ups alike. This recipe is inspired by the classic butter-corn topping on miso ramen, which is popular on the Japanese island of Hokkaido. It is sweet, salty, fatty, and a little bit spicy all at once. Honestly, if you just show up to a BBQ with a bowl of miso butter and a few ears of corn to throw on the grill, you will make everyone very happy in a matter of minutes.

INGREDIENTS

8 tablespoons (4 ounces/1 stick) unsalted butter, at room temperature
¼ cup white miso
2 tablespoons finely chopped fresh chives or scallions (optional)
½ teaspoon shichimi tōgarashi or chili powder
¼ teaspoon tamari or soy sauce
¼ teaspoon rice wine vinegar
Salt
4 ears corn, cut into thirds
Lime wedges, for serving

METHOD

In a medium bowl, whisk together the butter, miso, chives, shichimi, tamari, and vinegar until well combined. Season to taste with salt. Leave the butter mixture out, covered, for several hours, or store for up to 1 week in the refrigerator. Transfer the butter to a wide, shallow bowl and allow it to come to room temperature before using.

When you are ready to cook, preheat the grill to high heat, then clean and oil the grates well.

Lay the corn on the grill and char until blackened in spots, rolling and turning to get all sides, about 4 minutes total. Once each piece of corn is ready, roll it in the miso butter and serve it immediately, squeezed with lime.

DAD HACK

If you think you might be cooking these on a grill that doesn't get too hot, lightly coat the corn in oil before grilling, to aid in char and caramelization.

Buttered Soy Sauce Mushrooms

(in a Foil Pouch, with Lemon and Fresh Thyme)

SERVES
4

This is one of those "you're cheating" grill dishes, because you could absolutely just do this in the oven and it would not taste any different. But if you already have a grill going, this is an incredibly easy and delicious side to just throw onto an empty spot. Bunashimeji mushrooms (those somewhat small, long-stemmed mushrooms common in Japanese markets) are my favorite here, but any mushrooms, cut into bite-size pieces, will work. If your kids don't like these mushrooms, they don't like mushrooms.

INGREDIENTS

8 ounces bunashimeji mushrooms, tough stem end sliced off (or mushroom of choice, such as sliced shiitake caps, quartered cremini, or roughly torn oyster mushrooms)
2 tablespoons unsalted butter
2 tablespoons soy sauce
1 sprig fresh thyme (or any hard herb, such as rosemary)
1 slice lemon
Flaky salt
Freshly ground black pepper

METHOD

Preheat the grill to high or medium-high heat.

Lay out a foot-long sheet of aluminum foil. Place the mushrooms in a mound in the center of it, then top them with the butter and soy sauce. Lay the thyme sprig on top, followed by the slice of lemon. Fold up the foil on all sides, crimping it at the top to seal it so that steam won't escape.

Lay the foil pouch on the grill (even the top shelf of a grill is totally fine) and allow it to cook for 15 minutes. Remove the pouch and place it on a plate. When it is time to serve, open the pouch carefully to avoid being burned by trapped steam. Season the mushrooms immediately with a pinch of flaky salt and a few twists of pepper.

DAD HACK

If you don't want to cook in aluminum foil, you can use a small grill-safe metal pot with a lid—just keep the pot on the grill for an extra 5 minutes or so, to allow it to collect heat.

Baba Ghanoush

SERVES 6 TO 8

Baba ghanoush—the smoky, citrus-and-tahini-laden eggplant dip—is a great dish and, more important for me, one of my wife's favorites. The trick is to char whole eggplants all over to impart that smoky flavor while also making the flesh quite soft and tender, then drain off as much of the liquid as you can. While this recipe will taste just as good if you roast the eggplant in the oven, the grill makes this a whole lot easier with way less mess. Serve this with grilled pita or crudités; or alongside Shish Tawook (page 129) and "Kebab Plate" Rice (page 76).

Leftovers are a very good thing, making for an easy snack time (for kids or adults).

INGREDIENTS

2 medium Italian eggplants (2½ to 3 pounds total)
½ cup extra-virgin olive oil, plus more for drizzling
¼ cup tahini
¼ cup fresh lemon juice
2 garlic cloves, roughly chopped
Salt
2 tablespoons finely chopped fresh Italian parsley, plus more to finish
Smoked paprika, to finish

METHOD

Preheat the grill to medium-high heat, then clean the grates well (no need to oil).

Poke the eggplants all over, several times, with a fork. Place them on the grill and close the lid. Let them cook, turning occasionally, until they are charred all over and soft on the inside, 30 to 35 minutes.

Once finished, take them off the grill, and when they are cool enough to handle, cut them in half lengthwise. Place a fine-mesh strainer over a bowl, then scoop out the flesh and place it in the strainer, discarding the skin. Allow it to drain for 1 hour.

Once drained, take *half* of the eggplant and place it in a blender with the olive oil, tahini, lemon juice, and garlic. Add a hefty pinch of salt and blend it until it is fully combined and unified, then transfer it to a medium bowl. Add the remaining eggplant and the parsley. Whisk to combine, creating a smooth and chunky texture. Season to taste with more salt.

To serve, lay the baba ghanoush in a serving bowl and sprinkle with some smoked paprika, more chopped parsley, and a drizzle of olive oil.

Grilled Avocado Tostadas with Chipotle-Lime Crema

Once grilled, even so-so avocados get soft and luxurious. This recipe lays them atop a grill-crisped flour tortilla with melted cheese, with a smoky spicy, citrusy, chipotle-infused sour cream that gets drizzled over the top. This is a great, quick little appetizer or snack that you can easily scale up for a crowd.

MAKES 4 TOSTADAS

DAD HACK

Freeze leftover chipotle peppers in adobo sauce in a freezer bag, and simply slice off and chop whatever you need for future cooks.

INGREDIENTS

4 ounces (½ cup) sour cream
1 canned chipotle pepper in adobo sauce, very finely chopped
½ teaspoon adobo sauce (from the can)
A scant squeeze of lime juice
Kosher salt
1 large avocado
Extra-virgin olive oil or avocado oil
4 taco-size flour tortillas
2 ounces melting cheese (I prefer a mix of sharp cheddar and Monterey Jack), grated (about 1 cup, very loosely packed)
Flaky salt

METHOD

Set up a two-zone fire. If grilling with gas, set one side to high heat and the other to medium-low heat. Clean and oil the grates well.

In a medium bowl, combine the sour cream, chipotle, adobo sauce, and lime juice. Stir until well mixed and season to taste with salt. Set aside.

Cut the avocado in half lengthwise around the pit, then remove the pit. Cut each half again lengthwise through the middle, creating 4 long avocado quarters. Rub the cut sides with oil and place them with one of the cut sides down on the grill. Grill until they are browned with bits of blackening, about 2 minutes. Turn them and repeat with the other cut side.

Meanwhile, lay the tortillas down on the cooler side of the grill until the bottoms are golden brown and crisp, 2 to 3 minutes. Flip them over and, with the tortillas still on the grill, divide the grated cheese among the tortillas and allow it to cook until the other side is crisp and the cheese is melted.

Once off the grill, season the cooked avocados with flaky salt. Use a butter knife to cut them crosswise just through the flesh, into about 6 slices each. Once the tostadas are toasty and melted, transfer them to plates. Use a spoon to scoop out the avocado flesh and arrange it, with grill marks facing up, on the tostadas. Drizzle the tostadas with the chipotle-lime crema and serve immediately.

Fettunta

(The Best Way to Serve a Hunk of Bread)

SERVES 2 TO 3

Fettunta **(Italian for "oily slice") is, quite frankly, the best way to serve a hunk of bread: a thick slice of good bread, brushed with rather a lot of olive oil, grilled until crispy on the outside and fluffy on the inside, rubbed with raw garlic, drowned in yet more olive oil, and seasoned with flaky salt.**

People will keep asking you why it's so good, and you'll only be able to shrug. Frankly, I utterly and completely stole this recipe from one of the great chefs in the world, Nancy Silverton, when she made it at my house for an episode of our YouTube show ***Guest Chef.***

This bread goes with everything, but it's also a great thing to just put out and let the kids rip into while you sit down and enjoy a glass of wine—just remember to save yourself an oily slice.

INGREDIENTS

A 2-inch-thick slice of the best loaf of bread you can find
2 tablespoons extra-virgin olive oil, plus 2 tablespoons to finish
1 garlic clove, peeled but whole
Flaky salt

METHOD

Preheat the grill to high heat, then clean the grates well (no need to oil them).

Brush the bread thoroughly on both sides with about 2 tablespoons of the olive oil. Grill the bread, turning it every minute or so, until it is golden brown with bits of blackening at the edges, 6 to 8 minutes.

Remove it from the grill and take a raw whole garlic clove, and using either your hands or a fork, rub it all across both sides of the bread—almost like you're using the crispy bread as a grater for the garlic.

Cut the bread into thirds and place it on a plate. Drizzle it with the remaining 2 tablespoons olive oil and season it with flaky salt. Serve immediately.

OFF
LO

Mezcal Charro Beans

(with Charred Peppers and Onions)

SERVES 6 TO 8

I am a grill dad, but I am also very much a bean dad, and as such, I am a big believer in buying very good dried beans and cooking them with just water and salt to use throughout the week in everything from burritos to pastas to frijoles de olla. This recipe is an awesome way to add tons of charred vegetable flavor to a pot of hearty beans for the perfect vegetarian side dish for literally anything else in this book. You could cook this recipe with canned beans, but I *highly* recommend starting from dried. While pinto beans would be a classic move here, I use many different beans from Rancho Gordo, my favorite bean growers.

The dried beans can be cooked days in advance if necessary.

To Soak or Not to Soak: When it comes to beans, I do both! If I want beans today, I just simmer them with water and salt. If I remember that I want them tomorrow, I'll soak them before I go to bed. No matter what, as long as you cook dried beans gently in water until they are tender, you are doing a great job.

INGREDIENTS

- 1 pound dried medium beans, like pinto, King City Pink, or Caballero
- Salt
- 1 large white onion
- 1 red bell pepper
- 1 large mild-to-medium green chile, such as poblano or Anaheim
- 2 tablespoons extra-virgin olive oil, plus more to finish
- 1 garlic clove, roughly chopped
- 1 bay leaf
- 1 teaspoon smoked paprika
- 1 tablespoon mezcal or tequila
- Cotija cheese (optional), for serving

METHOD

Cook the dried beans according to the package directions, with just water and salt (see To Soak or Not to Soak, above). Set them aside.

Preheat the grill to high heat, then clean and oil the grates well.

Quarter the white onion by slicing directly through the root, keeping it attached. This will help to hold the onion together while you grill it, and give you three solid sides to char on each quarter. Remove the peels and discard them. Lay the onion quarters on the hot grill, flipping them over once each side is charred, 2 to 3 minutes per side. At the same time, add the bell pepper and chile to the grill as well, turning as needed until they are charred all over, about 6 minutes.

Transfer the peppers to a bowl and cover them with a plate, allowing them to steam until they are cool enough to handle. Meanwhile, roughly dice the charred onions, discarding the root. Once the peppers are cool enough to touch, peel the charred skin and discard it, then remove the stems and seeds. Dice the peppers.

In a large saucepot, heat the olive oil over high heat until shimmering. Add the onion, peppers, garlic, and bay leaf. Season them with salt and sauté, stirring occasionally, for about 2 minutes. Stir in the smoked paprika and let it toast for about 30 seconds, then add the mezcal and deglaze the pan. Once the mezcal is cooked off, reduce the heat to medium.

Use a slotted spoon or spider strainer to transfer the beans to the pot of onions and peppers, leaving most of the liquid behind. Once all of the beans are in the pot, add enough of the bean liquid to just barely cover them. Increase the heat to high and bring the pot to a strong simmer. Continue simmering until the liquid has thickened a bit, and the beans have a stew-like consistency, about 3 minutes. Season the beans to taste with salt.

Serve warm, drizzled with more olive oil and Cotija cheese if you desire.

“Kebab Plate” Rice

(with Charred Tomato, Shallot, and Green Chile)

SERVES 4 TO 6

I’ve eaten a lot of Lebanese and Armenian grill plates in my life, and they almost always come with rice, a grilled tomato, a grilled green chile, and some form of a grilled onion. I always end up cutting the vegetables up and mashing them together with the rice, and this is kind of my homage to that, as a complete rice side, with a few personal tweaks.

This recipe is also a bit of a Dad Hack unto itself: Once you have a pot of rice or a rice cooker going, all it takes is a few aromatics on the grill to make a near-instant, hearty side that everyone loves.

INGREDIENTS

1½ cups jasmine rice, washed
1 long mild-to-medium green chile, such as Anaheim or poblano
1 medium shallot
1 medium or 2 small Roma tomatoes
Salt
2 tablespoons extra-virgin olive oil
2 tablespoons fresh lemon juice
1 tablespoon soy sauce
Freshly ground black pepper

METHOD

Preheat the grill to high heat, then clean and oil the grates well.

In a pot or rice cooker, cook the jasmine rice according to the package directions and keep covered to stay warm.

Meanwhile, prepare the vegetables: Halve the chile lengthwise, then remove the stem and seeds. Cut the shallot in half through the root, keeping each half intact, and remove and discard the peels. Place the chile and shallot cut-side down on the grill, then lay the whole tomato (or tomatoes) down as well. Turn the tomato as it chars, until it is blackened in bits all over, 3 to 4 minutes total.

Once the cut side of the chile is charred and softened, about 3 minutes, flip it over and grill the other side just until the skin is blistered and browning but not charred (a minute or so), then remove it. Once the first side of the shallot is quite charred, 2 to 3 minutes, flip it over and repeat with the other side.

Once the vegetables are cool enough to handle, remove and discard the shallot root, then roughly dice the tomato, shallot, and chile and season them with salt. Fold them into the warm rice, along with the olive oil, lemon juice, and soy sauce. Season the rice to taste with salt and pepper and serve.

Big Salads

Southwest Veggie Chop 82
Spicy Grilled Chicken Caesar
with Garlic Bread Croutons 85
Grilled Chicken Tricolore
with Charred Pepperoncini Vinaigrette 88
Peanut-Miso Steak and Soba Salad 91
Grilled Shrimp Niçoise. 92
Sausage and Peppers Pasta Salad 95

Contrary to popular belief, one of the absolute best ways to incorporate everyday grilling into your life is with big, meal-size salads. An ordinary fridge salad takes on so much flavor once you throw some chicken breast, or a thin steak, or a slew of vegetables onto the fire to get some char, giving accent and texture.

This section shows off one of my favorite tricks for salads: dry-grilling certain vegetables with no oil or seasoning whatsoever. This gives them char and removes moisture, so that once you toss them in dressing, they become sponges, soaking up all of the extra flavor without leaking their own water into the salad.

This chapter shows you how to make Big Salads that are complete meals unto themselves (or a great side dish for a party), with supercharged flavor from things like grilled garlic bread croutons, a grilled pickled pepper vinaigrette, charred scallion Green Goddess dressing, or quick-charred proteins and vegetables.

Feel free to substitute any of the proteins for whatever you might prefer.

Southwest Veggie Chop

(with Charred Scallion Green Goddess)

SERVES
3 TO 4

This is one of the catchall salads that gets made all the time in my house. It is huge, loaded with veggies, lots of zip, and a hint of spice that fills you up and keeps you light on your feet (or at your desk). You can even get a head start on it when you have the time: The vegetables can be grilled a day in advance and served cold or at room temperature, and the dressing can be made up to a day in advance. I also like to grill any extra vegetables I have on hand while I'm at it, and set them aside for quick weeknight family meals, like tossing them into a quesadilla, a pot of beans, or a quick pasta.

Feel free to substitute any vegetables you like (or any leftover grilled vegetables) for this salad—it really is perfect for clearing out your fridge. I also try to cook as seasonally as possible, and have listed my favorite vegetables to add to the ones in the main recipe during each season.

INGREDIENTS

Seasonal Add-Ins

Fall: 1 delicata squash, cut into ½-inch-thick rings, seeded
Winter: 1 small-to-medium head broccoli or cauliflower, cut into florets
Spring: 1 bunch of asparagus, woody ends snapped off
Summer: 1 ear corn, shucked

Seasonal add-in vegetable
1 medium zucchini, quartered into spears
1 yellow squash, quartered into spears
4 scallions
1 serrano chile
1 ice cube
¼ cup extra-virgin olive oil
3 tablespoons mayonnaise
2 tablespoons fresh lime juice
2 tablespoons red wine vinegar
¼ cup tightly packed fresh cilantro leaves and tender stems
Salt
2 heads leafy lettuce, such as red leaf romaine, washed and roughly diced (or about 8 cups loosely packed washed lettuce)
1¾ cups cooked black beans or a 15-ounce can, drained and rinsed
1 English or 3 Persian (mini) cucumbers, medium-diced
1 orange bell pepper, medium-diced
1 avocado, medium-diced
¼ cup roasted pepitas (pumpkin seeds), either salted or unsalted
About ¼ cup finely grated Cotija, white cheddar, or Parmesan cheese

METHOD

Preheat the grill to high heat, then clean and oil the grates well.

Once preheated, place the seasonal vegetable, zucchini, squash, scallions, and serrano on the grill with no oil or seasoning whatsoever. Grill each until they are charred but tender, turning as needed, 2 to 4 minutes total, depending on the vegetable and its thickness. They are all fairly forgiving—just err on the side of undercooked rather than over (crunchy is better than mushy when it comes to salad). The exceptions are the serrano and scallions, which you want to make sure are fully charred all over.

Set the vegetables aside until cool enough to handle. Remove the stem and seeds from the serrano (or keep the seeds in for a spicier dressing) and then set about making the dressing.

In a blender, combine (in this order) the ice cube, olive oil, mayo, lime juice, vinegar, cilantro, scallions, and serrano. Season with a heavy pinch of salt and blend until smooth. Season to taste with salt.

Cut the remaining grilled vegetables into medium dice (or in the case of the corn, simply cut it off the cob).

Add the lettuce to a quite large bowl (or if necessary, a soup pot), along with the grilled vegetables, the black beans, cucumbers, bell pepper, and avocado. Pour in the dressing and toss until well mixed. Season to taste with salt and serve in a large serving bowl or individual salad bowls, topped with the pepitas and Cotija.

Spicy Grilled Chicken Caesar with Garlic Bread Croutons

SERVES
4

I adore a classic Caesar salad: all brightness and funk and crunch. But sometimes a recipe calls for maximalism, and this salad throws flavor at you from all sides while keeping the spirit of the original. Hot pickled peppers add spice and extra zing to the dressing, offering a punchy counterpoint to the charred, marinated chicken, and a garlic butter–soaked baguette gets grilled and chopped into simultaneously blackened, crunchy, and tender croutons.

This is also an ideal make-ahead dish or potluck recipe. The chicken can be hot, room temperature, or cold; the dressing can be made days in advance; and the croutons are great at room temperature. On a work-from-home day, I will often prep all the ingredients after my daughter goes to school, then fire up the grill about an hour before dinner. Then when it's time to eat, it's just a matter of tossing and serving.

INGREDIENTS

Marinated Chicken

3 garlic cloves, grated or very finely chopped
2 tablespoons fresh lemon juice
3 tablespoons extra-virgin olive oil
1½ teaspoons kosher salt
20 twists of freshly ground black pepper
1 pound boneless, skinless chicken breasts (usually about 2)

Marinated Garlic Bread Croutons

1 baguette, fresh or day-old is fine
½ teaspoon granulated garlic
1 teaspoon water
4 tablespoons (2 ounces/½ stick) unsalted butter
¼ cup extra-virgin olive oil
5 garlic cloves, grated or very finely chopped
1 tablespoon chopped fresh Italian parsley
½ teaspoon smoked paprika
½ teaspoon dried oregano
1 tablespoon fresh lemon juice

(continued)

METHOD

Marinate the chicken: In a wide resealable container or ziplock bag, combine the garlic, lemon juice, olive oil, salt, and pepper and stir it until well mixed.

Lay a chicken breast flat on a cutting board. Press your nondominant hand, palm down, on the top of the chicken breast. Starting on the thicker side, use a sharp knife to slice the chicken breast in half horizontally to make 2 cutlets. Repeat this with the second breast. Add them to the marinade, making sure each cutlet is fully coated. Marinate in the refrigerator, covered, for at least 1 hour and up to 12.

Marinate the garlic bread croutons: Use a bread knife to slice the baguette in half horizontally. Then slice the baguette crosswise into thirds (creating 6 total pieces of bread).

In a small saucepan, combine the granulated garlic and water and stir, allowing the garlic to bloom for about 30 seconds. Add the butter, olive oil, fresh garlic, parsley, smoked paprika, oregano, and lemon juice. Set over medium heat. Once the butter is melted, lower the heat to maintain a very bare simmer. Simmer for about 2 minutes, then turn off the heat.

If you are going to marinate the baguettes in a heatproof container (like a glass container or rectangular baking dish), pour the garlic butter right into the container. If you are using a ziplock bag, allow it to cool to room temperature.

Add the baguette slices to the container, then toss them until well coated. Cover them and allow them to marinate for at least 30 minutes and up to 6 hours, at room temperature.

Make the spicy Caesar dressing: In a blender or food processor (or in a tall narrow container, like a deli quart, if you want to use an immersion blender), combine the egg yolks, anchovies, Parmesan, lemon juice, garlic, pickled peppers, Worcestershire sauce, and mustard. Twist in the pepper and add a hefty pinch of salt. Blend the mixture until smooth, then, with the machine running, drizzle in the neutral oil until emulsified, 5 to 10 seconds. Transfer the dressing to a medium bowl and whisk in the olive oil. Season to taste with salt, pepper, and additional lemon juice. Keep the dressing refrigerated in an airtight container for up to 3 days.

Spicy Caesar Dressing
2 egg yolks
4 anchovy fillets
½ cup grated Parmesan cheese
¼ cup fresh lemon juice, plus more to taste
3 garlic cloves, roughly chopped
1 tablespoon chopped hot pickled peppers, such as Mama Lil's
½ teaspoon Worcestershire sauce
¼ teaspoon Dijon mustard
About 15 twists of freshly ground black pepper, plus more to taste
Salt
⅔ cup neutral oil, such as avocado or canola
3 tablespoons extra-virgin olive oil

To Finish
Flaky salt
Freshly ground black pepper
3 large heads romaine, leaves chopped into roughly 1½-inch pieces
1 large head bitter lettuce, such as frisée or radicchio, or 4 small heads Belgian endive, chopped into roughly 1½-inch pieces
Freshly grated Parmesan cheese

To finish: Set up a two-zone fire. If grilling with gas, set one side to high heat and the other to medium heat. Clean and oil the grates well.

Place the lettuces in a very large salad bowl (or soup pot, if you don't have a big enough salad bowl). Set aside while you grill the croutons and chicken.

Place the marinated baguette pieces over the medium heat, turning frequently, until the crust is crisp and the bread has some bits of blackening on the edges, about 5 minutes. Some flare-ups may occur thanks to all of the fat, so if that happens just be careful to move the baguettes away from those areas as needed. Once it comes off the grill, season the bread with flaky salt and pepper.

At the same time you are cooking the garlic bread (or after, if you would prefer), lay the chicken cutlets on the hottest part of the grill, making sure to lift them up and let the marinade drain from them before you lay them over the fire. Allow them to cook until they are well browned on the first side, about 4 minutes. Flip them over and grill until just cooked through, about 2 more minutes.

Once cooled, chop the baguette pieces into roughly 1-inch croutons and add them to the large salad bowl with the greens. When the chicken has rested for at least a minute, cut it into ½-inch-thick slices.

Toss the salad and croutons with the dressing until well mixed. Taste for seasoning, and adjust with more salt if needed. Top with the chicken breast and then finish it with more Parmesan and pepper. Serve immediately.

Grilled Chicken Tricolore with Charred Pepperoncini Vinaigrette

SERVES
4

I could eat this for lunch every day of the week and feel great about it. It has *lots* of different flavors and textures working together: chicken, radicchio, and skewered pickled pepperoncini get charred on the grill, then incorporated back into a shredded salad that gathers beautifully on your fork. Crunchy toasted almonds, fresh mozzarella and basil, torn dates and sliced sun-dried tomatoes, shaved Parmesan cheese, and a fast vinaigrette that incorporates the chopped-up grilled peppers—this is the salad you would plan a lunch date around, or a great afternoon meal for the whole family.

Note: If you are using a wooden skewer instead of a metal one for the pepperoncini, soak it in water for at least 30 minutes.

INGREDIENTS

1½ pounds boneless, skinless chicken breasts (usually 2 or 3)
2 tablespoons fresh lemon juice
1 tablespoon plus ¼ cup olive oil
Salt and freshly ground black pepper
1 teaspoon granulated garlic
½ cup sliced almonds
¼ cup sherry vinegar, champagne vinegar, or red wine vinegar
1 garlic clove, grated or finely chopped
1 teaspoon Dijon mustard
1 teaspoon honey
8 pickled pepperoncini
1 head radicchio, quartered through the stem
5 ounces arugula leaves
3 heads endive, sliced crosswise into ¼-inch or so ribbons
1 cup loosely packed sliced fresh basil leaves
8 ounces fresh mozzarella
¼ cup oil-packed sun-dried tomatoes, drained and thinly sliced
6 dates, pitted and quartered
Parmesan cheese

METHOD

Lay a chicken breast flat on a cutting board. Press your nondominant hand, palm down, on the top of the chicken breast. Starting on the thicker side, use a sharp knife to slice the chicken breast in half horizontally to make 2 cutlets. Repeat this with the remaining chicken breasts.

In a large bowl, combine the lemon juice and 1 tablespoon olive oil. Season the chicken liberally on both sides with salt and pepper, then sprinkle with the granulated garlic. Lay the chicken cutlets in the bowl and toss them to coat well. Allow the chicken to marinate in the refrigerator for at least 30 minutes and up to 6 hours.

In a small saucepan, toast the almonds over medium-high heat, stirring frequently, until they are golden brown, about 3 minutes. Set them aside.

When you are ready to grill, preheat the grill to high heat, then clean and oil the grates well.

In a medium bowl, whisk together the remaining ¼ cup olive oil, the vinegar, grated garlic, mustard, and honey. Season to taste with salt and pepper. Set the vinaigrette aside.

Meanwhile, spear the pepperoncini in a single row with a metal or soaked wooden skewer. Lay the pepperoncini on the grill, followed by the radicchio wedges (these are grilled totally dry). Allow the pepperoncini to cook until it is slightly blackened on one side, 3 to 4 minutes, then repeat with the other side for another 2 to 3 minutes. Set aside. Once the first side of the radicchio is nicely charred, about 2 minutes, flip it over and char the second side. Repeat with the third side of the wedge. Once they are all charred, remove them and set them aside.

Next, grill the chicken, discarding any remaining marinade. Allow it to cook until the first side of each cutlet is nicely browned with bits of blackening around the edges, about 4 minutes. Then flip it over and grill the other side until the chicken is cooked through, about 2 more minutes. Set it aside and let it cool.

Remove the pepperoncini from the skewers and give them a good chop, then fold them into the vinaigrette. Taste it again and season with salt as needed.

In a large salad bowl (or a big pot if need be), combine the arugula, endive, and sliced basil. Cut the radicchio into thin ribbons, discarding the stem end, and add it to the salad as well. Pull the mozzarella into shreds and add it to the salad, followed by the sun-dried tomatoes and dates. By now the chicken should be cool enough to handle. Pull it into shreds and add it to the salad. Pour in the vinaigrette and toss everything until it is well mixed. Season to taste with additional salt, then scatter the almonds over the top. Shave Parmesan cheese over the top with a vegetable peeler and finish it with a few more twists of pepper. Serve immediately.

Peanut-Miso Steak and Soba Salad

(with a Crunchy, Shredded Vegetable Rainbow)

SERVES
4

This simple steak is part of a complete meal in a bowl, loaded with protein, raw vegetables, fiber, starch, and a whisk-and-go nutty, spicy, bright dressing; and all of the components are perfectly chopstick grabbable. It's just a great way to feed your family with lots of flavor and nutrition. This feeds four full-grown adults (or probably two teenage boys), but you can make all of the components and keep them separate, just tossing together as much as you want to eat at a time, and setting the rest aside for future meals. Since the steak can be served cold or at room temperature, feel free to cook it in advance. You can also substitute any quick-cooking cut of steak you like for this, like a pounded sirloin, or a thinner rib eye or New York strip.

This would also make a *very* good vegetarian dish with the tofu from the Tofu Bánh Mì with Lemongrass BBQ Sauce (page 22).

INGREDIENTS

Peanut-Miso Dressing
¼ cup creamy peanut butter
¼ cup extra-virgin olive oil
3 tablespoons white or yellow miso
2 tablespoons rice wine vinegar
1 tablespoon soy sauce
1 tablespoon water
2 teaspoons chili crisp or chili oil
1 teaspoon honey

Veggie-Soba Mix
7 cups shredded red cabbage (from 1 small head)
4 medium or 2 large carrots, shredded
4 Persian (mini) cucumbers, cut into batons (a mandoline with a julienne setting speeds this up)
1 red or orange bell pepper, cut into thin strips
2 scallions, thinly sliced
1 bunch of cilantro, leaves and tender stems, thinly sliced
1 (9.5-ounce) package dried soba noodles

Grilled Steak and Salad
1 pound sirloin flap (bavette)
Neutral oil
Salt and freshly ground black pepper
1 teaspoon granulated garlic
¼ cup salted roasted peanuts
1 tablespoon toasted sesame seeds
1 lime, quartered

METHOD

Make the peanut-miso dressing: In a bowl, whisk together the peanut butter, olive oil, miso, vinegar, soy sauce, water, chili crisp, and honey. Set aside.

Make the veggie-soba mix: In a large salad bowl, combine the cabbage, carrots, cucumbers, bell pepper, scallions, and cilantro.

Bring a large pot of water to a boil and cook the soba according to the package directions. Drain and rinse under cold running water, then drain well and toss with the vegetables.

Grill the steak and assemble the salad: Preheat the grill to high heat, then clean and oil the grates well.

Rub the steak with just enough neutral oil to barely coat, then season it all over with salt and pepper and the granulated garlic. Grill the steak over high heat, flipping frequently, until it reaches an internal temperature of around 135°F, about 5 minutes. Remove the steak and allow it to rest.

Dress the soba and vegetables with the dressing and toss. Add the roasted peanuts and toss well to combine thoroughly. Divide the salad among four wide bowls, making sure to get a relatively even distribution of soba and vegetables.

Slice the steak thinly, against the grain, and divide it over the four salads. Garnish with sesame seeds and a lime quarter.

Grilled Shrimp Niçoise

(with Fresh Tarragon Vinaigrette)

SERVES
2

My wife loves a Niçoise salad—it is basically girl dinner, laid atop a bed of lettuce. This version follows that same principle, but uses the power of the grill to substitute beautifully charred shrimp and crispy-skinned potatoes for the more common tuna and boiled potatoes. To stand up to and contrast against the strong grill flavors, I love using snap peas, cucumbers, and a bright fresh herb vinaigrette with Dijon, shallots, champagne vinegar, and tarragon.

INGREDIENTS

Fresh Tarragon Dressing
½ cup extra-virgin olive oil
¼ cup champagne vinegar or white wine vinegar
2 tablespoons lightly packed fresh tarragon leaves
1 tablespoon sliced shallot
1 teaspoon Dijon mustard

Niçoise Salad
2 large eggs
8 ounces small fingerling potatoes
Salt
1 tablespoon mayonnaise
1 tablespoon Dijon mustard
1 teaspoon smoked paprika
12 ounces peeled large or jumbo shrimp

Assembly
6 ounces snap peas
4 heads Little Gem or 1 large head romaine, leaves cut roughly into large dice
½ cup Niçoise olives
1 English cucumber or 2 Persian (mini) cucumbers, cut into ½-inch pieces
½ cup halved cherry tomatoes, or 1 large tomato, cut roughly into large dice (whichever you can find the best, ripest version of)
Flaky salt
Freshly ground black pepper

METHOD

Make the fresh tarragon dressing: In a blender, combine the olive oil, vinegar, tarragon, shallot, and mustard and blend until smooth with specks of herb. This dressing will last for up to 3 days in the refrigerator, but is best the same day.

Make the Niçoise salad: Place the eggs in a medium pot and cover them well with water. Bring to a boil over high heat, then lower the heat to a simmer and cook for 7 minutes. Set up a bowl of ice and water and set it near the stove. Once the eggs are cooked, transfer them to the ice bath.

Add the potatoes to the pot and season very aggressively with salt. Return to a strong simmer and allow to simmer for 4 minutes. Drain the potatoes and let cool.

In a medium bowl, combine the mayo, mustard, smoked paprika, and a pinch of salt. Stir well, then add the shrimp and mix until they are well coated.

Preheat the grill to high heat, then clean and oil the grates well.

Place the potatoes on the grill and allow them to grill, turning as needed, until they are tender and the skin is crispy all over, about 4 minutes. Lay the shrimp on the grill, allowing it to get char and color on the bottom side, 2 to 3 minutes. Flip them over and allow them to finish grilling until just tender, 1 to 2 more minutes.

Assemble the salad: As the potatoes and shrimp cool, you can begin to assemble the salad. Peel the eggs and halve or quarter them lengthwise. Snap off the stem ends of the snap peas and peel the attached strand down the seam like a zipper and discard them. Cut the snap peas in half at an angle.

In a large bowl, toss the lettuce with half of the tarragon dressing.

Divide the lettuce between two large, wide salad bowls. Atop the lettuce, arrange the snap peas, potatoes, olives, cucumbers, and tomatoes. Drizzle the remaining dressing over the top and sprinkle with flaky salt. Finish with a few twists of pepper and serve immediately.

Sausage and Peppers Pasta Salad

SERVES 4 TO 8, DEPENDING ON HOW MUCH PASTA YOU EAT

This pasta is a far cry from mayo-loaded "macaroni salad," adding the char and smoky flavor of a backyard BBQ while playing off the classic Italian American combo of sausage and peppers. It gets loaded up with red wine vinegar, olive oil, soft herbs, and fresh mozzarella until it hits all the pleasure centers, and is great at room temperature or cold out of the fridge the next day. As a kid who grew up eating *a lot* of pasta (and as a dad who still cooks a lot of pasta), this is one of my favorite things to make for my family or bring to a potluck BBQ. It's also the recipe that taught me how much *both* of my kids like a smoky, grilled sausage.

Smoked sausage is ideal here—whether you smoke-grill it yourself (page 36) or buy it presmoked and throw it on a gas grill. My favorite sausage for this is a smoked salt-and-pepper pork sausage. But even a savory smoked chicken sausage would work really well here.

INGREDIENTS

- 2 red bell peppers
- 2 large mild green chiles, such as poblano or Anaheim
- 2 large or 4 medium shallots (about 8 ounces)
- 12 ounces smoked sausage, ideally salt-and-pepper smoked pork or chicken sausage
- Salt
- 1 pound dried pasta (I prefer fusilli)
- 3 tablespoons extra-virgin olive oil
- 3 tablespoons red wine vinegar
- ½ cup roughly chopped fresh basil leaves or other soft herbs, such as cilantro or Italian parsley
- Freshly ground black pepper
- 12 ounces small fresh mozzarella balls (ciliegine) or hand-torn fresh mozzarella
- A squeeze of lemon

METHOD

Set up a two-zone fire. If grilling with gas, set one side to high heat and the other to medium-low heat. Clean and oil the grates well.

While it is preheating, halve the bell peppers and mild chiles lengthwise. Remove and discard the stem and seeds and then slice the peppers in half again, lengthwise, to end up with long quartered strips.

Identify the root end of the shallots, then cut off the opposite tip and discard it. Slice the shallots in half lengthwise, through the root, then peel off and discard the skin.

Lay the sausage on the cooler side of the grill, turning them occasionally to keep from bursting.

On the hot side, lay down the shallots and peppers. Allow the peppers to grill until they are just starting to char around the edges, about 3 minutes. Flip them and repeat with the other side. Once the peppers are just tender and blackened in small bits, they can be removed from the grill.

Meanwhile, allow the shallots to cook until they are fully blackened, 5 to 6 minutes. Then flip them over and repeat with the other side until it is fully blackened, too. Remove them from the grill.

Once the sausages are warmed through (they should have an internal temperature of about 150°F), about 10 minutes, move them to the hotter part of the grill to char the outside, turning occasionally. Once they have some char and color to them, they can be removed from the grill.

Meanwhile, bring a large pot of heavily salted water to a boil. Add the pasta and cook until it is just al dente according to the package directions. Drain and add to a large bowl. Season it immediately with the olive oil and red wine vinegar.

Slice the peppers, crosswise, into roughly ½-inch-wide strips and add them to the pasta. Remove the roots from the shallots and discard them, then finely chop the charred shallots and add them to the bowl as well. Cut the sausage into ½-inch-thick slices and add that, too, along with the soft herbs. Mix well and season to taste with salt and pepper. Add the mozzarella and taste again, seasoning to taste.

Finish it with a squeeze of lemon and serve at room temperature.

Vegetarian
Mains

Mediterranean Quinoa with
Grilled Halloumi and Charred Fennel 100
Mabo-Stuffed Mushrooms with Yaki-Onigiri . . . 102
Stuffed Poblanos with Cilantro-Lime Tahini 105
Grilled Veggie Burritos 107
Huevos Divorciados 109
Salsa Ranchera and Salsa Verde 110
Grilled Spaghetti Squash with
Charred Cherry Tomato Sauce 112
Blackened Broccoli-Cheddar Split Pea Soup . . . 115
Smoked Potato Tacos 117

Growing up in Southern California with semi-hippie parents, I have had more than my fair share of '90s vegetarian health food. While I have a lot of fondness for that food, it also got *very* repetitive. Grilled vegetarian food was usually some combination of veggie burgers, tofu dogs, or a grilled portobello mushroom cap on a whole wheat bun. All of them came with an off-brand "health food" ketchup that was *definitely* worse than Heinz.

But as I will advocate over and over again, the grill is your opportunity to add texture and flavor to all kinds of food. This chapter is all about food that *anyone* will be happy to eat, regardless of whether they are a vegetarian. I also wanted to show off the myriad ways to use a grill to improve a vegetable: how even a pot of soup can be made more delicious with a little bit of direct fire. I want to teach my kids that *lots* of food can be delicious, and a lot of it happens to be vegetarian.

Mediterranean Quinoa with Grilled Halloumi and Charred Fennel

SERVES
4

This is the nutrient-dense, briny, veggie-loaded, light-but-filling meal that my wife "could eat every single day." Halloumi—a salty Cypriot cheese with an extremely high melting temperature—is perfect for grilling and adding a hot, "meaty" element to a totally vegetarian main course. The grilled fennel adds some beautiful charred, savory sweetness to this hot-and-cold dish that is a perfect lunch year-round, or a delightful thing to eat on a hot summer night. It also holds up surprisingly well in a kid's lunch box.

DAD HACK

If you can't find Halloumi, you can substitute paneer cheese (usually available in Indian markets)—just keep in mind it is frequently softer and far less salty than Halloumi. Meanwhile, if you can't find good, sweet cherry tomatoes, you can substitute a diced red bell pepper. In a pinch, you can also swap out a teaspoon of dried oregano leaves for the fresh ones.

INGREDIENTS

Fresh Oregano Vinaigrette

¼ cup extra-virgin olive oil
¼ cup fresh lemon juice
1 tightly packed tablespoon fresh oregano leaves
1 garlic clove, peeled but whole
½ teaspoon honey
Salt and freshly ground black pepper

Mediterranean Quinoa and Grilled Halloumi

1 cup quinoa, rinsed
1 fennel bulb, rinsed of any dirt
Extra-virgin olive oil
Salt
8 ounces Halloumi cheese, cut into 4 wide slices
1 English cucumber, diced
1 cup cherry tomatoes, halved
¼ cup pitted dry-cured black olives or Kalamata olives
1 tablespoon minced shallot
Freshly ground black pepper

METHOD

Make the fresh oregano vinaigrette: In a blender, combine the olive oil, lemon juice, oregano, garlic, and honey and blend until smooth. Season to taste with salt and pepper.

Make the Mediterranean quinoa and grilled Halloumi: Preheat the grill to high heat, then clean and oil the grates well.

Cook the quinoa according to the package directions, then leave it covered while you prepare the remaining ingredients.

Slice off and discard the fennel stalks, but set the fronds aside for later. Cut the fennel through the root end (to keep it intact) into wide planks roughly ¼ inch thick. Brush it all over with olive oil and season it with salt, then brush the Halloumi all over with olive oil as well.

Lay the fennel down on the grill and allow it to turn golden brown with some charring, about 3 minutes, then flip it over and repeat with the other side. At the same time, lay down the Halloumi and grill until is golden brown with some crisping at the edges, about 2 minutes, then flip it over and repeat with the other side.

Transfer the quinoa to a large bowl and add the cucumber, cherry tomatoes, olives, and shallot. Dice the grilled fennel, discarding the hard root end, and add it to the quinoa. Pour in the vinaigrette and toss until well mixed. Season to taste with salt and pepper. Lay the quinoa down in individual bowls or on a large serving platter, topped with the grilled Halloumi. Garnish with torn fennel fronds.

Mabo-Stuffed Mushrooms with Yaki-Onigiri

SERVES
4

Growing up, I ate a lot of portobello mushrooms in place of meat, almost always soaked with either pesto or balsamic vinegar. This is *not that.* Instead, I stuff portobello mushroom caps with a Japanese-style mabo tofu—using the natural juices of the mushroom to create a kind of vegetarian stock. Since mabo tofu is usually served with rice, this one comes with a grilled Japanese rice patty (yaki-onigiri), round instead of triangular because it shapes so easily with a cookie cutter or wide-mouth mason jar lid. The result is, I think, a whole lot better than the mushroom "steaks" of my childhood. As of this writing, this is too spicy for my kids to eat, but boy do they like chewing on the yaki-onigiri.

INGREDIENTS

3½ tablespoons soy sauce or gluten-free tamari
1½ tablespoons sake
1½ tablespoons mirin
1½ tablespoons white or yellow miso
3 scallions, finely chopped, whites and greens kept separate
1 teaspoon grated fresh ginger
1 teaspoon doubanjiang (chili bean sauce)
1 teaspoon neutral oil, plus more for brushing
1 garlic clove, grated or finely chopped
1 pound firm silken tofu, patted dry
4 portobello mushrooms
Salt
1½ teaspoons sugar
1 cup short-grain Japanese rice or sushi rice, cooked according to package directions
1½ teaspoons toasted sesame oil
Chili crisp, for garnish (I prefer Fly By Jing Sichuan Chili Crisp)

METHOD

Set up a two-zone fire. If grilling with gas, set one side to high heat and leave the other side off. Clean the grates well (no need to oil yet).

In a large bowl, combine 2 tablespoons of the soy sauce, the sake, mirin, miso, scallion whites, ginger, doubanjiang, neutral oil, and garlic. Whisk to combine the ingredients until well mixed. Cut the tofu into roughly ½-inch cubes and fold them into the mixture.

Remove the stems from the mushrooms and discard them. Brush the cap of each mushroom with neutral oil and season lightly with salt. Set the mushrooms, stemmed-side up, on a baking sheet and divide the tofu mixture among them, mounding the tofu in the center of each mushroom so that it sits relatively stable. Lay the mushrooms on the cooler side of the grill. Cover the grill and allow the mushrooms to cook until they are tender throughout and the tofu is warmed all the way through, 25 to 30 minutes.

Meanwhile, in a bowl in a microwave, or a small saucepan on the stove, combine the remaining 1½ tablespoons soy sauce and the sugar and warm it until the sugar is just dissolved. Place the warm cooked rice in a medium bowl and pour in the soy-sugar mixture and the sesame oil, along with a small pinch of salt. Mix it with a rice paddle or spoon using a slicing motion until it is all incorporated. Next, take a wide-mouth mason jar lid or 3-inch cookie cutter and lay it down on a flat surface. Lay a sheet of plastic wrap over it and then stuff some of the rice into it so that it fills the lid. Fold the plastic wrap over and then twist it to tighten it. Press on the rice through the plastic until it takes on the round shape of the lid, like a burger patty. Open the plastic and take out the onigiri and set it aside. Repeat with the remaining rice until you have 4 onigiri. (If you have extra rice, you can make additional onigiri.)

Once the mushrooms are cooked and ready, open the lid and oil the grill grates on the hot side, then lay the onigiri on the hot side of the grill. Cook until they are mostly golden brown with small bits of blackening, 60 to 90 seconds, then flip them over and repeat with the other side. Transfer the yaki-onigiri and mushrooms back to the baking sheet.

Lay each yaki-onigiri on a plate, then lay the mushroom next to it, lightly overlapping on top. Drizzle it to taste with chili crisp and sprinkle the scallion greens over the top. Serve immediately.

Stuffed Poblanos with Cilantro-Lime Tahini

SERVES
4

This a visual stunner of a main course, and perfect for a meal that wants a vegetarian option. Peppers get stuffed and wrapped in foil, which means they are incredibly easy to add to the grill and don't require any special attention. Meanwhile, the blender-simple cilantro-lime tahini is a nutty, bright, and gorgeous-green sauce that makes this a showstopping vegetarian riff on the classic Mexican dish of chiles en nogada (stuffed poblano peppers covered with a white walnut-cream sauce).

The peppers can be stuffed and left at room temperature for 3 or 4 hours before grilling.

INGREDIENTS

½ cup long-grain white rice
4 large poblano chiles
6 ounces tomatoes, diced
3 ounces Monterey Jack cheese or preferred melting cheese, diced or grated
Salt and freshly ground black pepper
2 tablespoons extra-virgin olive oil, plus more for drizzling
¼ cup tightly packed fresh cilantro leaves and tender stems, plus more leaves for garnish
¼ cup fresh lime juice
¼ cup water
3 tablespoons tahini
1 teaspoon agave or honey
Toasted sesame seeds, for garnish

DAD HACK
If you don't want to cook in aluminum foil, you can lay all four peppers in a single layer in a grill-safe metal pot with a lid—just keep the pot on the grill for an extra 5 minutes or so, to allow it to collect heat.

METHOD

Cook the rice according to the package directions.

Meanwhile, lay the poblanos on a cutting board. Cut a T-shaped slit in one of the peppers, with the horizontal cross going along the stem end of the pepper and the vertical line going down the length of it. Gently peel open the flaps at the top of the T and then slide the knife down and cut out the bulb of seeds and remove it. Repeat this with all four peppers.

Once the rice is cooked, add it to a medium bowl along with the diced tomatoes and cheese. Toss it well to mix and season it with salt and pepper. Stuff the rice mixture into the poblanos, filling each one as much as possible. Lay out 4 large sheets of aluminum foil and place a stuffed pepper in the center of each one. Drizzle them with olive oil and then season them liberally with salt and pepper. Lift up each edge of the foil and crimp it at the top, making sure that it is tightly sealed. Set the peppers aside until it is time to grill.

In a blender, combine the cilantro, lime juice, water, tahini, 2 tablespoons olive oil, and the agave. Blend until smooth and season to taste with salt. Set the sauce aside.

When you are ready to grill, preheat the grill to medium-high (or if you are already grilling, simply place the peppers in a medium-high area of the grill). Lay the peppers on the grill and allow them to cook for 20 minutes.

When it is time to serve, unwrap the peppers, discarding the foil, and lay each pepper in the center of a plate. Check the sauce. It should have body but be pourable. If it has thickened, simply stir in a splash of water and then season it again to taste with salt. Pour the sauce over each pepper, dividing the sauce among all four peppers, making sure to completely coat each one. Tilt the plates gently to coat them with sauce, then garnish with sesame seeds and cilantro leaves and serve immediately.

Grilled Veggie Burritos

("Christmas-Style," with Red & Green Salsas)

MAKES 4 LARGE BURRITOS

I grew up with a deep affection for big, sauce-covered fork-and-knife burritos, and I want my kids to enjoy the same. But I also have a perhaps controversial opinion: If I'm eating a big Tex-Mex burrito that's covered in sauce and melted cheese . . . I prefer a veggie one. It's a little bit lighter and brighter, with more textural variation, and you still get the nirvana point that is chewing through a saucy, cheese-melty flour tortilla. By grilling the veggies you get lots of smoke and char, with a mix of tenderness and crispness, then they all get tossed together with rice, beans, and more cheese, to make every bite great. Filling the plate with red and green salsa (or whichever you prefer), flavors the whole dish. This is a perfect thing to cook for the whole family at once, since the burritos can all be assembled together on a sheet pan and finished in the oven. For personal preference, feel free to substitute any other grilled vegetables that you would like.

Note: If you can't find extra-large burrito tortillas, this recipe works perfectly well with smaller ones—it will just make 6 smaller burritos instead of 4 larger ones.

INGREDIENTS

- 1 pound broccolini, baby broccoli, or sprouting cauliflower (sometimes called "caulini")
- 8 ounces green zucchini (about 2 small or 1 medium)
- 8 ounces yellow zucchini (about 2 small or 1 medium)
- 1 medium shallot
- 1 tablespoon neutral oil
- Salt and freshly ground black pepper
- 1 cup cooked long-grain white or jasmine rice
- 1¾ cups cooked black beans or 1 (15-ounce) can black beans, drained
- 4 large burrito-size flour tortillas
- 8 ounces medium yellow cheddar cheese, grated
- 8 ounces Monterey Jack cheese grated
- Salsa Ranchera (page 110), warmed
- Salsa Verde (page 110), warmed

METHOD

Preheat the grill to high heat, then clean and oil the grates well.

Place the broccolini in a large bowl. Halve the green and yellow zucchini lengthwise or if thick, quarter into long spears. Add them to the bowl. Peel the shallot and quarter it through the root end, keeping it attached at the root. Add it to the bowl as well, along with the neutral oil. Season the vegetables liberally with salt and pepper and give them a toss until well coated with the oil.

Grill the vegetables over high heat, turning as each side chars. Grill for 3 to 5 minutes total, depending on each vegetable and its thickness. Look for the broccolini to still have a little bit of crunch and the zucchini to still have a tiny bit of bite left. The shallot cannot be overcooked, as long as it is not burnt to the point of bitterness.

Meanwhile, preheat the oven to 450°F.

Once the vegetables are cool enough to handle, chop the broccolini and zucchini into a rustic medium dice. Finely chop the shallot, discarding the root end. Return the vegetables to the large bowl and then add the cooked rice and beans. Toss thoroughly and season to taste with salt.

Heat the tortillas on the grill or in a wide skillet over high heat, just until they are pliable and easy to fold without cracking. Lay them down on a clean work surface and add the filling mixture, dividing it among the tortillas. Add just a small handful of both cheeses to the top of each and roll them into burritos, saving most of it to top the burritos. Lay the burritos, seam-side down, in a row in a baking dish, sheet pan, or lasagna pan. Ladle some of the ranchera sauce on one side of each burrito and salsa verde on the other side—enough to coat the burritos (keeping most of the sauce reserved for later). Cover the burritos with a mixture of the remaining cheeses and place them in the oven. Bake until the cheese is melted and bubbling, about 10 minutes.

While the burritos are baking, line up four dinner plates. Ladle red and green salsa on each side of each plate, then tilt the plate to fill each half with a sauce. Once the burritos are ready, lift each one out with a spatula and set it on the plate with the salsa colors lining up with their corresponding sides. Serve immediately.

Huevos Divorciados

SERVES
2

The name of this Mexican breakfast dish of eggs, salsas, and black beans, with a side of tortillas, literally translates to "divorced eggs," but I feel like "split custody eggs" maybe makes more sense, since one egg lives with salsa verde and one egg with salsa ranchera. Okay, whatever, that's not the point. It's hearty but not too heavy, has spice and brightness, and is a wonderful weekend brunch dish that won't make you take a nap immediately after. Yes, it requires two pans (or four if you're trying to cook for a crowd), and the only thing grilled is the salsa you already made. But I don't care, because this is my favorite breakfast in the world and it's going in the book. Also, isn't a plate of beans, eggs, and salsa a great way to get your kids loaded up with protein and fiber for the day?

INGREDIENTS

2 tablespoons oil, such as corn, canola, vegetable, or avocado oil (or even extra-virgin olive oil)
¼ cup finely chopped white onion
Salt
1¾ cups cooked black beans with their cooking liquid, or 1 (15-ounce) can, undrained
2 tablespoons butter, either salted or unsalted
4 large eggs
1 cup Salsa Ranchera (page 110)
1 cup Salsa Verde (page 110)
About 2 tablespoons crumbled Cotija cheese
Corn or flour tortillas, heated and kept warm

METHOD

Place a stainless steel or well-seasoned cast-iron skillet over medium-low heat and allow it to preheat (if you are using a nonstick pan, there's no need to preheat it quite so long). At the same time, in a medium saucepan, heat the oil over medium heat until it is shimmering. Add the onions and a pinch of salt and cook, stirring occasionally, until they are just translucent but not browning, about 5 minutes. Add the beans and their liquid, and bring them to a simmer. Once simmering, reduce the heat to low, and cover the pan while you prepare the rest of the dish.

Add the butter to the skillet, tilting the pan so the butter melts across it. Once the butter is foaming, crack the first egg into a small bowl (making sure the yolk is intact) and pour it into one corner of the pan. Repeat with the remaining 3 eggs, putting one in each corner. Season the eggs with salt and allow them to cook until the whites are just set and the yolks are runny and bright, 3 to 4 minutes.

Set up two plates. Place 2 eggs on each plate, off to one side of the plate, and allow them to sit. Turn the skillet up to high heat and add the salsa ranchera to the pan. Allow it to come to a strong simmer, then spoon it over the whites of one of the eggs on each plate (leaving the yolks uncovered), letting the remaining sauce fill the plate. Wipe out the skillet, add the salsa verde to the skillet, and repeat, covering the unsauced egg whites with the salsa verde.

Taste the beans for salt and adjust as needed. Spoon equal amounts of the beans onto the empty sides of the plates. Sprinkle the plates with Cotija cheese and serve with warm tortillas.

Salsa Ranchera and Salsa Verde

MAKES 3 CUPS SALSA RANCHERA AND 2¼ CUPS SALSA VERDE

Charring ingredients on a grill is *so much easier* than doing it in a skillet or a baking sheet under a broiler. This recipe makes two delicious charred salsas, one red, one green, at the same time, with mostly overlapping ingredients. These are outstanding in Huevos Divorciados (page 109), Grilled Veggie Burritos (page 107), or even just to dip chips into. They could also be used for enchiladas, huevos rancheros, or chilaquiles.

The salsas will last for about 1 week in the refrigerator, but also freeze quite well. Doubling the recipe is easy, in case you want to have more on hand.

(Okay, technically these are sides and not mains, but they will be used in two of the main course dishes in this chapter.)

INGREDIENTS

- 1½ pounds meaty sauce tomatoes, such as Roma or San Marzano
- 1½ pounds tomatillos, husks removed and rinsed
- 1 large white onion, quartered through the root and peeled
- 2 serrano chiles
- 1 teaspoon plus 2 tablespoons neutral oil, such as avocado or canola
- Salt
- 1 bunch of cilantro, leaves and tender stems
- 2 garlic cloves, crushed with the side of a knife and peeled
- 2 tablespoons water

METHOD

Preheat the grill to high heat, then clean and oil the grates well.

Place the tomatoes, tomatillos, onion, and serranos in a large bowl. Add 1 teaspoon of the oil and a hefty pinch of salt and toss to combine. Lay the vegetables all on the grill and allow them to cook, turning as needed, until they are all completely charred on the outside, 6 to 8 minutes total. Once charred, return them to the bowl.

Cut the root end from the onions and discard them. If you want your sauces less spicy, remove the seeds from the serranos.

For the salsa ranchera: In a blender, combine the tomatoes, *half* of the onion, 1 serrano, *half* of the cilantro, one of the garlic cloves, a pinch of salt, and 1 tablespoon of the neutral oil. Blend until the mixture has a rustic texture. Pour the salsa into a medium saucepan.

For the salsa verde: Rinse the blender out and add the tomatillos and the remaining onion, serrano, cilantro, and garlic. Add the remaining 1 tablespoon neutral oil, the water, and a hefty pinch of salt. Blend until the mixture has a rustic texture, then pour into a second saucepan.

Place both pans over medium-high heat and once they are bubbling, reduce to a simmer and simmer for 5 minutes. Turn off the heat and season to taste with salt. Allow to cool completely before storing in the refrigerator.

Grilled Spaghetti Squash with Charred Cherry Tomato Sauce

SERVES 4 TO 6

Spaghetti squash was, for most of my childhood, the unofficial "gluten-free pasta" of the '90s, even though it's just a squash whose flesh shreds naturally into long strands when cooked and scooped out. Maybe it's just nostalgia, but it does hit a pleasure spot, and is a pretty unfussy gluten-free, vegetarian main course or side dish. I prefer this recipe in the fall, when spaghetti squash is in season and cherry tomatoes are just a little more acidic than at their summer peak.

Those cherry tomatoes, thanks to their higher pectin content, turn into an instantly thick-enough fresh tomato sauce when blended. If you don't have a grill pan, you can also make this recipe without grilling any of the tomatoes—simply blend them raw with the other ingredients (I actually prefer a half-raw, half-cooked tomato mixture).

Note: The squash can take anywhere from 30 minutes to 1 hour to cook, and will stay pretty darn hot for 10 to 15 minutes after you remove it from the grill, just as long as you don't scoop out the flesh.

INGREDIENTS

- 1 spaghetti squash (3 to 3½ pounds)
- About 2 tablespoons extra-virgin olive oil, plus more for brushing
- Salt and freshly ground black pepper
- 2 pints cherry tomatoes
- 2 garlic cloves, peeled but whole
- 1 tablespoon butter, either salted or unsalted
- A pinch of crushed red pepper
- 10 to 15 basil leaves
- Parmesan cheese

METHOD

Set up a two-zone fire. If grilling with gas, set one side to high heat and the other to medium heat. Clean the grates well (no need to oil them).

Cut the spaghetti squash in half crosswise, then use a spoon to scoop out the seeds and discard them. Brush the flesh of the squash with olive oil and season it well with salt and pepper.

Place the squash on the colder side of the grill, cut-side up, then place a grill pan on the hot side to preheat and close the lid. Allow the squash to cook until it is tender, up to 1 hour—start checking it at around 30 minutes as the time can vary. You'll be able to tell it is ready when a fork can easily flake the flesh of the squash all the way through.

Once tender, add half of the cherry tomatoes to the grill pan and grill until just charred, rolling them in the pan occasionally, about 2 minutes. Remove the grill pan, then flip the squash, flesh-side down, onto the hot side of the grill and allow it to char at the edges, about 2 more minutes.

Allow the squash to sit while you make the tomato sauce. In a blender, combine the cherry tomatoes (raw and/or grilled), garlic cloves, butter, crushed red pepper, and a pinch of salt and blend until smooth. Set aside.

When you are ready to serve, scoop the flesh from the spaghetti squash into a large bowl. Add about half of the basil leaves (the larger ones, if possible.) Pour in the cherry tomato sauce and stir well to combine. Season to taste with salt and then transfer to a serving plate. Top with Parmesan cheese, garnish with the remaining basil leaves, and then drizzle with the 2 tablespoons olive oil. Serve immediately.

Blackened Broccoli-Cheddar Split Pea Soup

SERVES 6 TO 8

This is a mashup of two great soups, forcing more fiber into my family's diet (split peas are one of the most fiber-dense foods on the planet). I never envisioned this as belonging in a grilling book, until I remembered a J. Kenji López-Alt recipe that called for hard-searing broccoli in the pan first for more flavor. Taking a page from one of the greats, I have used that idea here, grilling the broccoli, potatoes, and carrots before adding them to the soup. It imparts a smoky element that alludes to pork and split pea soup while keeping it vegetarian. Don't worry about fully cooking the vegetables on the grill—you just want some blackening—as they will finish in the soup.

INGREDIENTS

1½ pounds broccoli
2 medium carrots
12 ounces Yukon Gold or similar potato
2 tablespoons extra-virgin olive oil
1 medium yellow or white onion, diced
4 garlic cloves, chopped
Salt and freshly ground black pepper
1 cup split peas, rinsed
8 cups water, vegetable stock, or chicken stock (or any combination thereof)
4 ounces American or Velveeta cheese, grated
2 tablespoons butter, either salted or unsalted
1 pound sharp cheddar, grated
1 tablespoon soy sauce
Sour cream or yogurt, for serving
Hot sauce, for serving

METHOD

Preheat the grill to high heat, then clean and oil the grates well. If you are cooking with charcoal, a wood chunk placed on the edge of the charcoal bed will add some bonus smoky flavor.

Cut off the tough bottom part of the broccoli stem and discard it. Quarter the broccoli florets through the stem, keeping the quarters intact (or halve them, if the heads are especially small). Lay the broccoli, carrots, and potatoes on the grill with nothing else on them, turning as needed until they are somewhat charred on all sides but not fully burnt, about 6 minutes total.

Once they are cool enough to handle, dice the carrots and potatoes and set them aside. Break the broccoli florets off into bite-size pieces and set those aside, separate from the carrots and potatoes. Then dice the broccoli stems and put them with the potatoes and carrots.

In a soup pot or Dutch oven, heat the olive oil over medium-high heat until it is shimmering. Add the onion, garlic, potatoes, carrots, and broccoli stems. Season them with salt and pepper and continue cooking, stirring occasionally, until the onions are translucent, about 7 minutes.

Add the split peas and allow them to toast for about 2 minutes, then add the water or stock. Bring to a simmer, cover, and cook until the split peas are quite soft, about 1 hour.

Stir in the reserved broccoli florets. Transfer half of the soup to a blender or a large bowl with an immersion blender (you may need to work in batches if your blender is not big enough). Blend the soup until it is mostly smooth. If your blender is at capacity, pour some of the liquid back into the pot (you will be adding cheese to the blender momentarily).

Add the American cheese and butter and blend the soup until it is smooth. Set aside about one-quarter of the cheddar to garnish the soup and add the rest in batches to the blender. Blend until it is smooth and emulsified. Return the blended soup to the pot and stir to combine. Stir in the soy sauce and season to taste with salt and pepper.

Serve with yogurt, hot sauce, and the reserved cheddar (otherwise my wife will ask if there is cheese in it).

Smoked Potato Tacos

(with Smoked Tomatillo Salsa, Cotija, and Crunchy Red Cabbage)

SERVES 6 TO 8

One thing I learned when developing the cult-hit smoked potato breakfasts burritos for Cofax Coffee in Los Angeles is that potatoes and tomatillos take smoke *really* well. These are tacos that you might serve as a "vegetarian option" before everyone realizes that they're better than the meat option. Russet potatoes get smoke-grilled on a two-zone fire beside tomatillos, then fried up with onions and charred poblanos, and tossed with Cotija cheese to create the greatest spicy, acidic, smoky, cheesy potato hash imaginable. Served in lightly fried corn tortillas with lime-wilted red cabbage, this is not just one of the best vegetarian dishes in the book: It's one of the best dishes in this book, full-stop. This hash reheats *really* well, whether that's to make more tacos later, or to just fry up and eat with some eggs for breakfast with the kids.

I love these with lightly pan-fried corn tortillas, but they also work really well with hard-shell tacos, grilled corn tortillas, or even flour tortillas.

INGREDIENTS

Charcoal
Wood chunks (I prefer pecan, but oaks and even some fruitwoods will work fine here)
4 large russet potatoes (about 15 ounces each)
Neutral oil, such as canola or avocado oil
Salt
1½ pounds tomatillos, husks removed, rinsed
5 green poblano chiles (can substitute Anaheims)
½ cup extra-virgin olive oil or avocado oil
1 medium white onion, diced
12 ounces Cotija cheese, grated
1 medium head red cabbage, finely shredded
Juice of 1 good lime or 3 bad ones
About 24 small taco-size corn tortillas

METHOD

Set up a two-zone fire by lighting a full chimney of charcoal. Once they have turned gray, set them on one side of the grill. Place 2 chunks of pecan wood on top of the charcoal, then close the lid and allow them to burn off for about 5 minutes.

Meanwhile, pierce the potatoes several times with a fork. Toss them in a large bowl with enough oil to just barely coat and season them liberally with salt. In a medium bowl, coat the tomatillos with enough oil just to coat.

Once the grill is ready, lay the potatoes on the cooler side, with the tomatillos scattered around them. Close the lid, open the vent over the cooler side, and leave it closed over the hot side. (If you have bottom vents, open the one under the fire and close the one underneath the cold zone.)

Allow the potatoes and tomatillos to smoke, checking the grill every 40 minutes or so to add more wood and charcoal as needed, and rotating the positions of the potatoes if they start to darken too much in spots. Cook until the tomatillos have a khaki-green color and are soft like water balloons to the touch, about 1 hour. Remove them and set them aside in a bowl (being careful not to "burst" them and lose their liquor). Continue smoking the potatoes until they are cooked to an internal temperature of 208°F, 2 to 2½ hours total, depending on the grill and the potatoes.

DAD HACK

If you're tired of smoking your potatoes, after 1 to 1½ hours they will have plenty of smoke flavor and can be transferred to a 450°F oven and roasted until they are finished cooking.

Once the potatoes are finished, remove them and set aside to cool. Lay the poblanos on the hot side of the grill and allow them to cook until they are just barely charred on all sides, 2 to 3 minutes per side. Transfer them to a closed bag or a covered bowl to steam. Once steamed and cool enough to handle, remove the blackened skin and discard it. Then remove the stems and seeds and chop the chiles to a rustic dice. Finally, drop the tomatillos into a blender and blend until smooth.

Once the potatoes are cooled, cut them into a rustic, small dice as well, including the skins. It is okay if they get soft and a bit mashed in the process.

In a large skillet or Dutch oven, heat the olive oil over medium-high heat until it is shimmering. Add the onion, the poblanos, and a hefty pinch of salt. Fry, stirring occasionally, until the onions are translucent and softened, about 7 minutes.

Stir in the potatoes and another pinch of salt, stirring frequently until incorporated. Stir in the tomatillo puree and keep stirring, scraping the bottom with a wooden spoon as needed. Once the potatoes are warmed through and soft, stir in the Cotija and once it is all melted in, taste the mixture for seasoning, adding salt if needed.

In a large bowl, toss together the shredded cabbage, the lime juice, and salt to taste. Allow the cabbage to wilt while cooking the tortillas.

To heat the tortillas on the stove: For best results, heat a medium skillet with a thin layer of neutral oil over medium-high heat. Fry the tortillas on both sides for about 10 seconds, until lightly crisped, then fold them gently in half with tongs and lay them on paper towels to drain.

To heat tortillas on the grill: Simply grill them quickly over high heat on both sides until they begin to puff and lightly char, then transfer them to a plate, covered with a kitchen towel to stay warm.

To serve, spoon the potato filling into the tortillas and top them with a generous pinch of wilted cabbage.

Chicken
(and
a
Turkey
Breast)

Quick and Simple Grilled Chicken Breast 124
Achiote-Lime Chicken Breast 126
Shish Tawook 129
Ode to a Benihana Birthday Party. 131
Chicken “Gyoza” Eggplant 132
Ginger-Buffalo Wings 134
Pickle-Brined Drumsticks
with Spicy Honey 137
Shallot-Dijon Chicken Thighs 139
Smoke-Grilled Turkey Breast
(for Cold Cuts). 140
Smoke-Grilled Pollo
a la Brasa with Ají Verde 142

If it were up to my wife (and probably millions of other people), she (and they) would eat chicken breast pretty much every day. (Cue my rant about how everyone is obsessed with protein when they should be obsessed with fiber.) But the truth is, chicken is incredibly popular for a reason, and breast meat is versatile when seasoned well and not overcooked (it dries out incredibly quickly once it gets past 150°F). A simple grilled chicken breast is perfect for a light dinner with some grilled vegetables; and I love a thin, marinated breast for tacos, or with a plate of rice and beans.

If you have a little more time, it's hard to beat the flavor of bone-in, skin-on wings, thighs, and drumsticks. Dark meat is actually a *lot* harder to overcook. While it is "cooked" at 165°F, it gets more tender and stays juicy up to around 190°F. That means you can cook it longer, getting crispy charred bits without having to worry about it drying out.

This chapter will also teach you my absolute favorite way to grill chicken breast: as skewered, yogurt-marinated Shish Tawook (page 129), as well as how to make a way-better smoked turkey cold cut than you can get at the grocery store deli counter.

When shopping for chicken, small local farms can be a great option. Regardless, for the best flavor (and more humanely raised chickens), opt for pasture-raised and organic when you can.

Quick and Simple Grilled Chicken Breast

SERVES
4

If my family just wants "a piece of chicken," whether it's to throw together with some grilled vegetables and a side of rice, or to put in the fridge for easy school lunches, quesadillas, or a salad, this is the one I end up making. I prefer it with dried oregano, but you can easily omit if you want a more neutral salt-and-pepper flavor—or add any spices you prefer. If I'm grilling simple chicken breasts, I always cook more than I need and keep extras in the fridge.

Note: If they are especially small chicken breasts of even thickness, you can skip the pounding step.

INGREDIENTS

4 boneless, skinless chicken breasts (6 to 8 ounces each)
About 2 teaspoons extra-virgin olive oil
Kosher salt and freshly ground black pepper
1 tablespoon dried oregano
A squeeze of lemon (optional), to finish

METHOD

Preheat the grill to medium-high heat, then clean and oil the grates well.

Lay a long sheet of plastic wrap down on the counter and lay a chicken breast down on one side of it, with some extra space on all sides. Fold the other side of the plastic over it. (You could also use a large resealable bag and place the breast inside it.) Use a flat meat mallet or the bottom of a heavy skillet and pound it a few times with medium-strong force, just to create an even thickness. You're not looking for a thin breast—you're just trying to even it out so that it cooks at the same rate. Transfer to a plate or baking sheet and repeat with the remaining breasts.

Once pounded, drizzle the chicken breasts with the olive oil and toss them until evenly coated. Season them well with salt and pepper on all sides, followed by the oregano.

Lay the chicken down on the grill and cook until it is golden brown on the first side, 8 to 10 minutes. Flip it over and cook until the internal temperature of the chicken reads 150°F, 6 to 8 more minutes. Squeeze with lemon (if you desire) and then allow it to rest a couple of minutes before cutting.

Achiote-Lime Chicken Breast

(with Garlic and Fresh Cilantro)

SERVES 3 OR 4

Achiote (sometimes called annatto, and derived from the seeds of an evergreen shrub) is a very popular ingredient in parts of Mexico, South America, and the Caribbean. While it is often used to bring a bright red hue to foods, it also imparts a super-unique flavor that is earthy, slightly bitter, and a little citrusy. It has become my go-to ingredient when I want to make a quick marinade for butterflied chicken breasts, which I grill for tacos, quesadillas, or just serve with rice and beans. I keep a bag of achiote powder in my pantry at all times, and this chicken recipe is a regular staple in my house—it's become a big hit for literally every member of my family. Leftovers are *great* in a salad, too.

Note: If you don't feel confident butterflying a chicken breast, you can always ask the person behind the meat counter to do it. Similarly, you can marinate a whole breast instead, and cook as for Quick and Simple Grilled Chicken Breast (page 124).

INGREDIENTS

- 3 tablespoons fresh lime juice
- 3 garlic cloves, grated or very finely chopped
- 1 tablespoon dried oregano
- 1 tablespoon Diamond Crystal kosher salt, or 1½ teaspoons fine sea salt
- 1 tablespoon extra-virgin olive oil
- 1 teaspoon achiote (annatto) powder
- 1 teaspoon soy sauce
- Several twists of freshly ground black pepper
- 3 sprigs fresh cilantro
- 1¾ pounds boneless, skinless chicken breasts (3 to 4 breasts)

METHOD

In a resealable container that will fit the chicken comfortably, combine the lime juice, garlic, oregano, salt, olive oil, achiote, soy sauce, and pepper. Stir with a fork until fully combined, then add the cilantro sprigs and stir those in, too.

Lay a chicken breast flat on a cutting board. Press your nondominant hand, palm down, on the top of the chicken breast. Starting on the thicker side, use a sharp knife to slice the chicken breast horizontally through the center until you are about 1 inch from the other side, then open it like a book. Make small strokes of the knife to slice through to the "spine" of the book in any places necessary to help flatten it into an even thickness. Repeat this with the remaining chicken breasts.

Lay the chicken breasts in the marinade one by one, flipping them over to make sure each one is coated. Once they are all in the container, press them down to allow any marinade from the bottom to rise up to the top as well. Seal the container and place it in the refrigerator for at least 30 minutes and up to 8 hours.

When you are ready to cook the breasts, preheat the grill to high heat, then clean and oil the grates well.

When it is time to cook, lay the chicken breasts down in a single layer and cook until they lift easily from the grates and have a nice reddish-brown color with bits of blackening, 3 to 4 minutes. Flip them over and repeat with the other side. These are thin breasts, so as soon as you have some nice color, they should be ready to go, but if you are unsure, place an instant-read thermometer into the center of the breast and look for a temperature that is between 150° and 155°F. The breasts can be served immediately, whole or sliced.

100 YEARS OF
LOUISIANA'S
1923
NET 12 FL.

Shish Tawook

SERVES
4 TO 6

In Los Angeles, Lebanese takeout has always been a go-to week-night dinner option, and shish tawook, a tender, spiced, yogurt-marinated chicken kebab, might be my favorite way to eat grilled chicken breast. There are seemingly endless variations across the Middle East (and Los Angeles, too), and after many tasty trials, I've developed one I love to make at home. By cutting the chicken breasts into large cubes and then marinating them, you get *so much* surface area to coat and tenderize.

To avoid sticking, turn the kebabs frequently in the first 2 or 3 minutes of grilling, allowing some crust to form. This recipe works very well over gas, but does get a particularly good crust over a charcoal grill.

I love to serve these with "Kebab Plate" Rice (page 76) and any of the vegetable sides, especially Charred Cauliflower with Tahini-Yogurt Sauce (page 57) and Baba Ghanoush (page 68), to make a wonderful family dinner night at home.

Note: If you are using wooden skewers instead of metal skewers, soak them in water for at least 30 minutes.

INGREDIENTS

½ cup whole-milk yogurt
¼ cup fresh lemon juice
1 tablespoon extra-virgin olive oil
1 tablespoon tomato paste
1 tablespoon kosher salt
3 garlic cloves, grated or very finely chopped
2 teaspoons sumac, or 1 teaspoon smoked paprika
10 twists of freshly ground black pepper
1½ to 2 pounds boneless, skinless chicken breasts (3 to 4 breasts)
Flaky salt
Lemon wedges, for squeezing

METHOD

In a large bowl, combine the yogurt, lemon juice, olive oil, tomato paste, salt, garlic, sumac, and pepper and stir until well combined.

Cut the chicken breasts into rough cubes that are about 1 inch thick, not worrying too much about perfection. (Pieces from the thinner end of the breast can be folded over when they are skewered.) Add them to the marinade and toss until well mixed. Cover the chicken in the bowl and transfer to the refrigerator. Allow it to marinate for at least 2 hours and up to 12.

When you are ready to cook, preheat the grill to high heat, then clean and oil the grates well.

Meanwhile, skewer the chicken, keeping the cubes pressed against each other, while folding over any thin pieces as they are skewered. This should fill 2 to 3 skewers, depending on their length.

Once the grill is hot, lay the skewers down on the hottest part of the grill. Use tongs to turn them frequently, until they have gotten some color on all sides. Continue turning frequently until they are browned with small bits of char all over and the thickest parts of the largest pieces are registering an internal temperature of at least 155°F, 15 to 20 minutes.

Transfer to a serving platter, season with flaky salt, and serve with lemon wedges.

Ode to a Benihana Birthday Party

SERVES 4 TO 6

While I don't have a teppanyaki grill at my house, I've figured out a great way to throw a kid's Benihana-style birthday party at home, using a normal grill. But ultimately, this is all thanks to my friend Keisuke Akabori, a wonderful chef who created a copycat version of Benihana's signature ginger sauce, which you'll find below. There is also a version of their hot mustard sauce, in case you are #TeamMustard. A side of fried rice would not be a bad accompaniment, despite its very much not being a thing one should cook on a grill.

While this recipe is in the "chicken" section and uses both chicken and shrimp, you can feel free to substitute any proteins you like.

DAD HACK

If you have a grill pan, you can pre-cube all of the vegetables and grill them right on the pan to make life a little easier. But honestly, the method below works quite well.

INGREDIENTS

Keisuke's Ginger Sauce

⅔ cup roughly diced yellow onion
¼ cup roughly chopped fresh ginger
¼ cup soy sauce
2 tablespoons plus 2 teaspoons rice wine vinegar
1 tablespoon plus 1 teaspoon fresh lemon juice
½ teaspoon sugar

Mustard Sauce

2 tablespoons water
2 tablespoons heavy cream
1 garlic clove, smashed and peeled
1 tablespoon soy sauce
1 tablespoon toasted sesame seeds
1 teaspoon mustard powder

Benihana-Style Mix Grill

2 pounds boneless, skinless chicken thighs (8 to 10 thighs)
Neutral oil
Salt and freshly ground black pepper
1 pound peeled large or extra-large shrimp
½ teaspoon mayonnaise
1 pound zucchini, ends trimmed, quartered lengthwise into spears
8 ounces large button mushrooms
1 medium yellow onion, peeled and quartered through the root

METHOD

Make Keisuke's ginger sauce: In a blender, combine the onion, ginger, soy sauce, vinegar, lemon juice, and sugar and blend until smooth. Set aside and allow to settle before serving.

Make the mustard sauce: This is an incredibly powerful sauce, so you only need a little. As a result, I highly recommend blending it in a small blender, like a Nutribullet, or even a food processor, rather than a large, full-size blender. Combine all of the ingredients and blend them until smooth.

Make the Benihana-style mix grill: Preheat the grill to medium-high heat, then clean and oil the grates well.

Drizzle the chicken thighs with enough neutral oil to just barely coat them, then season them well on all sides with salt and pepper.

Meanwhile, in a bowl, combine the shrimp and mayonnaise and season liberally with salt and pepper. Toss together until well coated.

In a large bowl, combine the zucchini, mushrooms, and onion and toss them with just enough neutral oil to barely coat. Season liberally with salt and pepper.

Working in batches if necessary, grill the chicken, vegetables, and shrimp—starting with the chicken and cooking the shrimp last (since they cook the fastest). Grill the thighs until the first side is golden brown with bits of charring, about 5 minutes. Flip them and repeat with the other side until they are golden and crispy, with an internal temp of around 180° to 190°F—another 5 minutes.

Grill the vegetables until they are browned and tender with some light charring on each side, about 2 minutes per side for the zucchini, 3 minutes per side for the onion, and 4 for the mushrooms.

Grill the shrimp last, laying them down until browned with some char marks, about 2 minutes. Flip and repeat until just cooked through, about 2 more minutes.

Once cooked, transfer the chicken and vegetables to a cutting board and chop into a large dice. Serve everything together on a platter, family-style, with ramekins of the sauces for dipping.

Chicken "Gyoza" Eggplant

SERVES
4

I'm going to be honest: In my head, this seemed like a cool idea, and then when I made it . . . it was way better than I thought it would be. Eggplant gets scored and then stuffed and topped with what is essentially the filling for Japanese pan-fried dumplings. The eggplant becomes spoon-tender and the mixture of ground chicken, napa cabbage, ginger, and scallions get crispy and golden brown. Then the whole thing gets topped with a "dipping sauce" of soy sauce, rice wine vinegar, and chili oil to create a soft-and-crispy large appetizer that will be completely consumed before you know what happened. My daughter gave it a "What's *that*?" when she first saw it coming off the grill, and then thoroughly enjoyed it once I convinced her to try it.

Note: Just make sure to avoid using overly large eggplants. Around 12-ounce eggplants are ideal.

INGREDIENTS

"Dipping Sauce"
2 tablespoons rice wine vinegar
2 tablespoons soy sauce
A scant teaspoon of chili oil or chili crisp

Chicken "Gyoza" Eggplant
2 medium Italian eggplants (about 12 ounces each)
½ pound ground chicken thigh
¾ cup tightly packed finely chopped Napa cabbage
3 scallions, thinly sliced
4 garlic cloves, finely chopped
1 teaspoon finely chopped fresh ginger
1 teaspoon toasted sesame oil
1 teaspoon soy sauce
½ teaspoon kosher salt
½ teaspoon cornstarch
A pinch of ground white pepper or freshly ground black pepper

METHOD

Make the "dipping sauce": In a small bowl, stir together the vinegar, soy sauce, and chili oil and set aside.

Make the chicken "gyoza" eggplant: Set up a two-zone fire. If grilling with gas, set one side to high heat and the other to low heat. Clean and oil the grates well.

Cut the eggplants in half lengthwise through the stem. Score the flesh of each eggplant with a knife in a crosshatch pattern, with cuts about 1 inch apart. Try to cut deeply, being careful not to pierce the skin on the underside of the eggplant.

In a large bowl, combine the chicken, cabbage, scallions, garlic, ginger, sesame oil, soy sauce, salt, cornstarch, and pepper. Mix the ingredients together thoroughly (for best results, gloved or clean hands are the best tool, as you can kind of squeeze the mixture and really get it mixed together well).

Gently pull open the eggplant a bit and stuff a little of the "gyoza" mixture into the cut eggplant where you can. Divide the remaining filling across the top of the eggplants in an even layer.

Place the eggplant on the cooler side of the grill, cut-side up, and close the lid. Continue cooking them, rotating their positions every 15 minutes or so for even cooking, until they are tender and bubbling, and the "gyoza" filling is browned and crisp, about 40 minutes. If you are unsure if it is cooked, an instant-read thermometer should be registering between 175° and 185°F.

Place the eggplants on individual plates or a serving platter and pour the "dipping sauce" over the top of each eggplant. Eat with spoons.

Ginger-Buffalo Wings

SERVES 4 TO 6

I think that grilled wings are *wildly* underrated, since deep-fried ones seem to get all the attention. May I present these grilled wings, cooked over a two-zone fire until juicy and tender with crispy edges and bits of blackening. (Not for nothing, they are also a lot better for you when they aren't submerged in fry oil.) These are tossed in a Buffalo sauce steeped in ginger, garlic, and a touch of soy sauce. *This* is peak backyard party food.

You are more than welcome to eat them with blue cheese or ranch, but I find that grilled wings eat much lighter and don't need it.

INGREDIENTS

- 24 medium chicken party wings (a mix of flats and drumettes, or your preference), about 2 pounds
- Kosher salt and freshly ground black pepper
- 8 tablespoons (4 ounces/1 stick) unsalted butter
- ½ cup hot sauce (ideally Frank's RedHot)
- 3 ounces fresh ginger, finely chopped
- 3 garlic cloves, finely chopped
- ¼ teaspoon soy sauce

METHOD

Set up a two-zone fire. If grilling with gas, set one side to high heat and the other to low heat. Clean and oil the grates well.

Season the wings well with salt and pepper and lay them on the cooler side of the grill until they are cooked to an internal temperature of 165°F, about 20 minutes.

Meanwhile (or you can do this in advance), in a small saucepan, combine the butter, hot sauce, ginger, garlic, and soy sauce. Bring it to a bubble over medium-high heat, then reduce to a simmer and cook for 5 minutes. Pour the sauce through a fine-mesh strainer into a large bowl.

Once the wings are at 165°F, transfer them to the hot side of the grill and cook them, turning frequently, until they are golden brown with bits of charring all over, 2 to 3 minutes. Transfer them directly to the bowl of ginger Buffalo sauce and toss to combine. Serve immediately.

Pickle-Brined Drumsticks with Spicy Honey

SERVES 3 TO 4

This is my favorite thing to do with the leftover brine at the end of a jar of dill pickles. The marinade is *so* simple—you literally just put drumsticks in a container and cover them with pickle brine. Once they're grilled, they take on great color and really taste, unsurprisingly, like pickles. Drizzled with homemade spicy honey, they are brimming with Americana, or maybe a reversed, gluten-free Nashville hot chicken. This recipe is very easy to double if you save up your pickle brine. My kids are not teenagers yet, but if they're anything like me when I was, they will devour these with their friends after school.

INGREDIENTS

Spicy Honey
¼ cup honey
1 tablespoon crushed red pepper
½ teaspoon cayenne pepper
1 teaspoon red wine vinegar

Pickle-Brined Drumsticks
6 chicken drumsticks
About 1 cup dill pickle brine
Flaky sea salt

METHOD

Make the spicy honey: In a small saucepan, combine the honey, crushed red pepper, and cayenne and bring to a bubble over medium heat. Reduce the heat to low and cook for 7 minutes. Turn off the heat, then pour the mixture into a heatproof container. Stir in the vinegar and allow it to cool to room temperature. This will keep for several weeks, covered, at room temperature.

Make the pickle-brined drumsticks: In a resealable container or ziplock bag, combine the drumsticks and pickle brine, making sure that they are all submerged in the liquid. Place them in the refrigerator to brine for at least 6 hours and up to 24.

When it is time to grill, set up a two-zone fire. If grilling with gas, set one side to high heat and the other to medium-low heat. Clean and oil the grates well.

Place the drumsticks on the colder side of the grill and close the lid. Allow them to cook until the internal temperature reaches 175°F, 15 to 20 minutes. Move the drumsticks to the hot side of the grill and cook until they are browned with small bits of blackening, 3 to 5 minutes, turning them as needed to get even browning.

Once cooked, transfer the drumsticks to a serving plate and drizzle them with all of the spicy honey. Garnish with flaky salt and serve immediately, swiping the drumsticks through the spicy honey on the plate as you pick them up.

Shallot-Dijon Chicken Thighs

SERVES
4

Chicken thighs grill exceptionally well because they can get a lot of crisp and char while staying moist. These take on a marinade inspired by the classic French mustard-shallot vinaigrette. It makes them bright and savory at the same time, and they are quite lovely when paired with a quick-cooking vegetable, like Grilled Asparagus and Wilted White Cheddar (page 47). This would also make a nice light dinner with a side of simple greens.

Thanks to the fat content of chicken thighs, these reheat quite nicely in the oven at around 325°F.

INGREDIENTS

1 large or 2 small shallots, finely chopped
3 tablespoons Dijon mustard
3 tablespoons extra-virgin olive oil
3 tablespoons red wine vinegar
1 teaspoon soy sauce
6 bone-in, skin-on chicken thighs
Kosher salt and freshly ground black pepper

METHOD

In a resealable container or large ziplock bag that will fit all of the chicken thighs, combine the shallots, mustard, olive oil, vinegar, and soy sauce. Stir well to combine. Season the chicken liberally with salt and pepper and add to the marinade. Make sure that they are well coated, then place them in the refrigerator to marinate for at least 8 hours, but ideally 24.

When it is time to grill, set up a two-zone fire. If grilling with gas, set one side to high heat and the other to medium-low heat. Clean and oil the grates well.

Place the thighs, skin-side-up, on the colder side of the grill and close the lid. Allow them to cook until the internal temperature reaches 175°F, 15 to 20 minutes. Flip them over, skin-side down, onto the hot side of the grill and cook until the skin is browned with small bits of blackening, 3 to 5 minutes, turning them as needed to get even browning.

Let rest for at least 5 minutes before serving.

Smoke-Grilled Turkey Breast (for Cold Cuts)

SERVES 8 TO 10

This is the turkey cold cut upgrade your family will want to eat all week in sandwiches, wraps, salads, or straight out of the fridge.

I have smoked a lot of turkey in my life and ordered smoked turkey breast at many BBQ restaurants around the country. When it is good, it is very good. But the truth is, in most instances, it is exceptionally dry. That's because turkey breast is a fairly lean piece of meat that does not like to be kept warm or cooked any more than it needs to be. As a result, I have long since concluded that a smoked boneless, skinless turkey breast, cooked correctly, chilled, and sliced for cold cuts, is the best way to enjoy it. But while a low-and-slow smoke works well, I prefer this two-zone fire method, which creates a delicious smoked turkey breast in as little as an hour (or up to 2, depending on your grill). I like mine with only salt and pepper (and a little mustard just to help the seasonings adhere), but feel free to add additional spices, like Cajun seasoning or brown sugar, if that is more to your liking.

INGREDIENTS

1 large boneless, skinless turkey breast (3 to 4 pounds)
Kosher salt
Charcoal
2 chunks pecan, hickory, post oak, or wood of choice
2 chunks applewood or wood of choice
1 tablespoon yellow mustard
Freshly ground black pepper

METHOD

First, dry-brine the turkey breast. Season all sides liberally with salt, adding more to the thicker parts. Ideally, place the turkey breast on a wire rack set in a sheet pan. Otherwise, you could lay it across some skewers set over a plate or baking sheet. This will allow for airflow around the breast. Set it in the refrigerator, uncovered, for about 24 hours. (You can go as little as 8 hours in a pinch, or up to 36 if you have to.)

When you are ready to cook, set up a two-zone fire by lighting a full chimney of charcoal. Once it has turned gray, set it on one side of the grill. Place the wood chunks on top of the charcoal and then close the lid and allow them to burn off for about 5 minutes. Open the vent over the cooler side, and leave it closed over the hot side.

Meanwhile, pat the turkey breast dry, then rub it with a thin layer of mustard. Season liberally with pepper. Open the smoker and sort of shape the breast, tucking in the thin edges, almost like you're rolling a dough ball, or tucking it into itself—the goal is to keep it from having any thin edges that will cook faster than the thicker parts. Lay the tucked breast on the cooler side of the smoker and close it. After 30 minutes, turn the turkey 180° so that the end that was facing the back of the grill is facing the charcoal, then check the internal temperature. Continue cooking until the breast registers 145°F in the thickest part, adding more charcoal and wood if it is starting to burn out.

Once cooked, take the turkey off the grill and allow it to cool to room temperature. Transfer it to the refrigerator and allow it to chill through. Once chilled, I prefer to slice it to my desired thickness with a serrated knife and place in a resealable container. (You could slice it "to order," but nobody in my family will ever do that when they want some turkey.) It will last about 1 week in the refrigerator.

Smoke-Grilled Pollo a la Brasa with Ají Verde

SERVES
4 TO 6

Peruvian-style pollo a la brasa is my absolute favorite way of cooking a whole chicken, classically served with a spicy, acidic, herbaceous, creamy green sauce called ají verde. The version I grew up on came from a small restaurant in Koreatown (appropriately named Pollo a la Brasa) that did theirs over a wood-burning fire that you could smell from about a block away. This is my homage, using a two-zone fire with wood chunks for smoke, with the chicken split in half for easier grilling, served with ají verde and, ideally, Perfect Grilled Potatoes (page 58). The smoke really makes the dish on this one. Luckily, one of the key ingredients—ají amarillo paste, a Peruvian yellow chile paste—is very easy to find online these days.

It may not be easier than that grocery store rotisserie chicken that's ubiquitous in family fridges these days, but it is *a lot* better.

To Split a Chicken: If you ask your butcher, they will happily split a chicken in half for you. But if you want or need to do it yourself, start by taking out the chicken's backbone: To do that, flip it breast-side down onto a cutting board. Use a sharp knife or kitchen shears to cut along one side of the backbone, separating it from the rest of the chicken. Then cut out the other side. This backbone can now be saved in the freezer and used for stock. Flip the bird over and then press the palm of your hand down firmly on the breast to help flatten it. You will hear a little bit of a crunching sound. Take a heavy kitchen knife and drive the blade straight down between the two breasts, splitting them in half, then cut with force to completely separate them.

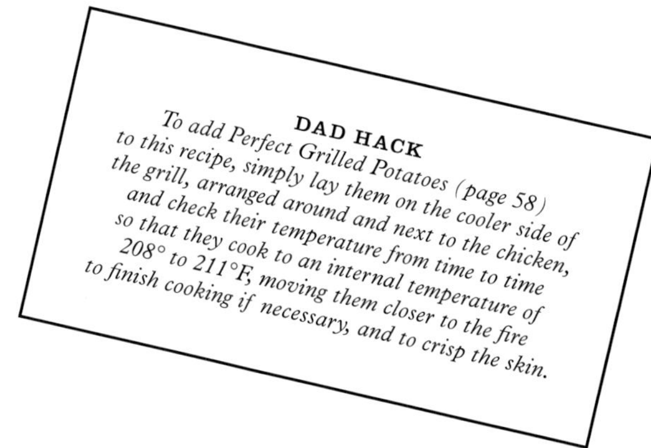

INGREDIENTS

1 whole chicken (4 to 5 pounds), split in half through the breast
Kosher salt
About 2 teaspoons extra-virgin olive oil
2 teaspoons smoked paprika
2 teaspoons dried oregano
2 teaspoons granulated garlic
Freshly ground black pepper
Charcoal
Pecan wood chunks or wood of your choice
Ají Verde (recipe follows), for serving

METHOD

First, dry-brine the chicken. Season the chicken all over, quite liberally, with salt. Lay the chicken pieces, skin-side up, on a wire rack set in a sheet pan. If you don't have a wire rack, you can also lay skewers across the baking sheet and lay the chicken on top. This process will create airflow to dry out the skin, season the chicken all the way through, and make for a better-tasting final product. (If necessary, you can also just lay the chicken on a baking sheet lined with paper towels.) Allow the chicken to dry-brine in the refrigerator, uncovered, for at least 18 hours and up to 48.

Once the chicken is brined, the skin should be quite dry. If any spots are not, simply pat them dry with a paper towel. Rub the chicken all over with olive oil just to barely coat, then season it on all sides with the paprika, oregano, granulated garlic, and pepper.

Meanwhile, set up a two-zone fire by lighting a full chimney of charcoal. Once they have turned gray, set them on one side of the grill. Place a chunk of pecan wood on top of the charcoal and then close the lid and allow the wood chunk to burn off for about 5 minutes.

Add the chicken to the cold part of the grill, arranging it so that the legs are facing the fire. Close the lid and open the vent over the chicken, and leave the vent closed over the hot side. (If you have bottom vents, open the one under the fire and close the one under the chicken.)

Allow the chicken to cook, checking it after about 40 minutes and rotating it if certain areas are getting darker than others. Add more charcoal as needed and add an additional chunk of wood once the first one has burned out. Continue cooking the chicken until the thickest part of the breast registers about 120°F.

Flip the chicken over and lay it skin-side down, with the breast side closer to the fire. Cover the grill and allow the chicken to continue cooking until the skin is crisp and the internal temperature of the breast reads 145° to 150°F in the thickest part, and the thigh registers at least 170°F, about 10 to 20 more minutes. Keep an eye on the color of the skin and move the chicken pieces as needed to get color all over to finish.

Take the chicken off the grill and allow to rest for at least 5 minutes.

Cut the chicken into serving pieces and serve with ají verde.

AJÍ VERDE

½ cup packed fresh cilantro leaves and tender stems
¼ cup fresh lime juice
¼ cup mayonnaise
2 tablespoons extra-virgin olive oil
3 ounces queso fresco
1 tablespoon ají amarillo paste
1 serrano chile, roughly chopped
2 scallions, roughly chopped
2 garlic cloves, peeled but whole
Pinch of salt, plus more to taste

In a blender, combine the cilantro, lime juice, mayo, olive oil, queso fresco, ají amarillo paste, serrano, scallions, garlic, and salt and blend until smooth. Taste for salt and add more as needed. Refrigerate for up to 3 days for best results and serve at room temperature.

BURBANK

Beef

Taverna Steak 150
California Tri-Tip Two Ways 152
Hermosillo-Style Carne Asada 154
Punchy, Funky Beef and Broccoli 166
Soy and Citrus Skirt Steak 169
Nước Chấm Brisket Noodle Bowl 170
Smoke-Grilled Bone-In Rib Eye
with Mansion Butter 172

Cows are big. As such, there are a *lot* of cuts of beef that are not optimal for quick-grilling, and there is a reason that beef grilling, for tons of people, starts and stops with steak. (Aaron Franklin and Jordan Mackay wrote an entire book on how to grill steak.)

This section does focus quite a bit on steaks, whether it is a quick-and-easy sirloin steak, a marinated skirt steak, a 2-inch-thick bone-in rib eye infused with wood smoke, or carne asada as made in Hermosillo, Mexico, the world capital of carne asada. Heck, even the tri-tip is a lot closer to a steak than it is to a roast. But these are all incredibly quick cooks compared to tougher cuts of meat that require a lot more time and attention, like a smoked whole brisket or a braised oxtail (which for obvious reasons I will not be getting into in this book).

But there are a couple of recipes that do call for traditionally tough cuts of meat like brisket and short ribs, slicing them thin and against the grain, then marinating them to create a lightning-fast grill time with tons of flavor and tenderness.

When shopping for beef to grill, I would only buy grass-fed beef if it came from a source that I really trusted—the grass-fed beef sold in most grocery stores just don't really have the fat content or flavor that is ideal for grilling. I try to look for beef from small local farms with beautiful fat, or I will shop with trusted local butchers. When in doubt, no matter where you're buying beef, it should have bright red color, firm texture, and no off-putting odor.

Taverna Steak

(Quick Sirloin with Oregano, Lemon, and Olive Oil)

SERVES 2 TO 3

One hot summer night, I ate dinner on the patio of a small taverna on a small island in Greece. I ordered a steak, which was seasoned only with oregano, olive oil, salt, and pepper. It showed up charred and rare, drizzled with more olive oil, and served with a wedge of lemon, which I immediately squeezed over it. It's still one of my favorite food memories, and proves my theory that almost anything is great with a squeeze of lemon.

This is now how I prefer to cook an affordable cut of steak, incredibly quickly and with lots of flavor—though this technique will certainly work with a more expensive cut, like rib eye or New York strip. For a quick family steak night at home, this goes really well with a side like Grilled Asparagus and Wilted White Cheddar (page 47), a side salad, and maybe a slice of Fettunta (page 73). In the summer, there may be no better pairing than sliced ripe tomatoes, drizzled with olive oil and flaky sea salt.

INGREDIENTS

1-pound sirloin steak, 1 inch thick
1 teaspoon extra-virgin olive oil, plus more for drizzling
Kosher salt
1 tablespoon dried oregano, ideally Greek
1 teaspoon granulated garlic
Freshly ground black pepper
½ lemon
Flaky salt, for serving

METHOD

Preheat the grill to high heat, then clean and oil the grates well.

Pat the steak dry with paper towels and rub it down with the olive oil. Season it aggressively with salt, then coat it in the oregano and granulated garlic, evenly dispersing it on all sides. Season with a few twists of pepper.

Place the steak right on the hottest part of the grill, flipping every 30 seconds or so, and even getting the sides, until it is charred on the outside and cooked to your liking. I prefer a rare to medium-rare temperature, about 130°F, when I take it off the grill.

Drizzle it with a little more olive oil and immediately squeeze the lemon juice over it. Allow it to rest for 5 minutes before serving. Either cut it into portions (I'll usually just cut it in half and split it with my wife), or cut into ½-inch-thick slices, cutting against the grain. Serve with flaky salt.

California Tri-Tip Two Ways

(Summer or Winter)

SERVES 4 TO 6

I'll admit that I've never been to Santa Maria, the namesake location of Santa Maria Tri-Tip. But tri-tip, a triangular cut of meat from the bottom of the sirloin, has been a staple meat in California grocery stores for as long as I can remember. It's a relatively affordable and truly delicious cut of beef that kind of functions halfway between a roast and a steak—an ideal option if you're cooking a piece of beef for the whole family. It works perfectly well over gas, but I highly recommended using a charcoal-and-wood grill. While classic Santa Maria Tri-Tip comes with a salsa that includes celery in it, mine does not. In fact, I find that I eat it differently during different times of year, so I present two seasonal sauces below.

In summer, I eat this steak with flour tortillas, Mezcal Charro Beans (page 75), and a salsa made with charred Hatch chiles. But in the winter, I eat it with crusty bread and an apple-horseradish sauce inspired by Cold Spring Tavern in Santa Barbara (which I have also never been to, but which brought about this dish thanks to rave reviews from my friend Kevin Faerkin).

INGREDIENTS

Mesquite charcoal (optional)
Wood chunks (optional), such as apple, oak and/or pecan
1 tri-tip roast (2 to 2½ pounds)
About 1 tablespoon extra-virgin olive oil
Salt and freshly ground black pepper
5 garlic cloves, finely chopped
Hatch Chile Pico de Gallo (recipe follows) or Apple-Horseradish Sauce (recipe follows)
Flour tortillas or crusty bread and butter

METHOD

Set up a two-zone fire. If grilling with gas, set one side to high heat and the other to low heat. If you are cooking with charcoal, a wood chunk placed on the edge of the charcoal bed will add some bonus smoky flavor. Once preheated, clean and oil the grates well.

Meanwhile, coat the tri-tip with the olive oil, then season it all over with salt and pepper. Rub in the garlic.

Lay the tri-tip on the cooler side of the grill. If operating on charcoal, close the lid, adjusting the vents so that they are closed over the fire and open over the cold spot. (If you have bottom vents, open the one under the fire and close the one underneath the cold zone.) Allow the tri-tip to cook until the thickest part reads about 115°F for medium-rare, about 15 minutes.

Flip the steak, transfer to the hot side of the grill, and cook, turning frequently, until it is nicely charred and reaches an internal temperature of 125° to 130°F. Due to the shape of the tri-tip, there will be some pieces that are slightly more well-done than others.

Let rest for about 10 minutes, then carve in slices against the grain, keeping an eye on the grain while you cut, as it shifts across the tri-tip. Serve with Hatch chile pico de gallo and warm flour tortillas. Or serve with the apple-horseradish sauce and crusty bread and butter.

HATCH CHILE PICO DE GALLO

3 Hatch chiles (can substitute poblanos or Anaheim chiles)
2 pounds best summer tomatoes you can find, finely chopped
¾ cup finely chopped white onion
½ cup finely chopped fresh cilantro leaves and tender stems (about 1 bunch)
Salt
A squeeze of lime

Lay the chiles on the hot side of the grill and allow them to cook until they are charred on all sides, 2 to 3 minutes per side. Transfer them to a bag or a covered bowl to steam. Once steamed and cool enough to handle, remove the blackened skin and discard it. Then remove the stems *and* seeds and chop the peppers to a rustic dice. Combine them in a medium bowl with the tomatoes, onion, and cilantro. Season to taste with salt and lime.

APPLE-HORSERADISH SAUCE

1 large crisp red apple, cored and finely diced (it can be a rough dice)
¼ cup heavy cream
¼ cup prepared horseradish (or finely grated fresh, if you can find it)
1 teaspoon fresh lemon juice

In a small pot, combine the apple with water to cover. Bring to a strong simmer over medium-high heat and cook until the apple is quite soft, about 30 minutes, adding more water if needed.

Once the apple is soft, increase the heat to high and boil off any extra liquid. Add the cream, horseradish, and lemon juice and reduce the heat to medium. Return the sauce to a simmer, stirring frequently. Allow it to simmer for about 30 seconds and then transfer to a large bowl. Whisk it thoroughly to help break up the apples. Serve cold or at room temperature.

Hermosillo-Style Carne Asada

SERVES 6 TO 8

* MESQUITE AND CHARCOAL ONLY*

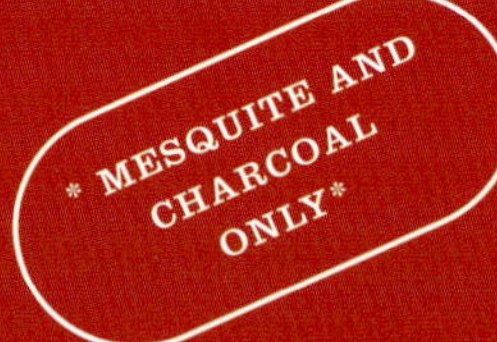

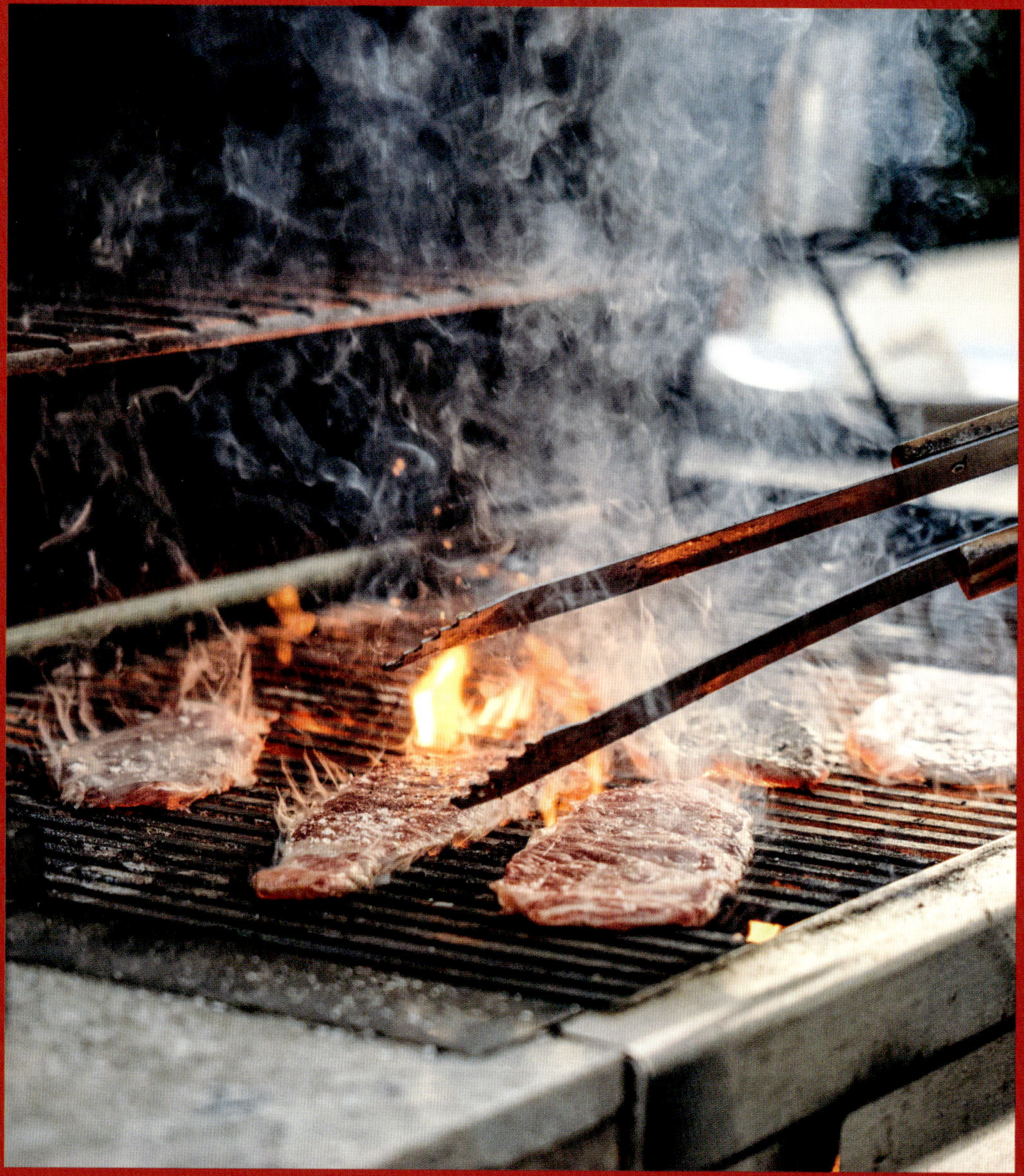

Why Hermosillo?

Growing up in Southern California, I thought I knew about carne asada. But when I set out to research it for this cookbook, I quickly learned that everything I thought I knew about carne asada was dead wrong.

"If you want to learn how to make carne asada," my colleague Bill Esparza wrote me over text, "we have to go to Hermosillo." Bill is one of the foremost experts on Mexican, Central American, and South American food in America. A few weeks after that text, we crossed the border from San Diego to Tijuana, then boarded a 4 a.m. flight to Hermosillo, the capital city in the northern Mexican state of Sonora. "Every region of Mexico grills carne asada for family gatherings," Bill told me, "but in Hermosillo, it's a lifestyle."

Hermosillo is not just a city with exceptional quality of beef and flour tortillas, it is the epicenter of carne asada. The taqueros and grillers in Hermosillo are experts at their craft, and the sheer breadth of carne asada establishments is unrivaled anywhere else in the world: There are roadside taco stands like Tacos El Chato, outdoor carne asada taquerias with craft beer and table service like Tacos del Chava, and high-end taquerias with full bars and an elaborate wine list like Tacos de Armando. There are sit-down carne asada paquetes (family-style combo "packets") like Asadero el Leñador and high-end full-blown steakhouses like Steaks del Herradero. There are even stands selling enormous burritos (percherones) filled with little more than carne asada, cheese, and avocado. Even the grocery stores have gorgeous cuts of steaks, hand-sliced, offered both aged and fresh. It is cooked in backyards, on street corners, and in the fanciest of restaurants. In Hermosillo, carne asada is a way of life.

There was incredible kindness shown to me by so many people on our trip—but none more so than chef, local legend, and a man I'm proud to call my friend: Eloy Aluri. Eloy and his cousin, "who is more like a brother," José Luis Hernández Uribe took us in and showed off Hermosillo, as well as some of the wonderful nearby cities in Sonora.

The recipes in this section are in no way my creations. I was given incredible context from the vast array of people and restaurants, but more than anything, these are the recipes and techniques of chef Eloy Aluri, taught to me in his backyard over coffee, bacanora, and cans of local beer from Buqui Bichi. This is the best carne asada I have ever eaten, re-created as best I can, so that I can cook it for myself, my friends, and my family.

Thank you to Bill, Eloy, José Luis, and our volunteer driver, Danny, for showing me why the best carne asada in the world resides in Hermosillo.

What Is Hermosillo-Style Carne Asada?

Carne asada in Hermosillo is actually fairly simple. The near-universal rule is that it is steak, seasoned only with salt, and grilled over mesquite charcoal. No marinades, no fuss: just steak, sea salt, and mesquite charcoal. This simplicity means that four things *really* matter: the steak, the cook, the tortillas, and the salsa bar.

THE STEAK

As chef Eloy Aluri told me, the primary cuts for carne asada come from along the loin of the cow. The most popular cut is the chuck roll, or diezmillo. But every good cut of steak is welcome for carne asada, whether that is rib eye, New York strip, sirloin, or picanha. The picanha and New York strip are my personal favorites.

THE COOK

Carne asada is cooked over mesquite charcoal once the coals have turned gray, so that the embers are hot but not smoking excessively. The grillers often will have a bottle of water at the grill to quiet flare-ups. Steaks are typically sliced to ¼ to ½ inch thick and cooked to a true medium-well and rested. Frequently, they are rested together to stay moist, often in a covered container, and then sliced to order. Eurocentric palates will tell you that steak is always supposed to be medium-rare, but visit Argentina and Hermosillo and you will learn that is definitely not true.

THE TORTILLAS

In Sonora, flour tortillas are king and Sonoran wheat (a nutty, sweet varietal grown primarily in the Sonoran Desert) from Los Gallos—a historic and iconic local company—is almost universally what they are made from. It is obviously not easy to find Sonoran tortillas in most of the world, but use the best flour tortillas you can possibly find.

THE SALSA BAR

The salsa bars can really vary in size and technique across Hermosillo, but as Bill and Chef Eloy explained, the core salsas are designed not just to complement the meat, but also the other salsas. That means that multiple salsas and condiments can go on a single taco without overwhelming or competing with each other. These are the core salsas that exist in some form at nearly every carne asada salsa bar in Hermosillo.

Tatemada

This is a rustic salsa made from roasted tomato and/or tomatillo, as well as roasted chiles, including serrano or jalapeño, and maybe Anaheim, typically made in a molcajete, or if necessary, pulsed in a food processor.

Salsa Bandera

This is known in much of the rest of Mexico and America as pico de gallo—a raw salsa made from chopped tomato, serrano, onion, cilantro, and occasionally some lime. It is important to not overchop this, which would make it too watery. It is often drained of excess liquid before being served.

A Spicy Salsa

There is usually a spicy salsa, or several of them, made using chiles like fresh habanero, or dried ones like chile de árbol (often called pico de *pájaro* for bird's beak in Hermosillo), or the incredibly popular small round dried chiltepin. For this book, I've included a recipe for a chiltepin salsa as well as a habanero.

Grilled Spring Onions and Wilted Red Onions

These are ubiquitous condiments as well—spring onions, their bulbs roasted over the charcoal, and red onions, wilted with vinegar and a bit of salt.

Shredded Cabbage, Cut Limes, Sliced Cucumbers, and Sliced Radish

A pinch of shredded cabbage and a squeeze of lime is a frequent addition to your taco, while the sliced cucumbers and radish are a refreshing complement to keep on the side.

Frijoles

Beans are a very popular side dish with carne asada, often used as a condiment to spread across the bottom of your tortilla. Everyone does it a little differently, but the most typical version takes beans cooked with just water, then seasoned with salt and mashed by hand. They are then topped with ground dried chile California. Smoking-hot pork lard is then poured over the beans and chile powder so that it fries the chile without burning it. Everything is then stirred together and a grated melting cheese is folded in, giving the beans a light brown-orange color and rich, delicious taste.

Avocado, Guacamole, or Avocado Salsa

Some form of avocado is very common as well. For this recipe, we are just going to serve our tacos with some diced fresh avocado, but a guacamole or avocado salsa would be a welcome addition, too.

JAAS-STYLE TACOS

Tacos Jaas and Jaas Light are iconic taquerias in Hermosillo, known for popularizing the Jaas-style taco technique of taking a roasted, peeled, and seeded Anaheim chile, topping it with cheese, and letting it melt on the grill. This is then put onto the tortilla as a base for a carne asada taco. This brilliant innovation is used throughout Hermosillo, usually honoring the name of its originator, but sometimes changing it to taco haas or even taco jazz.

A Carne Asada Party

(as made by Eloy Aluri in his backyard in Hermosillo)

This recipe is meant to be a bit of a party, a gathering of friends and family, whether born into or found later. As most people reading this recipe are probably not seasoned taqueros, I have tried to arrange this recipe in a way that will give you the easiest path to success. (But as you get better at it, you'll be able to multitask and throw the party together a little faster.)

A COMPLETE GROCERY LIST OF EVERYTHING YOU NEED FOR THE CARNE ASADA PARTY

Since there are a lot of components to this recipe, here is your one-stop-shop for all of the ingredients, for simpler shopping:

- ○ Mesquite charcoal
- ○ 3 to 4 pounds steak, sliced to ¼- to ½-inch thickness—chuck roll, New York strip, rib eye, or picanha are all very good options, but it can be any steak cut that you enjoy
- ○ About 8 ounces good white melting cheese, such as queso blanco, asadero, Monterey Jack, or even mozzarella, grated (plus more if you are making Jaas-style tacos)
- ○ About 2½ pounds Roma tomatoes
- ○ 1½ white onions
- ○ 4 or so spring onions
- ○ Several limes, ideally small Mexican limes
- ○ 3 or 4 avocados
- ○ 2 garlic cloves, unpeeled
- ○ 2 serrano or jalapeño peppers, plus more if you want to serve roasted whole chiles on the side
- ○ At least 1 Anaheim chile (or several more if you want to make Jaas-style tacos)
- ○ 1 habanero
- ○ Cucumbers
- ○ Radishes
- ○ 1 bunch of cilantro
- ○ ½ head green cabbage
- ○ Around 24 taco-size flour tortillas (the best you can find)
- ○ 1 pound dried pinto or mayocoba beans
- ○ ¼ cup pork lard
- ○ 1 tablespoon ground chile California
- ○ About 25 chiltepin chiles, or to taste
- ○ 1 black peppercorn
- ○ 1 cup strained tomatoes, either from a box or can
- ○ About 2 tablespoons distilled white vinegar
- ○ About 2 teaspoons dried oregano
- ○ 1 red onion
- ○ Sea salt
- ○ Flaky salt

First prepare the frijoles, and all of the parts of the salsa bar that do not require charcoal: salsa bandera, salsa chiltepin, salsa habanero, and wilted red onions. You can also prepare Maggi Onions (page 211) for a wonderful additional condiment.

FRIJOLES

1 pound dried pinto or mayocoba beans
Salt
¼ cup pork lard
1 tablespoon ground chile California
About 6 ounces good white melting cheese, such as queso blanco, asadero, Monterey Jack, or even mozzarella, grated

You can cook the dried beans any way you would like, but typically they are soaked in cold water for several hours, then simmered in enough water to comfortably cover them, until they are quite tender, 1 to 2 hours, depending on the age of the beans. Only season them with salt once they are just finished cooking.

When it is time to finish the beans, pour off most of the liquid, leaving just enough to barely cover the beans. Make sure the beans are still hot (reheating them if necessary), then mash them with a potato masher to create a roughly textured consistency but leaving no whole beans.

Meanwhile, in a small pot or pan, heat the lard over medium-high heat until is just beginning to smoke. Sprinkle the chile powder over the beans and then pour the hot lard over the chile powder, frying the powder in the lard. Stir well to combine, then fold in the cheese until it is all melted. Serve hot, rewarming to serve if need be.

SALSA BANDERA

1 pound Roma tomatoes, cut into roughly ½-inch pieces
1 small white onion, cut into roughly ½-inch pieces (about ¾ cup)
1 bunch of cilantro, leaves and tender stems, roughly chopped (about ¾ cup)
1 serrano chile, chopped into small pieces (seeded if you want it less spicy)
Sea salt
Lime, if needed

In a medium bowl, combine the tomatoes, onion, cilantro, and serrano. Season to taste with salt. If the tomatoes taste especially muted, a small squeeze of lime can help to wake them up. Before serving, drain any liquid from the salsa. Store at room temperature for several hours or in the refrigerator for up to a few days.

SALSA CHILTEPIN

1 cup strained tomatoes, from either a can or box
About 25 chiltepin chiles, or to taste
1 tablespoon distilled white vinegar
1 black peppercorn
About 1 teaspoon dried oregano
Salt

In a blender, combine the tomatoes, chiles, vinegar, peppercorn, oregano, and a pinch of salt and blend until smooth. Season to taste with more salt or chiltepin, if needed, and blend again. Just keep in mind that the salsa will get a little bit spicier as it sits. Store at room temperature for several hours or in the refrigerator for up to a few days.

SALSA HABANERO

2 Roma tomatoes, roughly quartered
1 habanero chile
1 garlic clove
Sea salt

In a blender, combine the tomatoes, habanero, garlic, and a pinch of salt. Add water, as needed, just to allow the blades to spin. Blend until smooth. Taste for salt and add more as needed. Store at room temperature for several hours or in the refrigerator for up to a few days.

WILTED RED ONIONS

1 red onion, halved and cut into roughly ½-inch-thick slices
Splash of distilled white vinegar
A pinch of dried oregano
Salt

In a bowl, toss together the onion, vinegar, oregano, and salt and let them wilt for at least 20 minutes before serving.

CUCUMBERS, RADISHES, LIMES, AND GREEN CABBAGE

Cucumbers (peeled, if they have a hard, waxy skin)
Radishes
Limes
About ½ head green cabbage

Cut the cucumbers into rounds or into bite-size chunks. Slice or cut the radishes into bite-size chunks as well. Cut the limes into quarters or wedges (depending on the size). Finely shred the green cabbage.

GRILLING FOR THE SALSA BAR

Mesquite charcoal
½ onion, to clean the grill
1 pound Roma tomatoes
4 or so spring onions
1 garlic clove, unpeeled (or 2, in case you're worried one might fall through the grill grates)
1 serrano or jalapeño chile, or more if you want to serve roasted whole chiles on the side
At least 1 Anaheim chile (or several more if you want to make Jaas-style tacos)

Fill a charcoal chimney or just make a pile of mesquite charcoal in the center of your grill, light the charcoal, and let it burn. Once it has begun to catch, arrange it in the center of the grill. Lay the grill grate over it and allow it to heat up.

Once hot, grab the ½ onion with a grill fork or tongs and rub the cut side against the grill to clean it. Lay the tomatoes around the edge of the grill, away from the direct heat. Lay the spring onions down around the edge, too, with their bulbs on the grill but the greens hanging off the edge.

Find a safe corner to lay your garlic clove without letting it fall through the cracks. You could also lay it on a piece of foil if that makes you feel more comfortable.

Place the serrano at the edge of the grill, but place the Anaheim(s) closer to the center. Turn the Anaheims frequently, just until all of the skin is browned but not burned, 4 to 5 minutes. You want the flesh to be cooked to "al dente." Once browned, transfer the Anaheims to a bag or a covered bowl to steam.

Cook and turn the remaining vegetables as the skins brown and blacken at the edges—they should all be tender and cooked through with some color. The serrano or jalapeño will take 5 or 6 minutes, the spring onions and garlic will take 6 to 7 minutes, and the tomatoes could take around 10. But it all depends on the heat of your charcoal and the distance from the heat. If the tomatoes are nicely charred but not cooked through and softened to the touch, move them closer to the flame and let them cook through.

Take the cooked vegetables off the grill and set them aside. Once cool enough to handle, peel and seed the Anaheim(s)—but do not run them under water to peel them, as it dilutes their flavor. Prepare to make the Tatemada, keeping an eye on your charcoal, adding more if needed to keep it hot for the final step: grilling the carne asada and warming the tortillas.

TATEMADA

1 garlic clove, roasted over mesquite charcoal
Sea salt
1 serrano chile or jalapeño, roasted over mesquite charcoal, stemmed
1 pound Roma tomatoes, roasted over mesquite charcoal until charred and cooked through
1 Anaheim chile, roasted over mesquite charcoal, then peeled and seeded

With a molcajete or mortar and pestle: Peel the garlic clove and place it in the molcajete with a pinch of salt. Pound it until it forms a paste. Add the serrano and pound it, too, making sure to leave no large pieces or long strings, while allowing it to retain some texture and small chunks.

Add the tomatoes, two at a time, with more salt and continue to pound, thinking about the final product, and making sure that you don't have any especially large pieces or big chunks of stem, while also keeping it chunky and textured. Slice the seeded Anaheim chile crosswise into about ½-inch-wide strips (rajas), then run your knife through them once, lengthwise, to shorten the strips. Fold them into the tatemada and then season to taste with salt. Store at room temperature for several hours or in the refrigerator for up to a few days.

With a food processor: Peel the garlic and add it to a food processor with a pinch of salt. Pulse it, scraping down the sides as needed, until it is fully broken down. Roughly chop the serrano and tomatoes, then add those as well, pulsing until you have a rustic texture with no big chunks. Transfer them to a bowl. Slice the seeded Anaheim chile crosswise into ½-inch-wide strips (rajas), then run your knife through them once, lengthwise, to shorten the strips. Fold them into the tatemada and then season to taste with salt. Store at room temperature for several hours or in the refrigerator for up to a few days.

JAAS-STYLE ANAHEIM CHILES

Anaheim chiles, roasted over mesquite charcoal, then peeled and seeded with the stem still attached
A good melting white cheese (1 to 2 ounces per chile), such as queso blanco, asadero, Monterey Jack, or even mozzarella, grated

Lay aluminum foil or a sheet pan on the grill (or in the oven at 400°F). Lay the roasted chiles on top, peeled open-face and flat. Sprinkle the cheese on top of the chiles to cover and place on the grill. Allow them to cook until the cheese is just melted. Serve hot.

CARNE ASADA AND TORTILLAS

3 to 4 pounds steak, sliced to ¼- to ½-inch thickness, such as chuck roll, New York strip, rib eye, or picanha (but it can be any steak cut that you enjoy)
Sea salt
Around 24 taco-size flour tortillas (the best you can find)
Flaky salt

As long as the charcoal is gray in color and still hot, you are ready to cook your carne asada. Season each steak on one side quite liberally with salt, then lay it seasoned-side down on the grill and season the other side with more salt. Repeat with more steaks, working in batches if necessary. You can use a meat thermometer if you would like to reach a specific desired internal temperature (I would target 140° to 145°F), or you can simply cook the steak until it has some color on the first side, then flip it over and let it cook until some reddish juices start to just pool at the top, 60 to 90 seconds per side, depending on the heat of the charcoal. Keep an eye out for flare-ups, moving the steaks to colder parts of the grill as needed.

Once cooked, remove the steaks and place them in a covered casserole dish to rest. Repeat this until all of the steaks are cooked. Allow them to rest briefly and stay warm while you grill the tortillas.

Grill the tortillas until they are warmed through, 5 to 10 seconds per side. If they puff up, they are definitely ready. Transfer them to a tortilla warmer or wrap them in kitchen towels to stay warm.

As a last step, cut the avocados and set it out for serving, along with your full salsa bar:

4 or 5 small avocados
Tatemada (page 164)
Salsa Bandera (page 161)
Shredded green cabbage
Cut limes, ideally halved, small Mexican limes
Salsa Chiltepin (page 161)
Salsa Habanero (page 163)
Wilted Red Onions (page 163)
Maggi Onions (page 211)
Grilled Spring Onions
Sliced, peeled cucumbers
Cut radishes
Frijoles (page 161), served warm
Jaas-Style Anaheim Chiles (page 164)

When you are ready to serve, cut the steaks as you desire, only cutting the ones that people are ready to eat right away—I tend to prefer to cut chuck roll into ¼-inch or so dice, but cut more expensive cuts like rib eye, picanha, or New York strip into slices ¼ to ½ inch thick. You can also give people their own steaks to cut with steak knives as they see fit. Once cut, season the steaks with some flaky salt and enjoy immediately.

Tacos are frequently assembled with a layer of beans across the bottom, followed by the Jaas-style Anaheim chile (if using), the carne asada, and condiments of choice (salsas, lime, onion, etc.), with cucumber and radish on the side.

Punchy, Funky Beef and Broccoli

(Flanken Short Rib with Broccolini and Green Olive Salsa Verde)

SERVES 4 TO 6

Flanken short rib is one of the great beef cut inventions of all time—you take a traditionally slow-cooking piece of meat and cut it thin for fast-grilling. It is most famous as LA galbi in Korean BBQ restaurants, but here I'm honoring this cut by dragging it through the flavors of the Mediterranean, with an anchovy-and-olive salsa verde packed with umami and citrus, hitting all the pleasure points and creating a fantastic California backyard crowd-pleaser.

While rational people would tell you to eat this with a fork and knife, I will stubbornly insist on this as a messy, party-time finger food. This was a "let's see what happens" idea that I'm fully in lust with.

INGREDIENTS

- ⅓ cup fresh lemon juice
- 10 garlic cloves, finely chopped
- 1 (1.73- to 2-ounce) can anchovies packed in oil, oil reserved and fillets finely chopped
- 4 tablespoons extra-virgin olive oil, plus more for coating
- 1 teaspoon crushed red pepper
- 1 tablespoon soy sauce
- 2 teaspoons kosher salt, plus more to taste
- 1 pound flanken short ribs, sliced ¼ to ½ inch thick
- 10 Castelvetrano or similar pitted green olives, finely chopped
- 2 tablespoons finely chopped fresh Italian parsley
- 1 tablespoon drained capers, roughly chopped
- 1 garlic clove, finely chopped
- Grated zest of 1 lemon
- 1 bunch of broccolini
- A squeeze of lemon juice

METHOD

In a large resealable container or ziplock bag, combine the lemon juice, garlic, anchovies and their oil, 2 tablespoons of the olive oil, crushed red pepper, soy sauce, and salt. Stir well to combine, then add the flanken short ribs, tossing to make sure they are fully coated. Transfer to the refrigerator, sealed. Allow the meat to marinate for at least 3 hours and up to 12. (The marinade can also be made up to a day in advance, then you can just add the short rib to it when the time is right.)

When you are ready to grill, preheat the grill to high heat, then clean and oil the grates well.

While the grill is preheating, in a medium bowl, combine the remaining 2 tablespoons olive oil, the olives, parsley, capers, garlic, and lemon zest. Stir well and season to taste with salt. Set the salsa verde aside.

In a large bowl, toss the broccolini with enough olive oil just to barely coat, then season lightly with salt.

When the grill is ready, lay down the short ribs, working in batches if necessary, and grill them until they are browned with bits of blackening on the first side, 2 to 3 minutes. Flip them and repeat with the other side. Either at the same time or after finishing the short ribs, grill the broccolini by laying it on the grill and cooking until it has bits of blackening at the edges, 2 to 3 minutes. Flip it and repeat with the other side, cooking until it is lightly blackened and tender to the touch, another 2 minutes or so. Return it to the large bowl.

Add about two-thirds of the salsa verde to the broccolini and toss it until well combined. Lay it on a serving platter. Cut the short ribs crosswise, between the bones, then toss them with the remaining salsa verde and serve them alongside the broccolini. Squeeze the lemon juice over the broccolini and consume immediately, ideally with your bare hands.

Soy and Citrus Skirt Steak

(with Chile de Árbol, Ginger, and Garlic)

SERVES
4

This is a recipe I've thoroughly enjoyed for years, since developing a menu for a charcoal-grilled rice bowl concept that never got off the ground. This was the flagship recipe—inspired by marinated arrachera from Los Angeles carnicerías, but with its flavors dragged through the Japanese grocery store.

In the end, this is California backyard cooking at its core. Citrusy, savory, lightly spicy, and super-tender marinated beef, which is great for almost all ages of eaters, and goes as well in a rice bowl as it does with a side of Perfect Grilled Potatoes (page 58), over a bowl of soba noodles, or in a flour tortilla with pico de gallo. I prefer a thicker piece of skirt steak if I can find it, as it's easier to char well and keep cooked to medium, but any skirt steak or even flap steak will work well.

INGREDIENTS

- 1½ pounds skirt or flap steak, ideally on the thicker side
- 2 chiles de árbol or other small dried hot chile, stemmed (or 1 teaspoon of any ground, dried red chile that you like)
- 5 garlic cloves, smashed and peeled
- 3 tablespoons tamari or soy sauce
- 2 tablespoons fresh lemon juice
- 2 tablespoons fresh lime juice
- 2 tablespoons extra-virgin olive oil
- 1 scallion, torn into rough pieces
- 1-inch knob fresh ginger, rinsed
- 2 teaspoons sake or dry white wine

METHOD

Lay your steak on a cutting board and cut it *with* the grain, into pieces that are roughly 6 inches long—this is just to optimize its size for grilling, to be sliced again (against the grain) after it is cooked.

In a small saucepan, toast the chiles over high heat just until they are fragrant, shaking the pan frequently, about 60 seconds once the pan is hot. Transfer them to a blender and add the garlic, tamari, lemon juice, lime juice, olive oil, scallion, ginger, and sake. Blend until smooth.

Pour the marinade into a resealable container, add the steak pieces, and turn to make sure all of the pieces are coated in marinade. Marinate in the refrigerator for at least 3 hours and up to about 18.

When you are ready to grill, preheat the grill to high heat (the hotter the better), then clean and oil the grates well.

Lay the steaks on the grill in a single layer and let them cook until they are nicely charred on the first side, 3 to 4 minutes. Flip the steak and cook the other side until cooked to your desired internal temperature. I prefer about 135°F for a medium steak, 1 to 3 more minutes depending on the thickness of the steak and the heat of the grill.

Transfer the steaks to a cutting board. For best results, slice against the grain and serve immediately.

Nước Chấm Brisket Noodle Bowl

SERVES
4

This recipe is a riff on a riff on a riff—like a game of recipe telephone. It's inspired by a late-night snack cooked for me by the award-winning photographer Eric Wolfinger, who was in turn inspired from his time working with chef James Syhabout on his cookbook *Hawker Fare.*

The result is a wonderful way to grill brisket: sliced paper-thin and marinated in nước chấm, a classic Vietnamese dipping sauce comprising lime juice, hot chiles, sugar, garlic, and fish sauce. It doubles as both marinade and sauce for a variation on a Vietnamese noodle bowl that is typically served with pork (bún thịt nướng) with lots of herbs, cucumbers, and pickled vegetables. This is a nice dish to prep out in advance because once you are ready to grill, it comes together in mere minutes.

Notes: Paper-thin sliced brisket can be found in many Korean markets, and more recently, I've noticed it in the frozen section of a wide variety of supermarkets. In a pinch, however, you can buy a piece of raw brisket, partially freeze it, and hand-slice it with a serrated or very sharp knife. Some butchers will also do it for you with some advance notice.

Fried shallots are frequently available in Thai, Japanese, and Korean grocery stores, or readily available online.

INGREDIENTS

Nước Chấm and Brisket Marinade

½ cup sugar
½ cup fresh lime juice
⅓ cup fish sauce
4 garlic cloves, finely chopped
3 Thai chiles, thinly sliced
1 tablespoon neutral oil
1¼ pounds brisket, sliced very thin (see Notes)

Brisket Noodle Bowl

¼ cup water
1 (14-ounce) package vermicelli rice noodles
2 English cucumbers or 4 Persian (mini) cucumbers, cut into strips
About 2 cups loosely packed soft herb leaves and tender stems, any mix of cilantro, Thai basil, and mint
About 1 cup Đồ Chua (page 23)
1 or 2 jalapeños, sliced into thin rings (optional, if you want it less spicy)
Fried shallots (see Notes)

METHOD

Make the nước chấm and marinate the brisket: In a large bowl, combine the sugar, lime juice, and fish sauce. Whisk until the sugar is mostly dissolved. Measure out ½ cup of the mixture then transfer it to a small mixing bowl and set it aside for the noodle bowl. The large bowl is for the marinade.

To the large bowl, add 3 of the garlic cloves, 2 of the chiles, and the neutral oil. Stir to combine and then add the thinly sliced brisket, making sure to separate the slices, allowing the marinade to touch all of the beef. Toss together to combine and place the bowl in the refrigerator to let the meat marinate for at least 30 minutes and up to 3 hours.

Assemble the brisket noodle bowl: In the bowl with the reserved sauce, add the water, and the remaining garlic and chile. Stir it well and set it aside while you grill the brisket.

Preheat the grill to high heat, then clean and oil the grates well. (If you have a grill pan, this will reduce the quantity of brisket that might fall through the grates.)

In a large pot of boiling water, cook the vermicelli according to the package directions. Drain and rinse thoroughly in cold water. Set aside.

When the grill is ready, cook the brisket, in batches if necessary, until all of the raw color is gone, with some crisping at the edges, 1 to 2 minutes depending on the heat of your grill. Don't worry if your brisket is clumping as you gather, flip, and turn it—variety in texture is a good thing. Just make sure all the raw color is cooked out.

Once all of the brisket is cooked, refresh the vermicelli in cold running water and use your fingers to break up any clumps. Drain it well and then divide it into individual bowls. Top each bowl with the brisket, cucumbers, herbs, đồ chua, and sliced jalapeño if you desire. Sprinkle with fried shallots and serve with the reserved nước chấm. Eat immediately.

Smoke-Grilled Bone-In Rib Eye with Mansion Butter

SERVES
2 TO 3

WOOD & CHARCOAL ONLY

This is the best steak I have ever cooked in my life. It is essentially a "reverse-sear," cooking the steak slowly and gently to your exact specifications before crisping and charring the outside. But instead of the more common method using an oven or a sous-vide machine, this grilled version adds a buttery smokiness to the fat, which infuses throughout the entire steak. Right after it is finished charring on the grill, I slather it with an amped-up compound butter, which I'm calling mansion butter, because it is way more luxurious and flavor-packed than the more classic hotel butter. If you want to use a "cowboy" or "tomahawk" rib eye, with the big bone on it, you absolutely can. It is a fun showstopper and gives you an easy handle for flipping the steak.

Note: For best results, season the steak with salt 24 to 48 hours in advance.

INGREDIENTS

2-inch-thick bone-in rib-eye steak (about 2 pounds)
Kosher salt
Charcoal
Wood chunks (I prefer a mix of post oak and pecan)
Freshly ground black pepper
A hefty pat of Mansion Butter (recipe follows)

METHOD

For best results, season the steak liberally with salt on all sides, patting it into the steak and then place the steak on a wire rack set in a sheet pan. Ideally, you want it to sit in the refrigerator for 1 to 3 days, but if you are in a hurry, you can certainly skip this step and season it right before cooking.

Set up a two-zone fire by lighting a full chimney of charcoal. Once they have turned gray, set them on one side of the grill. Place 2 wood chunks on top of the charcoal and then close the lid. Open the vent over the cooler side, and leave it closed over the hot side.

Season the steak quite liberally on all sides with pepper, patting it into the steak.

Once the wood has burned for about 5 minutes, add the steak to the cooler side of the grill, with the bone facing the fire.

Cover the grill and allow the steak to cook, adding another handful of charcoal and 2 additional chunks of wood if the wood or charcoal is burning off (check after about 30 minutes).

Cook the steak to about 15°F below your desired final temperature. For me, that is about 120°F, which usually takes 30 to 45 minutes. (This will finish the steak at a nice medium-rare.) When checking the internal temperature of the steak, don't check too close to the bone, or it will temp much colder than the majority of the steak. When the steak is ready, move it to the hot side of the grill. Allow it to cook and brown and char at the edges, flipping quite frequently and moving it as needed to avoid flare-ups.

Once the steak is browned all over to your liking, 90 seconds to 2 minutes, transfer it to a cutting board and spread the mansion butter over the steak. Allow it to rest for at least 2 minutes, then slice against the grain and serve immediately.

MANSION BUTTER

Makes a generous ½ cup

In addition to its role on a wood-grilled rib eye, mansion butter is outstanding with sautéed shrimp, steamed clams, or spooned into a baked sweet potato. Note that it is very important that the butter be quite soft, otherwise the ingredients won't combine properly.

1 stick (4 ounces) unsalted butter, at room temperature
3 tablespoons finely chopped fresh Italian parsley
2 garlic cloves, grated or finely chopped
1½ tablespoons finely chopped shallots
1½ teaspoons finely chopped jalapeño (seeded, if you desire)
1 teaspoon fresh lemon juice
¾ teaspoon soy sauce or gluten-free tamari
⅛ teaspoon fine sea salt
Several twists of freshly ground black pepper

In a medium bowl, combine the butter, parsley, garlic, shallot, jalapeño, lemon juice, soy sauce, salt, and pepper and mix quite well, using either a rubber spatula or gloved hands. Store at room temperature for a few hours, or in an airtight container in the refrigerator for up to 3 days. Allow the butter to come to room temperature before using.

Pork

Buttermilk-Brined Pork Chop
with Grilled Lemon 178
Pork Secret 180
Sausage and Lentils with Grilled Leeks 183
"Pretend It's the '90s" Honey-Balsamic
Pork Tenderloin 185
Coconut-Crusted Tiki Pork Ribs 186
Smoke-Grilled Baby Backs 188
BBQ Pork Belly Bossam 190

Pork is probably the most versatile protein on the planet. It is nuanced enough to taste great with little more than salt and pepper, but can *also* handle a ton of spices, brines, cures, and marinades. Even some cuts that are typically more common in slow-cooked BBQ, like ribs and pork belly, I actually prefer on the grill, as it creates a crispier bite with a faster cook (especially if you smoke-grill it using a two-zone fire with wood chunks). The grill is also great for a leaner cut, like pork tenderloin. And of course, the classics, like sausage and pork chops, are classics for a reason.

I've found that pork from small local farms tastes *leaps and bounds* better than the commodity stuff you often find at grocery stores. But when you're shopping from local farms, it is important to take a look at the cuts you're going to be working with before you buy them. Since commodity pigs are typically quite large, the cuts from small farms might be smaller and leaner than the ones you see at the grocery store. Make sure your ribs have some thickness and meatiness, and make sure that your pork chops and bellies have enough fat on them to keep from drying out.

Buttermilk-Brined Pork Chop with Grilled Lemon

SERVES 3 OR 4

Pan-seared pork chops get a lot of love, and with good reason—they get to cook in their own rendered fat. But while a pan-seared chop prefers a dry brine, a grilled pork chop does well with a wet one. That's because a wet brine will add extra water to the pork chop, making it harder to brown in a pan. This is not a problem on the grill, as that extra water falls right out. You also get to add a ton of flavor and tenderness to the pork chop itself, as demonstrated by this buttermilk/orange juice brine loaded with fresh herbs and a little bit of soy sauce. A lot of people might add brown sugar here, but I think the orange juice adds just the right amount of mellow sweetness.

This recipe is great with any of the sides, but I particularly enjoy it with the Broccolini with Preserved Lemon (page 42) and some Mezcal Charro Beans (page 75).

INGREDIENTS

- 1 cup buttermilk
- ½ cup orange juice
- 2 tablespoons Diamond Crystal kosher salt, or 1 tablespoon Morton kosher or table salt
- 1 tablespoon soy sauce or gluten-free tamari
- 3 sprigs fresh thyme
- 6 fresh sage leaves
- 2 garlic cloves, grated
- About 15 twists of freshly ground black pepper
- 2 bone-in pork rib chops (12 to 16 ounces each), about 1½ inches thick
- 1 lemon
- Extra-virgin olive oil

METHOD

In a resealable container or large ziplock bag that will fit both pork chops, combine the buttermilk, orange juice, salt, and soy sauce. Whisk thoroughly to help dissolve the salt, then rub the thyme sprigs and sage leaves to release the oils and drop them into the container. Add the garlic, pepper, and pork chops. Make sure they are both fully coated with liquid and seal the container. Place it in the refrigerator to marinate for at least 6 hours and up to 24. (I find that 12 to 18 hours is the sweet spot.)

When you are ready to grill, set up a two-zone fire. If grilling with gas, set one side to high] heat and the other to medium-low heat. Clean and oil the grates well.

Lift the pork chops from the brine and allow the liquid to drain off. Lay them on the cooler side of the grill, with the bones facing the fire. Allow them to cook until they reach an internal temperature of 115°F, 12 to 15 minutes.

Move them directly over to the hot side of the grill, turning frequently. Cook them until they have beautiful brown coloring on the outside and an internal temperature between 130° and 140°F, 3 to 5 more minutes. Take them off the heat and allow them to rest.

Meanwhile, cut the lemon in half and rub the cut sides with oil. Lay the halves cut-side down on the hot side of the grill and allow them to grill until they have a golden-brown color with some bits of blackening, about 3 minutes.

Serve the pork chops whole or sliced, garnished with the grilled lemon.

Pork Secret

(Secreto with Rosemary, Garlic, Chile de Árbol, and Tangerine Zest)

SERVES 4 TO 6

Pork secreto, the "secret cut" of the pig, has been showing up for a while at "cool guy" restaurants across the country. But here's the deal: It's delicious. It is well-marbled but not overly fatty, can be cooked to a nice medium to medium-rare, and does not take a lot of effort to have wonderful flavor. I get mine from a beloved local farm here in California called Peads & Barnetts, but you can often find it through local butchers or specialty stores. Different butchers cut it slightly differently, but my friends at Peads "take it from where the belly runs into the lower shoulder, essentially from the brisket area of the pig."

My version is inspired by the great chef Suzanne Goin, who cooked at my house for a goofy little YouTube show called *Guest Chef.* It is prepared with a simple rub of fresh and dried ingredients, pounded or chopped, and rubbed all over the salted secreto. This dish pairs perfectly with Jimmy Nardellos with Red Yuzu Vinaigrette (page 60).

INGREDIENTS

- 1 pork secreto (about 1½ pounds)
- Kosher salt and freshly ground black pepper
- About 12 inches of rosemary sprigs
- Grated zest of 1 tangerine (try your best to avoid the white pith)
- 3 garlic cloves, smashed and peeled
- 1 chile de árbol
- 1 tablespoon extra-virgin olive oil
- Charcoal (optional)
- Wood chunks (optional)
- Flaky salt

METHOD

Season the pork secreto liberally with salt and pepper on all sides.

Strip the leaves from the rosemary and add it to a mortar and pestle along with the tangerine zest, garlic, chile de árbol, and olive oil. Pound until a fine paste forms. (Alternatively, you could very finely chop all of the ingredients and stir them into a bowl with the olive oil.) Rub the pork secreto all over with the paste and set it aside while you light the grill.

Set up a two-zone fire. If grilling with gas, set one side to high heat and the other to medium-low heat. If you are using charcoal, light a chimney full of charcoal and when it turns gray, push it to one side. Add a chunk of wood and allow it to smolder for 5 minutes, covered. Clean and oil the grill grates well.

Lay the secreto over the hot side of the grill and allow it to cook, turning frequently, until it is nicely browned all over with bits of charring around the edge, about 15 minutes.

Transfer it to the cooler side of the grill and check the internal temperature. Continue cooking until the thickest part of the secreto reaches an internal temperature between 130° and 140°F, another 10 to 20 minutes, depending on the thickness.

Remove it from the grill and let it rest for 10 minutes. Carve into slices, against the grain on a bias, and serve with flaky salt.

Sausage and Lentils with Grilled Leeks

SERVES
4

As a fiber evangelist and lover of lentils, I'm always trying to find a way to cook them for my kids. I find that both sausage and leeks benefit from poaching before hitting the grill, for perfectly cooked ingredients with great char. This recipe doubles down on flavor efficiency by poaching the leeks and sausage together, then using that same liquid to cook the lentils.

Note: It is worth looking for delicious, less common lentils if you can. Umbrian Castelluccio di Norcia would be wonderful, as would French green lentils, Puglia lentils, or black caviar lentils—but simple brown lentils will work as well. Also, feel free to sub a savory chicken sausage if that's your preference.

INGREDIENTS

2 medium leeks (or 1 leek, if it is quite large)
4 pork sausages, such as salt-and-pepper, sweet Italian, or hot Italian
2 garlic cloves
1 sprig fresh rosemary
1 bay leaf, fresh or dried
Salt
1 cup small green, brown, or black lentils (see Note), rinsed
Freshly ground black pepper
Freshly grated Pecorino Romano or Parmigiano-Reggiano cheese
Extra-virgin olive oil, for drizzling

METHOD

Cut the dark green parts from the leeks and discard (or save for another use, like making stock). Slice off as much of the root as you can while keeping the base of the leek intact. Cut the leeks in half lengthwise, then remove the outermost layer and rinse the leeks under cold water, gently peeling back layers as necessary to remove any mud and dirt.

In a Dutch oven or deep sauté pan with a lid, lay the sausages down in a single layer. Lay the halved leeks on top and add the garlic, rosemary, and bay leaf to the pot. Fill the pot with cold water just until the leeks are almost covered. Season with a hefty pinch of salt and place the pot over medium-high heat. Keep an eye on the pot so that it does not boil, but just reaches a gentle simmer. Simmer for 5 minutes, then remove the leeks and set them aside. Insert an instant-read thermometer into the end of one of the sausages. If they are 145°F or over, you can remove them, otherwise keep simmering until they are between 145° and 150°F (at most, this will take about 20 minutes, but it is frequently much less). Leave the garlic, rosemary, and bay leaf in the pot.

Add the lentils to the pot and bring to a boil. Reduce the heat to low, cover, and cook until the lentils are tender, 25 to 45 minutes depending on the type and age of the lentil. Once the lentils are tender, discard the bay leaf and rosemary sprig and turn off the heat, keeping the pot covered.

Meanwhile, preheat the grill to high heat, then clean and oil the grates well.

When the lentils are tender or *almost* tender, you can grill the sausages and leeks. Add the sausages to the grill and cook, turning as needed, until the skins are browned and crisped, about 3 minutes. Set aside. Allow the leeks to char on the first side, about 2 minutes, then flip them over and repeat with the other side.

Roughly chop the leeks, then season them with salt and fold them into the pot of lentils. Place the pot over medium-high heat and bring to a simmer. The lentils should have a stew-like consistency at this point, but if they are especially dry and stiff, simply add a splash of water. Conversely, if they are quite wet, continue simmering until they reduce to a stew-like consistency. Season to taste with salt and pepper.

Spread the lentils on a serving platter and top with the sausages. Sprinkle grated cheese over the top and drizzle with olive oil. Serve immediately.

“Pretend It’s the ’90s” Honey-Balsamic Pork Tenderloin

(with Grilled Red Onion and Arugula)

SERVES
4

This is the ’90s Italian restaurant main course of my childhood. The tenderloin is a lean cut of pork that takes on a marinade relatively quickly, and is delicious on the grill. It also, for whatever it’s worth, might be the easiest cut of meat to carve and serve. For this version, I like to marinate the tenderloin along with quartered red onions and rosemary in balsamic vinegar, olive oil, and honey. The result is a tangy, sweet, umami-rich piece of meat that will take on excellent caramelization—that’s why I prefer to cook it hot and fast with lots of char. The big trick here is to not overcook it, since it is so lean. The tenderloin is complemented beautifully by the balsamic-grilled onions and a bed of arugula, along with some lemon and Parmesan.

INGREDIENTS

½ cup balsamic vinegar
2 tablespoons extra-virgin olive oil, plus more to finish
1 tablespoon honey
1 tablespoon Diamond Crystal kosher salt, or 1½ teaspoons Morton kosher or table salt
10 twists of freshly ground black pepper, plus more to finish
1- to 1¼-pound pork tenderloin
1 red onion, peeled and quartered through the root
1 sprig fresh rosemary
2 ounces arugula (or two handfuls)
1 lemon
Flaky salt
Parmesan cheese

METHOD

In a resealable container or ziplock bag large enough to fit the full tenderloin (it is best to be able to pack it in tightly), add the vinegar, olive oil, honey, salt, and pepper. Stir to help dissolve the salt.

Trim any excess fat from the tenderloin and add it to the marinade along with the red onion. Rub the rosemary with your fingers to release the oils and drop it in the bag as well. Make sure the tenderloin is covered with liquid. Allow it to marinate in the refrigerator for at least 1 hour and up to 8.

When you are ready, preheat the grill to high heat, then clean and oil the grates well.

Lift the pork from the marinade and let any excess liquid drain off. Lay the pork on the grill and let it cook, turning frequently until it registers between 135° and 140°F in the thickest part (this will be a proper medium cook—but feel free to cook it further if you desire), about 15 minutes.

At the same time, lift out the onions as well and add them to the grill, turning them as they char. Remove them when they are charred on all sides and tender, 10 to 15 minutes.

Let the pork rest for 10 minutes, then arrange the arugula on a serving platter. Slice off the root ends from the red onion and scatter the petals across the arugula. Squeeze some lemon over the arugula, drizzle it with olive oil, and season it with flaky salt and pepper. Slice the tenderloin against the grain and lay it on top of the arugula. Drizzle any juices from the cutting board over the top and top with freshly shaved or grated Parmesan cheese. Serve immediately.

Coconut-Crusted Tiki Pork Ribs

SERVES 2 TO 4

I have always been a firm believer that to make good ribs, wood smoke needs to be involved somewhere along the way. But with these ribs, I have successfully convinced myself otherwise, since these are *delicious* on a gas grill. (That being said, they are *even* better using the same method with a charcoal grill and wood chunks.)

These ribs are a party. (I will *always* enjoy watching my kids' faces get smeared with sauce while chewing on ribs.) The trick is a sweet-and-spicy tiki-inspired pineapple BBQ sauce, with a heavy dusting of shredded coconut that goes on toward the end, getting browned and crunchy at the finish.

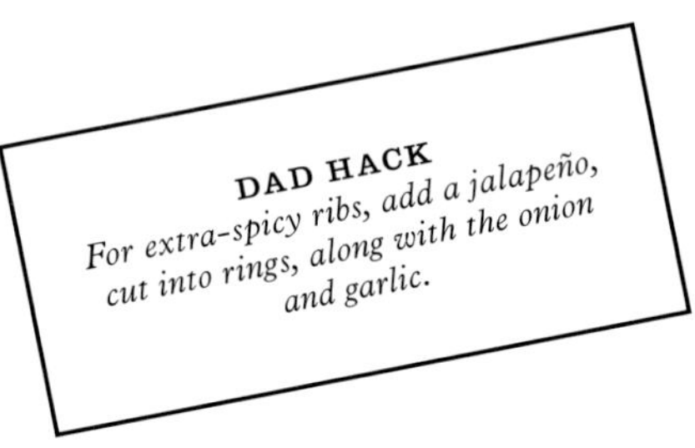

INGREDIENTS

½ cup firmly packed light brown sugar
½ cup pineapple juice
¼ cup ketchup
¼ cup apple cider vinegar
½ red onion, roughly chopped
3 garlic cloves, roughly chopped
2 tablespoons soy sauce
Freshly ground black pepper
½ teaspoon granulated onion
½ teaspoon granulated garlic
¼ teaspoon mustard powder
1 tablespoon chili crisp (I prefer Fly By Jing Sichuan Chili Crisp)
Charcoal (optional)
Wood chunks (optional)
1 rack St. Louis–style pork spare ribs (with some nice fat and marbling on top)
Kosher salt
3 tablespoons unsweetened finely shredded coconut

METHOD

In a medium saucepan, combine the brown sugar, pineapple juice, ketchup, vinegar, onion, garlic, soy sauce, 10 twists of pepper, the granulated onion, granulated garlic, and mustard powder. Bring to a simmer over medium-high heat, stirring frequently. Reduce the heat to a gentle simmer and cook, stirring occasionally, just to soften the onions and garlic, about 5 minutes. Remove from the heat, cover, and let steep for at least 30 minutes.

Pour the BBQ sauce through a sieve into a bowl. Stir in the chili crisp and set aside until you are ready to cook the ribs. Set aside about half of the BBQ sauce for basting and reserve the rest for serving. The pineapple BBQ sauce will last up to a full week in the refrigerator.

When you are ready to cook, set up a two-zone fire. If grilling with gas, set one side to high heat and the other to medium-low heat. If you are using charcoal, light a chimney full of charcoal and when it turns gray, push it to one side. Add a chunk of wood and allow it to smolder for 5 minutes, covered. Clean and oil the grill grates well.

Pat the ribs dry with a paper towel and then season both sides with salt and pepper.

Lay the pork ribs, meaty-side up, on the cooler side of the grill. Baste them thoroughly with the BBQ sauce, close the lid, and grill for 20 minutes.

Baste the ribs again and let them cook for another 15 minutes.

Baste once again and check the internal temperature at the thickest part. Continue checking the ribs, basting every time you check, until they have reached an internal temperature of about 170°F in the thickest part (this will usually take about 40 minutes).

Baste the ribs one last time, then close the lid and let them sit for 5 minutes. Move the ribs closer to the fire and then coat the top of them thoroughly with an even layer of the shredded coconut. Allow it to toast and cook until the ribs have an internal temperature of 195°F, about 15 more minutes. If they are fully cooked but the coconut is not browned, gently lift and tilt them toward the fire, being careful not to scrape off the coconut, and allow it to finish browning.

Remove the ribs, carve them between the bones, and serve immediately with additional BBQ sauce.

Smoke-Grilled Baby Backs

(with Aleppo Pepper, Mirin, and Cider Vinegar)

SERVES 2 TO 4

WOOD & CHARCOAL ONLY

This recipe is inspired by the great Kevin Bludso's grilled ribs from *Bludso's BBQ Cookbook*, which we wrote together a few years back. By grilling the ribs over indirect heat with charcoal and wood chunks, you get the flavor of smoke along with the char of the grill to create juicy, addictive ribs that cook in around an hour (as opposed to the 3 or 4 hours it takes to cook them in an offset smoker). I am both proud and a little frightened of how much my daughter loves eating these right off the bone.

I love the pure flavors these get from a dry rub of just salt, granulated garlic, and the unique fruity-spicy Aleppo pepper. The Aleppo, along with a spray of mirin (sweet Japanese cooking wine) and cider vinegar throughout the cook, gives perfectly subtle sweetness to complement the smoke.

Note: If you have a bigger grill, you can easily double this recipe, as long as you can keep a two-zone fire.

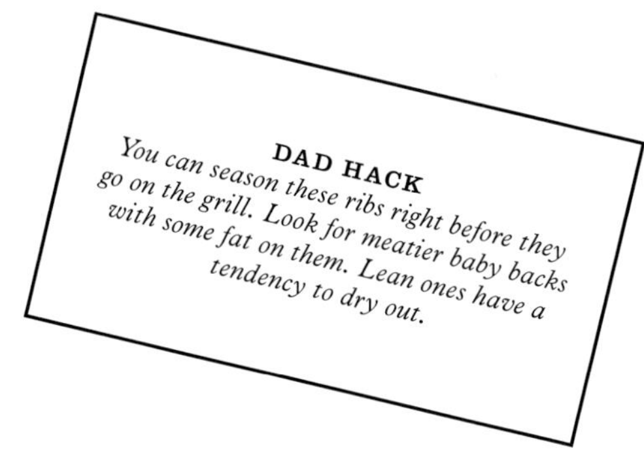

INGREDIENTS

1 rack baby back ribs
Yellow mustard
Kosher salt
1 tablespoon granulated garlic
2 teaspoons Aleppo pepper
Mesquite or lump charcoal
Wood chunks (I prefer a mix of post oak or hickory, with apple or pecan)
¼ cup mirin
¼ cup apple cider vinegar

METHOD

Pat the rack of ribs dry with a paper towel. Rub it down with enough yellow mustard to just barely coat it. Season liberally all over with salt, then sprinkle it all over with the granulated garlic and Aleppo, seasoning heavier on the front (the meatier side) of the ribs than the back.

Set up a two-zone fire by lighting a full chimney of charcoal. Once they have turned gray, set them on one side of the grill. Place 2 wood chunks on top of the charcoal, then close the lid and open the vent over the cooler side and leave it closed over the hot side. Let the wood burn for about 5 minutes.

Add the ribs to the cooler side of the grill, with the thick side facing the fire. Close the lid and smoke the ribs undisturbed for the first 30 minutes. Meanwhile, combine the mirin and vinegar in a clean spray bottle.

After 30 minutes, open the lid and give the ribs a spray, adding more charcoal or wood if either are nearly burned off. Continue cooking until the ribs are just tender, anywhere from 10 minutes to 1 hour, depending on your grill and the thickness of the ribs. Spray the ribs every time you open the lid to check them. They should have some bend to them when you lift the ribs up with tongs, and feel tender to the touch. (Alternatively, you can use a meat thermometer inserted into the thickest part of the ribs—it should register between 190° and 195°F.)

Once cooked, transfer them to a cutting board, meat-side down—it is much easier to see where the bones are this way. Find the curvature of the bones and use a chef's knife to cut between the bones through the middle of the meat. Turn them over and serve immediately.

BBQ Pork Belly Bossam

SERVES
6

WOOD & CHARCOAL ONLY

Bossam is a classic Korean dish and beloved drinking food, usually involving simmered pork belly or pork shoulder, served with lots of pickles, rice, and condiments (often including freshly shucked oysters), and eaten in Napa cabbage or lettuce wraps. My friend Kevin Faerkin used to make the David Chang Momofuku version of this, and we kept evolving it, eventually using a pit-smoked pork shoulder. I've now taken even more orthogonal turns, blending in yet more cultures and dragging the bossam further through the American South into this hybrid dish that has become a heck of a party trick. In fact, we throw an annual family backyard potluck centered around this dish now (or a larger-format version, using a whole bone-in, skin-on pork shoulder).

Skin-on pork belly gets scored and dry-brined, then smoke-grilled over indirect heat until it is tender and smoky with crispy pork skin. Served in lettuce wraps with steamed rice and (optional) oysters, it is the pickles and the BBQ sauce that take the whole thing to a beautiful place that feels *very* backyard SoCal.

INGREDIENTS

Dry-Brined Pork Belly

2 pounds skin-on pork belly
2 tablespoons kosher salt
2 tablespoons granulated sugar

Jalapeño and Onion Soy Sauce Pickles

1 medium white onion, cut into ½-inch half-moons
2 jalapeños, sliced into ½-inch rings
1 cup rice wine vinegar
½ cup soy sauce
½ cup water
2 tablespoons firmly packed light brown sugar
1 bay leaf
1 cinnamon stick
1 dried chile de árbol or other small hot red chile
A strip of lemon zest

Miso-Mustard BBQ Sauce

1 teaspoon neutral oil, such as avocado or canola
2 garlic cloves, grated or very finely chopped
1 teaspoon grated or very finely chopped fresh ginger
¼ cup white miso
1 tablespoon tomato paste
1 tablespoon mirin
½ cup apple cider vinegar
½ cup yellow mustard
¼ cup firmly packed light brown sugar
A pinch of cayenne pepper
1 teaspoon mustard powder
1 teaspoon soy sauce
1 teaspoon toasted sesame oil
1 teaspoon honey or agave
¼ teaspoon Worcestershire sauce

To Grill and Serve

Mesquite or lump charcoal
Wood chunks (I like to use pecan and either apple or hickory)
Toasted sesame oil
Flaky salt
Freshly cooked short- or medium-grain white rice
About 2 heads Bibb or butter lettuce, large lettuce leaves pulled off and rinsed
6 scallions, thinly sliced
12 small briny oysters (optional), freshly shucked

METHOD

Dry-brine the pork belly: Use a sharp or serrated knife to score the pork belly skin into a crosshatch pattern, with the cuts about 2 inches apart. You don't need to worry about the cuts being too deep; you just want to break through the skin. That said, pork skin can be tough, so if you cut a little deeper, that's okay, too.

In a small bowl, combine the salt and sugar and whisk until well combined. Season the pork belly all over with the mixture, allowing it to get into the cuts on the skin as well. Allow the pork to brine in the refrigerator, uncovered, for between 8 and 48 hours. For best results, set it on a wire rack over a quarter-sheet pan, for more air circulation.

Make the jalapeño and onion soy sauce pickles: Place the onion and jalapeños in a heat-proof container, like a medium stainless steel bowl.

In a small saucepan, combine the vinegar, soy sauce, water, brown sugar, bay leaf, cinnamon, chile, and lemon zest. Bring to a boil over high heat. Reduce the heat to a gentle simmer and stir to make sure the sugar is dissolved. Pour the mixture over the onions and jalapeños. Allow it to sit until it comes to room temperature. It can be eaten right away, or stored in a sealable container in the refrigerator for up to 1 month.

Make the miso-mustard BBQ sauce: In a small saucepan, heat the neutral oil over medium heat until shimmering. Add the garlic and ginger, stirring frequently. Allow it to sizzle for about 30 seconds, then add the miso and tomato paste. Toast, stirring constantly, for another 30 seconds. Add the mirin and deglaze the bottom of the pan. Once the mirin is evaporated, add the vinegar, mustard, brown sugar, cayenne, mustard powder, soy sauce, sesame oil, honey, and Worcestershire sauce and whisk to combine. Continue stirring occasionally until the mixture comes to a strong simmer. Turn off the heat and allow it to cool to room temperature. Rewarm gently to serve, being careful not to burn it. The sauce will keep for up to 1 week in an airtight container in the refrigerator.

When you're ready to grill: Set up a two-zone fire by lighting a full chimney of charcoal. Once they have turned gray, set them on one side of the grill. Place 2 wood chunks on top of the charcoal and then close the lid and allow them to burn off for about 5 minutes. Open the vent over the cooler side, and leave it closed over the hot side. Clean the grates well.

Lay the pork belly, skin-side up, on the cooler side of the grill. Cover the grill and allow the meat to cook until the pork belly is tender and has an internal temperature of around 190°F, about 2 hours, occasionally checking the charcoal and wood and refilling as needed to maintain heat and smoke—usually adding 2 more chunks of wood and a handful of charcoal every 30 to 45 minutes.

Once finished, open the lid and move the pork belly closer to the charcoal, turning it on its side with the skin facing the coals. Cook carefully to avoid burning and watch for pork-fat flare-ups over the fire. When in doubt, you can always take the belly off the grill until the fire dies down. Continue flashing the skin near the grill until the skin gets crisp, 3 to 5 minutes.

Set the pork on a cutting board and use a heavy knife to chop it all up into fairly small pieces, making sure to cut up the crispy pork skin. The whole thing should have a chopped BBQ pork feel, with little bits of crispy skin throughout. Drizzle it with about a tablespoon of sesame oil and sprinkle it with flaky salt. Serve immediately.

Make-your-own wraps: Lay warm rice into a lettuce leaf and top with the chopped pork, BBQ sauce, pickles, scallions, and a shucked oyster (if using).

Sea food

Grilled Clams with Cocktail Butter 196
Grilled Oysters with Miso-Ginger
Calabrian Chili Butter 198
Grilldas (or Grilled Squid Gildas) 201
Charred Garlic-Butter Sriracha Shrimp 203
Quick-Grilled Fish Steak 204
Crispy-Skinned Fish Fillet 206
Grilled Fish Tacos with Chile Crunch 208
Whole Grilled Fish Tacos
with Maggi Onions 211
Smoke-Grilled Miso Black Cod 212

Halibut
Snapper

The most common complaint I hear about cooking seafood is that "it makes the house smell like fish." While I think good fish will make a house smell good, I understand the sentiment. Enter: the grill. Grilling fish outside prevents the lingering smell of fish or fish-tinted oil spattering across your stove and kitchen walls.

Grilling is also the *easiest* way to cook seafood. The key comes from my friend Ari Kolender, the highly acclaimed chef of LA restaurants like Found Oyster and Queen's Raw Bar & Grill, who taught me that painting your seafood with a thin veil of mayonnaise will make it virtually nonstick on the grill. The trick to grilling a piece of fish is to lay it on the grill, leave it alone, and flip it just once. Or as Ari says, "Messing with it messes with it."

When you are shopping for seafood, I cannot encourage you enough to follow two simple principles:

1. **DIVERSIFY THE SEAFOOD THAT YOU EAT.**
   There is so much more out there than tuna and salmon. Think about the health of the planet and open your mind to all of the delicious sea creatures that are not overfished and overconsumed.

2. **BUY AMERICAN.**
   The United States is historically the best country in the world at regulating its own seafood supply, but we are not great at regulating what we import. We have some of the best and most sustainable seafood in the world, yet we export 80 percent of it to other countries and import 80 percent of the stuff we do eat. That seafood is overly cheap for a reason. It is frequently overfished, unsustainable, and in many cases, caught by ships that engage in horrifying human rights violations. So . . . buy American.

Grilled Clams with Cocktail Butter

SERVES 4 TO 6

Clams are my favorite seafood in the world. Also . . . I might care *a little too much* about my kids liking them. This recipe has you lay whole clams right on the grill and, when they open just a little, take them off the grill, pry off the top shell, top them with cocktail sauce and butter, then return them to the grill until they bubble and start to char around the edges. This recipe is inspired by a restaurant I have never been to, but have always been obsessed with: The Place, in Guilford, Connecticut. My good friend Kevin Faerkin swears they make the best grilled clams, and this is an homage to those. For the cocktail sauce, I have unashamedly stolen the recipe from *How to Cook the Finest Things in the Sea,* the cookbook I wrote with my friend Ari Kolender, because it is the best cocktail sauce.

Topneck or littleneck clams are ideal for this, but I have also made it with Manila clams, which are smaller (and more annoying because you have to grill so many of them). Whatever clam you choose, it will be unbelievably delicious.

INGREDIENTS

- 24 live topneck or littleneck clams or 48 Manila clams, well cleaned
- Ari Kolender's Cocktail Sauce (recipe follows)
- 2 sticks (8 ounces) unsalted butter, melted

METHOD

Preheat the grill to high heat, then clean the grates well (no need to oil them).

Once the grill is hot, lay half of the clams on the grill. Once they are just starting to open, 2 to 3 minutes, transfer them to a platter or baking sheet. Once they are cool enough to handle, pry off one of the half shells and discard it, scraping the meat with a spoon or knife to release it from the shell if need be.

Once all the clams are off the grill and open, give each clam a 1 teaspoon or so dollop of cocktail sauce and butter. Return them to the grill, in batches, until they are bubbling and, ideally, blackening slightly at the edges, 1 to 2 more minutes. Serve immediately and repeat with the remaining clams.

ARI KOLENDER'S COCKTAIL SAUCE

Makes a scant ⅓ cup

I've included gram weights here,
because it's way easier to measure into a bowl on a scale.

- *⅓ cup (100g) Heinz ketchup*
- *2 tablespoons (35g) prepared horseradish*
- *1 tablespoon (18g) Dijon mustard*
- *1½ teaspoons (9g) Worcestershire sauce*
- *1½ teaspoons (9g) vodka*
- *1 teaspoon (6g) fresh lemon juice*

In a medium bowl, combine the ketchup, horseradish, mustard, Worcestershire sauce, vodka, and lemon juice and whisk until well combined. Store covered, in the refrigerator, for up to 3 days for best results.

Grilled Oysters with Miso-Ginger Calabrian Chili Butter

SERVES 4 TO 6

One of my favorite things in the world is a tiny raw oyster, fresh from Hama Hama Oyster Company in western Washington, one of the great oyster farms in the world. But once the oysters get a little bigger, I prefer them topped with this sweet-and-spicy drawn butter, then cooked on an open grill until the edges are bubbling, the oyster liquor intertwining with fat, umami, and heat. These are gateway oysters for anyone who thinks they don't like them.

Note: The butter can be made in advance and kept in the fridge for 4 days or the freezer for months, then warmed before topping the oysters. Extra butter is great for finishing an array of dishes, from seafood to meat, a roasted sweet potato, or even a simple pasta.

To Shuck Oysters: Make sure that the flat side of the shell is facing up. Insert the tip of an oyster knife into the hinge of the oyster, then twist the blade to separate the shells. Glide the knife across the outer edge and then scrape the top shell to separate it from the adductor muscle. Remove the top shell, then clean the blade and scrape under the oyster to free it as well. Keep it in the half shell, preserving as much of the oyster liquor as you can.

INGREDIENTS

Miso-Ginger Calabrian Chili Butter

- 1 stick (4 ounces) unsalted butter
- 2 tablespoons white or yellow miso
- 1½ tablespoons finely chopped Calabrian chili peppers in oil, drained
- 1 tablespoon finely chopped fresh ginger
- 2 garlic cloves, finely chopped
- ½ teaspoon soy sauce or gluten-free tamari

Grilled Oysters

- 12 fresh oysters (I love the "grillers" from Hama Hama Oyster Company)
- Lemon wedges, for serving

METHOD

Make the miso-ginger Calabrian chili butter: In a medium saucepan, melt the butter over medium heat. Add the miso, Calabrian chili peppers, ginger, garlic, and soy sauce. Stir thoroughly to combine the ingredients. Once simmering, reduce the heat to a gentle simmer and cook for 5 minutes. Turn off the heat and allow to sit until the mixture is room temperature. Leave it out for several hours, or store in an airtight container in the refrigerator or freezer.

Grill the oysters: Preheat the grill to high heat, then clean the grates well (no need to oil them).

Meanwhile shuck the oysters, placing them on a baking sheet. (To keep the oyster liquor from spilling out, it sometimes helps to crimp some pieces of aluminum foil into rings to sit them on, keeping the shucked oysters upright.)

Dollop each oyster with a teaspoon or so of the butter, then place them on the grill, working in batches if necessary. Close the lid and grill until the oyster juices are bubbling, about 2 minutes. Remove them from the grill and serve immediately, with lemon.

Grilldas (or Grilled Squid Gildas)

MAKES
12 GRILLDAS—
ENOUGH TO
SERVE 6 TO 8

The Gilda is an iconic pintxo from the Basque region of Spain (supposedly named after the 1946 Rita Hayworth movie). It is a wonderful snack to serve with a drink—an anchovy, a pickled guindilla pepper, and an olive, together on a toothpick, meant to be eaten in one bite.

This is my backyard riff, created one night with my yet again mentioned friend Kevin Faerkin (who may or may not have trademarked the word "Grillda"), that highlights the beauty of a grilled olive and replaces the anchovy with delicious and underutilized squid. Squid is actually one of the *easiest* things in the world to grill, as it tends not to stick much, cooks quickly, and tastes great. So yeah: It's time to become the cool dad who offers people Grilled Squid Gildas as a cocktail hour appetizer, alongside some nice, chilled dry vermouth.

Note: If you are using wooden skewers, soak 2 to 3 of them in water for at least 30 minutes.

INGREDIENTS

- 4 whole squid (about ½ pound total), cleaned, bodies separated from tentacles
- 1 teaspoon extra-virgin olive oil, plus more for drizzling
- ½ teaspoon ground Espelette pepper or smoked paprika
- Salt
- 12 pitted Castelvetrano olives
- A squeeze of lemon
- 12 small or 6 large pickled guindilla peppers or pickled pepperoncini
- Flaky salt

METHOD

Preheat the grill to high heat, then clean and oil the grates well.

Place the squid bodies and tentacles in a medium bowl and add the olive oil, Espelette, and a healthy pinch of salt. Toss until well combined. Skewer the olives through the opening, packing them together on 1 or 2 skewers, depending on the length. Place the 4 squid tentacles on the remaining skewer.

Lay the olives on the grill, turning occasionally until they have spots of blackening, about 4 minutes. Meanwhile, place the squid bodies and skewered tentacles on the grill, turning occasionally until the bodies are lightly charred, heated through, and firmed up very slightly, 2 to 3 minutes total. The tentacles also take 2 to 3 minutes, and will char a bit more and turn slightly more purple in hue.

Once cooked, place the squid on a cutting board and squeeze the lemon over it. Slice the bodies in half, lengthwise. Begin skewering your Grilldas on toothpicks. If the guindilla peppers are too large to eat in a single bite, they can be torn in half. Skewer a pepper first, followed by either a squid tentacle or body. If you are skewering a body, fold it in half lengthwise as you skewer. Finish with a grilled olive on top. Repeat with the remaining Grilldas. Lay them on a plate with the charred side of the squid facing up. Drizzle with more olive oil and sprinkle with flaky salt. Serve immediately.

Charred Garlic-Butter Sriracha Shrimp

SERVES
4 TO 6

I love the char of a grilled shrimp, but I also firmly believe that shrimp-served-hot loves to be in a sauce. This recipe marries these two ideas, with the shrimp tossed in a Sriracha-mayo to add flavor and that nonstick mayo effect on the grill, while also adding some delightful little char marks. But what really takes it over the top is tossing the cooked shrimp in a bowl of melted butter, simmered with lots of garlic and soy sauce. These shrimp are saucy, fatty, lightly spiced, and versatile enough to go with pretty much anything else in the book. But I really enjoy them alongside some steamed rice, Bonus Shrimp Stock Rice (see Dad Hack, below), or "Kebab Plate" Rice (page 76), along with any of the grilled veggie sides.

INGREDIENTS

6 garlic cloves, finely chopped
3 tablespoons butter
3 tablespoons soy sauce or gluten-free tamari
1 tablespoon mayonnaise
1 tablespoon Sriracha
1¾ pounds peeled large shrimp, tails removed, or 2 pounds shell-on shrimp, peeled and tails removed
1 lime

METHOD

Preheat the grill to high heat, then clean and oil the grates well.

In a large metal bowl that can go on the grill (no rubber grippers on the bottom), combine the garlic, butter, and soy sauce. (Alternatively, if you don't have a bowl for this, combine these ingredients in a small saucepan and simmer them over medium-high heat until the garlic is wilted, about 3 minutes. Then transfer to a large bowl.)

In a medium bowl, combine the mayo and Sriracha and stir until well combined. Add the shrimp and mix thoroughly, so that all of the shrimp are coated.

Place the bowl with the garlic mixture directly on the grill and allow the butter to melt and the garlic to wilt and soften a bit. Once the butter is melted and the garlic is sizzling, about 3 minutes, remove it from the heat with a kitchen towel and set it aside.

Working in two batches, lay half of the shrimp directly on the grill, keeping track of the order in which you laid them down. Allow them to grill until they have blackened grill marks on the bottom side, 60 to 90 seconds. Flip them over and repeat with the other side, another 60 to 90 seconds. Once cooked, transfer them to the bowl of garlic/soy sauce/butter and repeat with the remaining shrimp. If your grill has residue on it from the first round, give it a quick clean and another layer of oil, then repeat with the remaining shrimp.

Once they are all in the bowl, give it a squeeze of lime and then toss the shrimp thoroughly and serve immediately.

DAD HACK
BONUS SHRIMP STOCK RICE

To add flavor to a side of rice, place all of your shrimp shells in a medium saucepot along with 2 onion quarters. Cover with water and bring to a boil over high heat. Reduce to a simmer and cook for about 10 minutes. Turn off the heat and allow to sit for 5 more minutes. Strain the shrimp stock (discard the solids) and use it to cook a batch of rice, substituting the stock for water. (If you don't have enough shrimp stock, just make up the difference with more water.)

Quick-Grilled Fish Steak

(with Lemon and Herbs)

MAKES 1 FILLET

This is Feed My Family a Healthy Piece of Fish 101—a recipe that's about getting it from the grill to the table as quickly and easily as possible, with little to no mess. Ideally, you are looking for what my friend Ari Kolender and I refer to as a "steaky fillet"—something skin-off and not too delicate, like swordfish, mahi-mahi, vermilion, halibut, snapper, or sea bass. As always, look for fish caught in the United States to give you the best chance of eating as sustainably as possible.

Thickness matters more than weight here. I tend to look for a piece of fish that is about 1 inch thick and aim for 4 to 6 ounces per serving. Anything less than an inch might not get quite as much char as you would like before getting cooked through.

INGREDIENTS

1 skinless steaky fish fillet (see Headnote), about 1 inch thick
Mayonnaise
Kosher salt and freshly ground black pepper
1 teaspoon dried oregano
Lemon wedge

METHOD

Preheat the grill to high heat, then clean and oil the grates well.

Pat the fish dry and paint it with a very thin veil of mayonnaise. Season it aggressively on both sides with salt and pepper, then sprinkle it with the oregano.

Lay the fish on the grill and then do not touch it. After about 2 minutes, try to gently lift it with a spatula. If it is giving you resistance, let it go a little longer until it does not. Once it releases easily, flip the fish over and continue cooking the other side until the internal temperature registers 140°F, about 2 more minutes. Remove the fillet and serve it with a wedge of lemon.

Crispy-Skinned Fish Fillet

(with Parsley Pesto)

MAKES
1 FILLET

Yes, this recipe works with salmon. But here's the thing: Isn't it weird that pretty much every single restaurant in America offers the same kind of fish? It's time to open up your eyes to the wider world of seafood, and realize that there are lots of other great fish that come with skin that can get crispy and delicious, like vermilion, snapper, halibut, arctic char, amberjack, rockfish, and turbot.

Okay, rant over. This is a great way to make a crispy-skinned fish on the grill—it's so much cleaner, faster, and easier than doing it pretty much any other way. Look for fish of relatively even thickness for a more even cook. These get served with a simple blender-made parsley pesto, which will be enough for 4 to 5 servings. Scale up with multiple fillets as you desire.

INGREDIENTS

1 skin-on fish fillet (4 to 6 ounces), of relatively even thickness (see Headnote)
Mayonnaise
Salt and freshly ground black pepper
Parsley Pesto (recipe follows)

METHOD

Preheat the grill to medium-high heat, then clean and oil the grates well.

Pat the fish dry and then paint it with a very thin veil of mayonnaise. Season it on all sides with salt and pepper.

Lay the fish on the grill, skin-side down. After 30 seconds, press down gently with your fingers on the far edges of the fish to help it make better contact with the grill. Continue grilling until the skin is crisp and releases easily from the grill, about 3 minutes. Flip the fish over and cook until the internal temperature reaches 140°F, about 1 more minute.

Serve immediately, skin-side up with the parsley pesto.

PARSLEY PESTO

Besides being great with Crispy-Skinned Fish Fillet, this is a great condiment for a side of grilled potatoes.

2 ice cubes
¼ cup extra-virgin olive oil
2 tablespoons fresh lemon juice
1 garlic clove, smashed and peeled
1 cup tightly packed fresh Italian parsley and tender stems (about 1 bunch)
Salt and freshly ground black pepper

In a blender, combine (in this order) the ice cubes, olive oil, lemon juice, garlic, and parsley. Season with a pinch of salt and a few twists of pepper. Blend until rustic but well blended and then season to taste with more salt. Store, covered, in the refrigerator. It's best the same day, but will last 2 to 3 days before the garlic and lemon start overpowering.

Grilled Fish Tacos with Chile Crunch

MAKES
6 TACOS—ENOUGH TO SERVE 3 OR 4

I am slightly prejudiced against grilled fish tacos. To me, they conjure images of tourist-trap beachside restaurants, where they arrive alarmingly wet and with some kind of fruit salsa, their fish juices dripping onto your plate and shirt the entire time. (For reference: The best fish tacos in the world are deep-fried in Ensenada, Mexico.) It is with this level of skepticism that I worked on this fish taco: It is bright and refreshing from fresh lime, with heat and crunch from fried almonds, garlic, and chiles de árbol. It's served on a flour tortilla that has been smeared with crushed avocado to mercifully prevent excessive wetness. This is the Southern California grilled fish taco that I would be thrilled to eat, even at an overpriced tourist beach restaurant with my in-laws.

INGREDIENTS

4 large garlic cloves or 6 smaller ones, thinly sliced
¼ cup extra-virgin olive oil
¼ cup sliced almonds
4 dried chiles de árbol, thinly sliced
Salt
About 2 cups finely shredded green cabbage (¼ to ½ small head)
About 12 ounces steaky fish fillet (see Headnote, page 204), like swordfish, rockfish, halibut, or mahi-mahi
Mayonnaise
Freshly ground black pepper
6 taco-sized flour tortillas (usually 6 to 8 inches)
A squeeze of fresh lime (about 2 tablespoons)
6 cherry tomatoes, quartered
About 3 tablespoons crumbled Cotija cheese, plus more for serving
1 large avocado

METHOD

Place the garlic cloves in a small heatproof bowl and pour the olive oil over them. Place the almonds in small deep saucepan (like a narrow 2-quart saucepan) and set over medium-high heat. Shake the pan frequently to dry-toast the almonds until they become fragrant and take on some light browning, about 3 minutes. Add the chiles de árbol and allow them to toast for 30 seconds. Pour in the oil and garlic mixture and stir it well. Cook until the garlic is browned, about 30 more seconds. Turn off the heat and pour everything back into the heatproof bowl. Season liberally with a nice pinch of salt and set aside.

When you are ready to grill, preheat the grill to high heat, then clean and oil the grates well.

Place the cabbage in a large bowl and set it aside. Next, cut the fish into 6 roughly equal pieces (they will each be around 2 inches wide). Use a brush to paint the fillets on both sides with the thinnest veil of mayonnaise that you can. Season the fish on both sides with salt and pepper.

Lay the tortillas on the grill and allow them to cook until they have light grill marks, about 15 seconds, then flip them over and repeat with the other side. Good flour tortillas should puff up when they're ready, but even if they don't, you can remove them once they have some color on both sides. Lay them in a stack in a tortilla warmer, or onto an open kitchen towel, then fold it over them to allow them to steam and retain heat.

Lay the fish fillets down on the grill and leave them until you get a nice grill mark on the first side and are easy to flip without sticking, about 90 seconds. Flip them over and repeat with the other side, about 1 more minute. Remove the fish from the grill. If you are nervous about undercooking fish, you can use an instant-read thermometer to make sure it is above 140°F. Set the fish aside while you assemble the tacos.

Set a fine-mesh sieve over the cabbage and pour the almond/garlic/árbol oil through it. Reserve the crispy bits in the sieve. Add the lime juice, cherry tomatoes, and Cotija to the cabbage. Toss until well combined, then taste for seasoning, adjusting with more salt as needed.

Place the tortillas on plates and then open the avocado, dividing the flesh among the 6 tortillas, smashing the avocado with a fork and spreading it across the tortillas. Lay a fillet atop each tortilla, followed by a handful of the cabbage mixture. Divide the crispy topping from the sieve between them, then top with more Cotija and serve immediately.

Whole Grilled Fish Tacos with Maggi Onions

SERVES
4

This recipe is my favorite way to eat a whole fish: with friends and family, tortillas, and lots of condiments for customization, including onions that have been wilted down in Jugo Maggi (see Notes) and soy sauce—a classic condiment found all over Mexico. Consider it a PSA about how easy it is to grill a whole fish, especially when it has already been scaled and gutted. Flip it as little as possible and otherwise just leave it alone. If you try to poke it or move it more than necessary, you are likely to break the skin, releasing juices and causing the fish to stick.

Notes: Look for a 2-pound or so fresh fish, with a mild, flaky flesh, such as rockfish or branzino. If you go to a quality fish market, they can always just tell you what looks good to them.

Maggi is a seasoning that comes in different forms in different countries. In Mexico, it's called Jugo Maggi, which is almost like a more robust cross between Worcestershire sauce and soy sauce. Look for it in Mexican grocery stores and online.

INGREDIENTS

Maggi Onions

1 medium-to-large white onion, halved and cut into ½-inch-thick slices
¼ cup Jugo Maggi (see Notes)
¼ cup soy sauce

Grilled Whole Fish Tacos

1 whole fish (about 2 pounds), such as rockfish, sea bass, or branzino, scaled and gutted
Mayonnaise
Kosher salt
Corn tortillas
Lime wedges
Flaky salt

Salsas and Condiments of Your Choice, Such As

Tatemada (page 164)
Salsa Bandera (page 161)
Salsa Chiltepin (page 161)
Salsa Habanero (page 163)
Sliced avocado

METHOD

Make the Maggi Onions: In a medium saucepan, combine the onion, Jugo Maggi, and soy sauce and bring to a simmer over medium-high heat. Reduce the heat to a gentle simmer and cook for 5 minutes. Remove from the heat and allow to cool to room temperature.

Make the grilled whole fish tacos: Preheat the grill to high heat, then clean and oil the grates well.

Use scissors or a sharp knife to cut off any parts of the fish that will burn, such as fins and tail fin, and discard them. Lightly brush the fish all over the outside with a thin veil of mayonnaise. Season it aggressively inside and outside with salt.

When you are ready to cook, lay the fish on the grill, leaving space to flip it either forward or backward on the grill when you want to cook the other side (you want to be able to flip it while handling it as little as possible). Allow the fish to grill, untouched—unless you have a charcoal fire that is really out of control and smoking, in which case remove the fish from the grill and control the fire, then try again. After about 5 minutes, you can begin to gently lift the edge of the fish to look for color. Once the fish is taking on some golden-brown color and small black marks, 6 to 8 minutes on the grill, use two spatulas (or a spatula and tongs) to gently flip it over.

Continue grilling until the other side is golden brown with blackened edges, 6 to 8 more minutes. Flip it again to recrisp the first side, continuing to cook until an instant-read thermometer registers at least 130°F in the thickest parts of the fish. If you're in doubt, err on the side of overcooked, as a whole fish is quite forgiving on the grill.

Transfer the fish to a serving platter. Quickly grill the tortillas for about 30 seconds per side, then transfer them to a towel or tortilla warmer and cover to allow them to steam and stay warm. Serve immediately with the Maggi Onions, limes, flaky salt, and any condiments of choice, flaking the fish into your tortillas and watching for pin bones.

Smoke-Grilled Miso Black Cod

SERVES
4

Miso Black Cod is perhaps the most famous dish from Nobu Matsuhisa, one of the most celebrated chefs in Los Angeles history. But black cod (also known as sable in Jewish delis and bagel shops), with its high fat content, is also a fish that takes beautifully to being smoked. With my BBQ background and love of Japanese food, a wood-smoked riff on this LA classic was a no-brainer. In our house, we often just end up picking at it right when it comes off the grill. But if it survives long enough to eat with sides, it is lovely with rice and any number of vegetable sides like Buttered Soy Sauce Mushrooms (page 66), Grilled and Glazed Baby Bok Choy (page 52), Broccolini with Preserved Lemon (page 42), or Jimmy Nardellos with Red Yuzu Vinaigrette (page 60). In a pinch, you can marinate it for as little as 2 hours, but I find that 2 days nets the best results.

Note: If your black cod has pin bones, I recommend keeping them in when you cook, and eating around them to preserve the beautiful, flaky flesh.

INGREDIENTS

1 pound skin-on black cod (sable) fillets, cut into 4 portions
Kosher salt
6 tablespoons white miso
3 tablespoons sake
3 tablespoons mirin
1 tablespoon sugar
1 tablespoon grated fresh ginger
1 teaspoon neutral oil
Mesquite or lump charcoal
Wood chunks (I prefer pecan)

METHOD

Season the fillets lightly with salt on all sides, then transfer them to the refrigerator to sit for 30 minutes.

Meanwhile, in a resealable container or ziplock bag, combine the miso, sake, mirin, sugar, ginger, and neutral oil and whisk thoroughly to combine.

After the 30 minutes are up, use paper towels to pat the fish dry. Transfer it to the resealable container and toss the fillets until they are thoroughly coated. Place them in the fridge to marinate for at least 2 hours, but ideally closer to 48 hours.

When you are ready to cook, set up a two-zone fire by lighting a full chimney of charcoal. Once they have turned gray, set them on one side of the grill. Place 2 wood chunks on top of the charcoal, then close the lid and open the vent over the cooler side and leave it closed over the hot side. Let the wood burn for about 5 minutes.

Remove the fillets from the marinade and wipe off any excess with a paper towel. Add the fillets to the cooler side of the grill. Close the lid and allow the fish to cook until it reaches an internal temperature between 145° and 155°F, about 25 minutes.

Remove the fillets and serve hot for best results. Serve cold or at room temperature for very, very good results.

WEEKEND VIBES
A BOAT BEER
SALTY CREW
BLONDE ALE
WEEKEND VIBES
CORONADO BREWING CO.
IPA
ORANGE AVE WIT
California original since 96
Coronado, California

B&B
CHARCOAL

ACKNOWLEDGMENTS

Neither this book nor my last one would exist without my wonderful editor, Lexy Bloom, who I hope is so overwhelmed with emotion upon reading this that she immediately green-lights my next one. I hope to write many more books in my life, and for Lexy to be my editor for all of them.

Thank you to my agent Alison Fargis at Stonesong, who I hope is so overwhelmed with emotion upon reading this that she immediately waives her commission. You have always fought for me and believed in me, and are a much bigger part in shaping the books you pitch than you ever get credit for.

Kristin Teig, Carrie Anne Purcell, David Peng, Alicia Buszczak, and Daniela Swamp—the incredible team behind the photography for this book. You have made this book what it is and have made me look far better than I deserve. You kept the set a wonderful, collaborative, and fun place to work every single day, no matter how many bone-dry martinis or heavy pours of fancy French vermouth I fed you the previous night.

To the whole team at Knopf: thank you to Jordan Pavlin, Tom Pold, Deb Wood, Kelly Blair, Nicole Pedersen, Kathryn Ricigliano, Isa Connolly, Sarah New, and Sara Eagle. You have helped me make something I truly love, and to have the job I never knew to even dream of having when I was a kid.

Thank you to Bill Esparza for your unrelenting standards and constant beliefs in fighting the good food fight. But perhaps most of all, thank you for taking me to Hermosillo and showing me the way. I am also proud to say that a video documenting our trip called *I Found the Best Carne Asada in the World* (for our Tasted YouTube Channel) was shown at the Cineteca Sonora in Hermosillo.

Finally, to all of the culinary mentors and friends who have made me a far better cook than I deserve to be. Thank you to Eloy Aluri, Nyesha Arrington, Erik Black, Kevin Bludso, Kevin Faerkin, Jeremy Fox, Suzanne Goin, Ari Kolender, Sarah Minnick, Nancy Lyons, Frank Pinello, Josh Scherer, Nancy Silverton, and so many more who will go unnamed likely due to forgetfulness.

My photo crew, clockwise from top left: Alicia Buszczak, David Peng, Kristin Teig, Daniela Swamp, and Carrie Anne Purcell

INDEX

Page numbers in *italics* refer to illustrations.

A
achiote (annatto) powder, 126
Chicken Breast, Achiote-Lime (with Garlic and Fresh Cilantro), 63, 126, *127*
ají amarillo paste, 142
Pollo a la Brasa with Ají Verde, Smoke-Grilled, 142–4, *143*
Akabori, Keisuke, 131
Aleppo pepper:
Baby Backs, Smoke-Grilled (with Aleppo Pepper, Mirin, and Cider Vinegar), 188, *189*
All-American Burger chain, 11
almonds:
Fish Tacos with Chile Crunch, Grilled, 208, *209*
Aluri, Eloy, xxviii, 155, 156, 160
anchovy fillets:
Beef and Broccoli, Punchy, Funky (Flanken Short Rib with Broccolini and Green Olive Salsa Verde), 166, *167*
Chicken Caesar with Garlic Bread Croutons, Spicy Grilled, *84,* 85–6
appetizers and snacks:
Avocado Tostadas with Chipotle-Lime Crema, Grilled, 70, *71*
Baba Ghanoush, 68, *69,* 129
Caprese Sandwich, Smoky Grilled, 24, *25*
Cauliflower with Tahini-Yogurt Sauce, Charred, *56,* 57, 129
Chicken "Gyoza" Eggplant, xxv, 132, *133*
Grilldas (or Grilled Squid Gildas), *200,* 201
Wings, Ginger-Buffalo, 134, *135*
Apple-Horseradish Sauce, 152, *152,* 153
Ari Kolender's Cocktail Sauce, 196, *197*
Arrington, Nyesha, xxviii
Artichokes alla Garlic Knots, Grilled, *48,* 49
arugula:
Chicken Tricolore with Charred Pepperoncini Vinaigrette, Grilled, 88, *89*
Pork Tenderloin, "Pretend It's the '90s" Honey-Balsamic (with Grilled Red Onion and Arugula), *184,* 185
Asadero el Leñador, 155
asparagus:
Grilled Asparagus with Wilted White Cheddar, *46,* 47, 139, 150
Southwest Veggie Chop (with Charred Scallion Green Goddess), 82–3, *82*
avocado(s):
Avocado Tostadas with Chipotle-Lime Crema, Grilled, 70, *71*
Citrus and Fennel Salad (Grilled and Raw, with Avocado), *54,* 55
Fish Tacos with Chile Crunch, Grilled, 208, *209*
Fish Tacos with Maggi Onions, Whole Grilled, *210,* 211
guacamole, 158
Hermosillo-Style Carne Asada, *154,* 155, 158, *162,* 165
Veggie Wraps, Better Grilled (with Avocado Hummus, Sprouts, and Feta), 26

B
Baba Ghanoush, 68, *69,* 129
Bacon Cheeseburgers, Backyard, 8, *9*
balsamic vinegar:
Brussels Sprouts, Charred (with Soy and Balsamic), 50, *51*
Pork Tenderloin, "Pretend It's the '90s" Honey-Balsamic (with Grilled Red Onion and Arugula), *184,* 185
Zucchini Spears and Balsamic, Mint, and Garlic, 44, *45*
beans:
canned beans Dad Hack, 75
Frijoles, 158, 161, 165
Huevos Divorciados, *108,* 109
Mezcal Charro Beans (with Charred Peppers and Onions), xii, *74,* 75, 152, 178
soaking/not soaking decision, 75
Southwest Veggie Chop (with Charred Scallion Green Goddess), 82–3, *82*
Veggie Burritos, Grilled ("Christmas-Style," with Red & Green Salsas), *106,* 107
beef, 146–73
Bacon Cheeseburgers, Backyard, 8, *9*
Beef and Broccoli, Punchy, Funky (Flanken Short Rib with Broccolini and Green Olive Salsa Verde), 166, *167*
Brisket Noodle Bowl, Nước Chấm, 170, *171*
cuts for grilling, 149
internal temperature guide, xxvii
shopping for, 149
Tri-Tip Two Ways, California, 149, 152–3, *152*
See also steaks
Beer Brats (with Grilled Onions, Sauerkraut, and Spicy Brown Mustard), *34,* 35
Big Green Egg, xiv
binco/hibachi grills, xv
Bitzinger Sausage Stand, Vienna, Austria, 36
Bludso, Kevin, xi, xix, xxviii, 188
Bludso's BBQ Cookbook (Bludso), 188
Bok Choy, Grilled and Glazed Baby (with Tamari Vinaigrette), 52, *53,* 212
Bossam, BBQ Pork Belly, 190–1, *190*

bread and buns:
Fettunta (The Best Way to Serve a Hunk of Bread), *72*, 73, 150
fresh baguette Dad Hack, 22
Garlic Bread Croutons, Marinated, *84*, 85–6
poppy seed hot dog buns, 12, *13*, 15
breakfast dishes:
Cofax Coffee's smoked potato breakfast burritos, 117
Huevos Divorciados, *108*, 109
broccoli:
Broccoli-Cheddar Split Pea Soup, Blackened, xii, *114*, 115
Southwest Veggie Chop (with Charred Scallion Green Goddess), 82–3, *82*
Veggie Burritos, Grilled ("Christmas-Style," with Red & Green Salsas), *106*, 107
broccolini:
Beef and Broccoli, Punchy, Funky (Flanken Short Rib with Broccolini and Green Olive Salsa Verde), 166, *167*
Broccolini with Preserved Lemon, 42, *43*, 178, 212
Veggie Burritos, Grilled ("Christmas-Style," with Red & Green Salsas), *106*, 107
Brussels Sprouts, Charred (with Soy and Balsamic), 50, *51*
burgers, 7
Bacon Cheeseburgers, Backyard, 8, *9*
Lamb Burgers, Cumin (with Gruyère, Curry Ketchup, and Dill Yogurt), *20*, 21
patty-size Dad Hack, 8
Turkey Burgers, The Juiciest (with Goat Cheese, Pickled Peppers, and Sprouts), *18*, 19
type of beef to use for, 8
butter:
Clams with Cocktail Butter, Grilled, 196, *197*
Mansion Butter, Smoke-Grilled Bone-In Rib Eye with, 172–3, *172*
Miso-Butter Corn, *64*, 65
Miso-Ginger Calabrian Chili Butter, 198, *199*
Sriracha Shrimp, Grilled Garlic-Butter, *202*, 203
Buttermilk-Brined Pork Chop with Grilled Lemon, 178, *179*

C
cabbage:
Chicken Teriyaki Sandwiches with Jalapeño-Cabbage Slaw, 16, *17*
Fish Tacos with Chile Crunch, Grilled, 208, *209*
Hermosillo-Style Carne Asada, 158, 163, 165
Peanut-Miso Steak and Soba Salad (with a Crunchy, Shredded Vegetable Rainbow), *90*, 91
Potato Tacos, Smoked (with Smoked Tomatillo Salsa, Cotija, and Crunchy Red Cabbage), xi, *116*, 117–18
Calabrian chili peppers:
Oysters with Miso-Ginger Calabrian Chili Butter, Grilled, 198, *199*
Caprese Sandwich, Smoky Grilled, 24, *25*
Carne Asada, Hermosillo-Style, xvi, 149, 154–65, *154*, *156*, *157*, *159*, *162*
Carne Asada Party grocery list, 160
Salsa Bar, 158, *159*, 161, *162*, 163–4
steak cuts and thickness of slices, 156, 165
carrot(s):
Đồ Chua (Pickled Daikon and Carrot), 22–3, *22*, 170, *171*
Peanut-Miso Steak and Soba Salad (with a Crunchy, Shredded Vegetable Rainbow), *90*, 91
cauliflower:
Southwest Veggie Chop (with Charred Scallion Green Goddess), 82–3, *82*
Tahini-Yogurt Sauce, Charred Cauliflower with, *56*, 57, 129
Veggie Burritos, Grilled ("Christmas-Style," with Red & Green Salsas), *106*, 107
Chang, David, 190
charcoal:
types of and choosing which to use, xvi, *xvii*
wood and charcoal together, xvi, xix
See also mesquite charcoal
"charcoal and wood only" recipes, xxviii
Baby Backs, Smoke-Grilled (with Aleppo Pepper, Mirin, and Cider Vinegar), 188, *189*
Cod, Smoke-Grilled Miso Black, 212, *213*
Hermosillo-Style Carne Asada, xvi, 149, 154–65, *154*, *156*, *157*, *159*, *162*
Pollo a la Brasa with Ají Verde, Smoke-Grilled, 142–4, *143*
Pork Belly Bossam, BBQ, 190–1, *190*
Potato Tacos, Smoked (with Smoked Tomatillo Salsa, Cotija, and Crunchy Red Cabbage), xi, *116*, 117–18
Rib Eye with Mansion Butter, Smoke-Grilled Bone-In, xi, 172–3, *172*
Turkey Breast, Smoke-Grilled (for Cold Cuts), 123, 140, *141*
charcoal grills:
charcoal basket for, xiv
chimney fire starter for, xxi, xxiv
how to clean, xxiv
how to light, xxiv
tools for cleaning out, xxii
variables and choosing, xiv–xv
cheese:
Asparagus with Wilted White Cheddar, Grilled, *46*, 47, 139, 150
Bacon Cheeseburgers, Backyard, 8, *9*
Broccoli-Cheddar Split Pea Soup, Blackened, xii, *114*, 115
Caprese Sandwich, Smoky Grilled, 24, *25*
Jaas-Style Anaheim chiles, 158, 164, 165
people eating things with cheese on top, 47
Poblanos with Cilantro-Lime Tahini, Stuffed, *104*, 105
Quinoa with Grilled Halloumi and Charred Fennel, Mediterranean, 100, *101*
Turkey Burgers, The Juiciest (with Goat Cheese, Pickled Peppers, and Sprouts), *18*, 19
Veggie Burritos, Grilled ("Christmas-Style," with Red & Green Salsas), *106*, 107
Veggie Wraps, Better Grilled (with Avocado Hummus, Sprouts, and Feta), 26
See also Cotija cheese; mozzarella cheese; Parmesan cheese
Chicago-Style Char Dogs, 12, *13*, 15
chicken, 120–44
Breast, Achiote-Lime (with Garlic and Fresh Cilantro), 63, 126, *127*
Breast, Quick and Simple Grilled, 124, *125*, 126
butterflying, 126
Caesar with Garlic Bread Croutons, Spicy Grilled, *84*, 85–6
Drumsticks with Spicy Honey, Pickle-Brined, *136*, 137
"Gyoza" Eggplant, xxv, 132, *133*
internal temperature guide, xxvii, 123
Nashville hot chicken, reversed, gluten-free, 137
Ode to a Benihana Birthday Party, *130*, 131
Pollo a la Brasa with Ají Verde, Smoke-Grilled, 142–4, *143*
popularity of chicken breast, 123
Shish Tawook, xxii, 68, 123, *128*, 129
shopping for, 123
splitting a whole chicken, 142
Teriyaki Sandwiches with Jalapeño-Cabbage Slaw, 16, *17*
Thighs, Shallot-Dijon, 50, *138*, 139
Tricolore with Charred Pepperoncini Vinaigrette, Grilled, 88, *89*
Wings, Ginger-Buffalo, 134, *135*
chile(s):
Beans, Mezcal Charro (with Charred Peppers and Onions), xii, *74*, 75, 152, 178
Brisket Noodle Bowl, Nước Chấm, 170, *171*
Hatch Chile Pico de Gallo, 152, *152*, 153
Jaas-Style Anaheim chiles, 158, 164, 165
"Kebab Plate" Rice (with Charred Tomato, Shallot, and Green Chile), xii, 68, 76, *77*, 129, 203
Oysters with Miso-Ginger Calabrian Chili Butter, Grilled, 198, *199*
Poblanos with Cilantro-Lime Tahini, Stuffed, *104*, 105
Pollo a la Brasa with Ají Verde, Smoke-Grilled, 142–4, *143*
Pork Secret (Secreto with Rosemary, Garlic, Chile de Árbol, and Tangerine Zest), 180, *181*
Potato Tacos, Smoked (with Smoked Tomatillo Salsa, Cotija, and Crunchy Red Cabbage), xi, *116*, 117–18
Salsa Bandera (pico de gallo), 158, 161, *162*, 165, 211
Salsa Chiltepin, 158, 161, 165, 211

Salsa Habanero, 158, 163, 165, 211
Salsa Ranchera, xii, *106,* 107, *108,* 109, 110, *111*
Salsa Verde, xii, *106,* 107, *108,* 109, 110, *111*
Sausage and Peppers Pasta Salad, *94,* 95
Tatemada, 158, 164, 165, 211
See also chipotle peppers in adobo sauce
chiles de árbol:
Fish Tacos with Chile Crunch, Grilled, 208, *209*
Kabocha Macha (Grilled Kabocha Squash with Salsa Macha and Lime), *62,* 63
Skirt Steak, Soy and Citrus (with Chile de Árbol, Ginger, and Garlic), 149, *168,* 169
chili crisp:
Peanut-Miso Steak and Soba Salad (with a Crunchy, Shredded Vegetable Rainbow), *90,* 91
Pork Chop Sandwiches with Grilled Pineapple and Chili Crisp Mayo, 32, *33*
Chiltepin, Salsa, 158, 161, 165, 211
Chimichurri Mayo, xxi, 11
chimney fire starter, xxi, xxiv
chipotle peppers in adobo sauce:
Avocado Tostadas with Chipotle-Lime Crema, Grilled, 70, *71*
freezing leftovers Dad Hack, 70
cilantro:
Chicken Breast, Achiote-Lime (with Garlic and Fresh Cilantro), 63, 126, *127*
Pollo a la Brasa with Ají Verde, Smoke-Grilled, 142–4, *143*
Salsa Bandera (pico de gallo), 158, 161, *162,* 165, 211
Salsa Ranchera, xii, *106,* 107, *108,* 109, 110, *111*
Salsa Verde, xii, *106,* 107, *108,* 109, 110, *111*
Citrus and Fennel Salad (Grilled and Raw, with Avocado), *54,* 55
Clams with Cocktail Butter, Grilled, 196, *197*
Cocktail Sauce, Ari Kolender's, 196, *197*
Coconut-Crusted Tiki Pork Ribs, 186, *187*
Cofax Coffee's smoked potato breakfast burritos, 117
Cold Spring Tavern, Santa Barbara, 152
corn:
Miso-Butter Corn, *64,* 65
Southwest Veggie Chop (with Charred Scallion Green Goddess), 82–3, *82*
Cotija cheese:
Fish Tacos with Chile Crunch, Grilled, 208, *209*
Huevos Divorciados, *108,* 109
Potato Tacos, Smoked (with Smoked Tomatillo Salsa, Cotija, and Crunchy Red Cabbage), xi, *116,* 117–18
cucumber(s):
Brisket Noodle Bowl, Nước Chấm, 170, *171*
Hermosillo-Style Carne Asada, 158, 163, 165
Peanut-Miso Steak and Soba Salad (with a Crunchy, Shredded Vegetable Rainbow), *90,* 91
Quinoa with Grilled Halloumi and Charred Fennel, Mediterranean, 100, *101*
Shrimp Niçoise, Grilled (with Fresh Tarragon Vinaigrette), 92, *93*
Southwest Veggie Chop (with Charred Scallion Green Goddess), 82–3, *82*
Tofu Bánh Mì with Lemongrass BBQ Sauce, 22–3, *23*
Tzatziki, 30–1, *30*

D
daikon:
Đồ Chua (Pickled Daikon and Carrot), 22–3, *22,* 170, *171*
dates:
Chicken Tricolore with Charred Pepperoncini Vinaigrette, Grilled, 88, *89*
Dill Yogurt, 21
Đồ Chua (Pickled Daikon and Carrot), 22–3, *22,* 170, *171*

E
eggplant(s):
Baba Ghanoush, 68, *69,* 129
Chicken "Gyoza" Eggplant, xxv, 132, *133*
Veggie Wraps, Better Grilled (with Avocado Hummus, Sprouts, and Feta), 26, *27*
eggs:
Huevos Divorciados, *108,* 109
Shrimp Niçoise, Grilled (with Fresh Tarragon Vinaigrette), 92, *93*
emotions, importance of in feeding family, xxix
endive:
Chicken Caesar with Garlic Bread Croutons, Spicy Grilled, *84,* 85–6
Chicken Tricolore with Charred Pepperoncini Vinaigrette, Grilled, 88, *89*
Ensenada, Mexico, fish tacos, 208
Esparza, Bill, 155, 158

F
Faerkin, Kevin, 152, 190, 196, 201
fennel bulb(s):
Citrus and Fennel Salad (Grilled and Raw, with Avocado), *54,* 55
Quinoa with Grilled Halloumi and Charred Fennel, Mediterranean, 100, *101*
feta cheese:
Veggie Wraps, Better Grilled (with Avocado Hummus, Sprouts, and Feta), 26
Fettunta (The Best Way to Serve a Hunk of Bread), *72,* 73, 150
fiber, importance of, xxviii, 123
fish, *See* seafood and fish
fish sauce:
Brisket Noodle Bowl, Nước Chấm, 170, *171*
foil/foil pouch recipes:
aluminum foil replacement Dad Hack, 66, 105
Buttered Soy Sauce Mushrooms (in a Foil Pouch with Lemon and Fresh Thyme), 66, *67,* 212
Poblanos with Cilantro-Lime Tahini, Stuffed, *104,* 105
food:
cooking for and feeding family, importance of nutrition and emotions in, xxviii–xxix
internal temperature guide, xxvii
leftovers are your friend, xii
rule about trying new things, xii
Found Oyster, 195
Fox, Jeremy, xxviii
Franklin, Aaron, xv, 149
Frijoles, 158, 161, 165
fuel choices, xvi–xix
charcoal, xvi, *xvii,* xix
charcoal and wood together, xvi, xix
natural gas and propane, xvi
wood chunks, *xvii, xviii,* xix

G
garlic:
Artichokes alla Garlic Knots, Grilled, *48,* 49
Brisket Noodle Bowl, Nước Chấm, 170, *171*
Chicken Breast, Achiote-Lime (with Garlic and Fresh Cilantro), 63, 126, *127*
Chicken Caesar with Garlic Bread Croutons, Spicy Grilled, *84,* 85–6
Fettunta (The Best Way to Serve a Hunk of Bread), *72,* 73, 150
Fish Tacos with Chile Crunch, Grilled, 208, *209*
Mansion Butter, Smoke-Grilled Bone-In Rib Eye with, 172–3, *172*
Parsley Pesto, 58, 206, *207*
Pork Secret (Secreto with Rosemary, Garlic, Chile de Árbol, and Tangerine Zest), 180, *181*
Salsa Ranchera, xii, *106,* 107, *108,* 109, 110, *111*
Salsa Verde, xii, *106,* 107, *108,* 109, 110, *111*
Skirt Steak, Soy and Citrus (with Chile de Árbol, Ginger, and Garlic), 149, *168,* 169
Sriracha Shrimp, Grilled Garlic-Butter, *202,* 203
Zucchini Spears and Balsamic, Mint, and Garlic, 44, *45*
gas grills:
convenience of, xi, xiv
extra propane tank recommendation, xiv
how to clean, xxiv
how to light, xxiv
natural gas and propane, xvi
toast test for hot and cold spots, *xxiii*
variables and choosing, xiv
ginger:
Chicken "Gyoza" Eggplant, xxv, 132, *133*
Keisuke's Ginger Sauce, *130,* 131
Oysters with Miso-Ginger Calabrian Chili Butter, Grilled, 198, *199*
Skirt Steak, Soy and Citrus (with Chile de Árbol, Ginger, and Garlic), 149, *168,* 169
Wings, Ginger-Buffalo, 134, *135*
Goat Cheese Spread, *18,* 19
Goin, Suzanne, 180
Golden State, The, 21

grapefruits:
Citrus and Fennel Salad (Grilled and Raw, with Avocado), *54*, 55
grease fires, xxiv
grill brush, xxi
grilling:
advantages and benefits of, xi–xii
being a grill dad, xi
convenience grilling, xi
cooking for a lot of people, xii
extension of kitchen, grill as, xii
signifiers in recipes for wood and/or charcoal, xxviii
Weekend Project Grilling, xi
See also smoke-grilling; two-zone fires
grill pan, xxii, 131
grills:
fuel choices, xvi–xix
how to clean, xxiv
how to light, xxiv
temperature guide, xxii, xxvii
types of, xiv–xv
See also charcoal grills; gas grills
guacamole, 158
Guest Chef show, 73, 180

H
Habanero, Salsa, 158, 163, 165, 211
Halloumi cheese:
Quinoa with Grilled Halloumi and Charred Fennel, Mediterranean, 100, *101*
substitution Dad Hack, 100
Hama Hama Oyster Company, 198
Hatch Chile Pico de Gallo, 152, *152*, 153
Hawker Fare (Syhabout), 170
Hermosillo, Mexico, xvi, 155–6, 158, 160
Hermosillo-Style Carne Asada, xvi, 149, 154–65, *154*, *156*, *157*, *159*, *162*
Carne Asada Party grocery list, 160
Salsa Bar, 158, *159*, 161, *162*, 163–4
steak cuts and thickness of slices, 156, 165
Hernández Uribe, José Luis, 155
hibachi/bincho grills, xv
Hollywood Farmers' Market, 55
honey:
Drumsticks with Spicy Honey, Pickle-Brined, *136*, 137
Pork Tenderloin, "Pretend It's the '90s" Honey-Balsamic (with Grilled Red Onion and Arugula), *184*, 185
horseradish:
Apple-Horseradish Sauce, 152, *152*, 153
Cocktail Sauce, Ari Kolender's, 196, *197*
Smoke-Grill a Sausage, How to, 36, *37*
hot dogs, 7
Chicago-Style Char Dogs, 12, *13*, 15
How to Cook the Finest Things in the Sea (Kolender and Galuten), 196
hummus:
Veggie Wraps, Better Grilled (with Avocado Hummus, Sprouts, and Feta), 26

J
Jaas Light taqueria, 158
Jaas-Style Anaheim chiles, 158, 164, 165
jalapeño pepper(s):
Brisket Noodle Bowl, Nước Chấm, 170, *171*
Chicken Teriyaki Sandwiches with Jalapeño-Cabbage Slaw, 16, *17*
Jalapeño and Onion Soy Sauce Pickles, 190–1, *190*
Mansion Butter, Smoke-Grilled Bone-In Rib Eye with, 172–3, *172*
JJ's Lone Daughter Ranch, 55
Jugo Maggi, 211

K
Kabocha Macha (Grilled Kabocha Squash with Salsa Macha and Lime), *62*, 63
kamado-style grills, xiv
"Kebab Plate" Rice (with Charred Tomato, Shallot, and Green Chile), xii, 68, 76, *77*, 129, 203
Ketchup, Curry, 21
kettle-style charcoal grills, xiv, xv
Kolender, Ari, xxi, xxviii, 195, 196, 204

L
Lamb Burgers, Cumin (with Gruyère, Curry Ketchup, and Dill Yogurt), *20*, 21
leeks:
Sausage and Lentils with Grilled Leeks, *182*, 183
Lemongrass BBQ Sauce, Tofu Bánh Mì with, 22–3, *23*
lemon(s) and lemon juice:
Baba Ghanoush, 68, *69*, 129
Broccolini with Preserved Lemon, 42, *43*, 178, 212
buying preserved lemons, 42
Citrus and Fennel Salad (Grilled and Raw, with Avocado), *54*, 55
Parsley Pesto, 58, 206, *207*
Pork Chop with Grilled Lemon, Buttermilk-Brined, 178, *179*
Shish Tawook, xxii, 68, 123, *128*, 129
Skirt Steak, Soy and Citrus (with Chile de Árbol, Ginger, and Garlic), 149, *168*, 169
lentils:
Sausage and Lentils with Grilled Leeks, *182*, 183
types to buy, 183
lettuce, Bibb or butter:
Pork Belly Bossam, BBQ, 190–1, *190*
lettuce, romaine:
Chicken Caesar with Garlic Bread Croutons, Spicy Grilled, *84*, 85–6
Southwest Veggie Chop (with Charred Scallion Green Goddess), 82–3, *82*
lighter, long-necked, xxi
lime(s) and lime juice:
Avocado Tostadas with Chipotle-Lime Crema, Grilled, 70, *71*
Brisket Noodle Bowl, Nước Chấm, 170, *171*
Chicken Breast, Achiote-Lime (with Garlic and Fresh Cilantro), 63, 126, *127*
Hermosillo-Style Carne Asada, 158, 163, 165
Kabocha Macha (Grilled Kabocha Squash with Salsa Macha and Lime), *62*, 63
Poblanos with Cilantro-Lime Tahini, Stuffed, *104*, 105
Pollo a la Brasa with Ají Verde, Smoke-Grilled, 142–4, *143*
Skirt Steak, Soy and Citrus (with Chile de Árbol, Ginger, and Garlic), 149, *168*, 169
López-Alt, J. Kenji, 115

M
Mackay, Jordan, xv, 149
Maggi Onions, 161, 165, *210*, 211
Mansion Butter, Smoke-Grilled Bone-In Rib Eye with, 172–3, *172*
masculinity, actions, and emotions, importance of in feeding family, xxix
Matsuhisa, Nobu, 212
mayonnaise:
Chimichurri Mayo, xxi, 11
Fish Fillet, Crispy-Skinned (with Parsley Pesto), 206, *207*
Fish Steak, Quick-Grilled (with Lemon and Herbs), 204, *205*
Pork Chop Sandwiches with Grilled Pineapple and Chili Crisp Mayo, 32, *33*
Sriracha Shrimp, Grilled Garlic-Butter, *202*, 203
uses when grilling, xxi, 195
mesquite charcoal, xvi, xix
Hermosillo-Style Carne Asada, xvi, 149, 154–65, *154*, *156*, *157*, *159*, *162*
Mezcal Charro Beans (with Charred Peppers and Onions), xii, *74*, 75, 152, 178
Minnick, Sarah, xxviii
miso:
BBQ Sauce, Miso-Mustard, 190–1, *190*
Cod, Smoke-Grilled Miso Black, 212, *213*
Corn, Miso-Butter, *64*, 65
Oysters with Miso-Ginger Calabrian Chili Butter, Grilled, 198, *199*
Peanut-Miso Steak and Soba Salad (with a Crunchy, Shredded Vegetable Rainbow), *90*, 91
Momofuku, 190
mozzarella cheese:
Caprese Sandwich, Smoky Grilled, 24, *25*
Chicken Tricolore with Charred Pepperoncini Vinaigrette, Grilled, 88, *89*
Sausage and Peppers Pasta Salad, *94*, 95
mushrooms:
bunashimeji, 66
Buttered Soy Sauce Mushrooms (in a Foil Pouch with Lemon and Fresh Thyme), 66, *67*, 212
Mabo-Stuffed Mushrooms with Yaki-Onigiri, xxv, 102, *103*
Ode to a Benihana Birthday Party, *130*, 131
mustard:
Chicken Thighs, Shallot-Dijon, 50, *138*, 139
Miso-Mustard BBQ Sauce, 190–1, *190*
Mustard Sauce, *130*, 131

N
Napa cabbage:
Chicken "Gyoza" Eggplant, xxv, 132, *133*

Nashville hot chicken, reversed, gluten-free, 137

O
oil, neutral, xxi
olives:
Beef and Broccoli, Punchy, Funky (Flanken Short Rib with Broccolini and Green Olive Salsa Verde), 166, *167*
Grilldas (or Grilled Squid Gildas), *200,* 201
Quinoa with Grilled Halloumi and Charred Fennel, Mediterranean, 100, *101*
Shrimp Niçoise, Grilled (with Fresh Tarragon Vinaigrette), 92, *93*
Za'atar-Blackened Mahi-Mahi Pitas, *28,* 29
onion(s):
Beans, Mezcal Charro (with Charred Peppers and Onions), xii, *74,* 75, 152, 178
Beer Brats (with Grilled Onions, Sauerkraut, and Spicy Brown Mustard), *34,* 35
Caprese Sandwich, Smoky Grilled, 24, *25*
Fish Tacos with Maggi Onions, Whole Grilled, *210,* 211
Hatch Chile Pico de Gallo, 152, *152,* 153
Jalapeño and Onion Soy Sauce Pickles, 190–1, *190*
Maggi Onions, 161, 165, *210,* 211
Ode to a Benihana Birthday Party, *130,* 131
Pork Tenderloin, "Pretend It's the '90s" Honey-Balsamic (with Grilled Red Onion and Arugula), *184,* 185
Red Onions, Wilted, 158, *159, 162,* 163, 165
Salsa Bandera (pico de gallo), 158, 161, *162,* 165, 211
Salsa Ranchera, xii, *106,* 107, *108,* 109, 110, *111*
Salsa Verde, xii, *106,* 107, *108,* 109, 110, *111*
Spring Onions, Grilled, 158, *159, 162,* 163–4, 165
Steak Sandwich 2.0, Nostalgia (with Chimichurri Mayo and Tomato-Onion Salad), xxi, *10,* 11
Veggie Wraps, Better Grilled (with Avocado Hummus, Sprouts, and Feta), 26, *27*
orange(s) and orange juice:
Citrus and Fennel Salad (Grilled and Raw, with Avocado), *54,* 55
Pork Chop with Grilled Lemon, Buttermilk-Brined, 178, *179*
variety recommendations, 55
oysters:
with BBQ Pork Belly Bossam, 190–1, *190*
how to shuck, 198
Miso-Ginger Calabrian Chili Butter, Grilled Oysters with, 198, *199*

P
Parmesan cheese:
Chicken Caesar with Garlic Bread Croutons, Spicy Grilled, *84,* 85–6
Spaghetti Squash with Charred Cherry Tomato Sauce, Grilled, 112, *113*
parsley:
Artichokes alla Garlic Knots, Grilled, *48,* 49
Chicken Teriyaki Sandwiches with Jalapeño-Cabbage Slaw, 16, *17*
Chimichurri Mayo, xxi, 11
Mansion Butter, Smoke-Grilled Bone-In Rib Eye with, 172–3, *172*
Pesto, Parsley, 58, 206, *207*
pasta:
Brisket Noodle Bowl, Nước Chấm, 170, *171*
Sausage and Peppers Pasta Salad, *94,* 95
Steak and Soba Salad, Peanut-Miso (with a Crunchy, Shredded Vegetable Rainbow), *90,* 91
Peads & Barnetts farm, 180
peanut butter:
Steak and Soba Salad, Peanut-Miso (with a Crunchy, Shredded Vegetable Rainbow), *90,* 91
peanuts:
Salsa Macha, *62,* 63
Steak and Soba Salad, Peanut-Miso (with a Crunchy, Shredded Vegetable Rainbow), *90,* 91
pellet smokers, xv, xix
peppers:
Beans, Mezcal Charro (with Charred Peppers and Onions), xii, *74,* 75, 152, 178
Jimmy Nardellos with Red Yuzu Vinaigrette, 60, *61,* 180, 212
Sausage and Peppers Pasta Salad, *94,* 95
Veggie Wraps, Better Grilled (with Avocado Hummus, Sprouts, and Feta), 26, *27*
See also chipotle peppers in adobo sauce; jalapeño pepper(s)
Pickle-Brined Drumsticks with Spicy Honey, *136,* 137
pickled peppers:
Chicago-Style Char Dogs, 12, *13,* 15
Chicken Caesar with Garlic Bread Croutons, Spicy Grilled, *84,* 85–6
Chicken Tricolore with Charred Pepperoncini Vinaigrette, Grilled, 88, *89*
Grilldas (or Grilled Squid Gildas), *200,* 201
Turkey Burgers, The Juiciest (with Goat Cheese, Pickled Peppers, and Sprouts), *18,* 19
pickles:
Chicago-Style Char Dogs, 12, *13,* 15
pineapple:
Pork Chop Sandwiches with Grilled Pineapple and Chili Crisp Mayo, 32, *33*
Pinello, Frank, xxviii
pitas, 7
Pork Souvlaki Pitas, 30–1, *30*
Za'atar-Blackened Mahi-Mahi Pitas, *28,* 29
PK Grill, xv, xxv
Place, The, 196
Pollo a la Brasa restaurant, 142
Pollo a la Brasa with Ají Verde, Smoke-Grilled, 142–4, *143*
poppy seed hot dog buns, 12, *13,* 15
pork, 174–91
Belly Bossam, BBQ, 190–1, *190*
Chop Sandwiches with Grilled Pineapple and Chili Crisp Mayo, 32, *33*
Chop with Grilled Lemon, Buttermilk-Brined, 178, *179*
internal temperature guide, xxvii
Secret (Secreto with Rosemary, Garlic, Chile de Árbol, and Tangerine Zest), 180, *181*
shopping for, 177
Souvlaki Pitas, 30–1, *30*
Tenderloin, "Pretend It's the '90s" Honey-Balsamic (with Grilled Red Onion and Arugula), *184,* 185
See also sausage(s)
pork ribs:
Baby Backs, Smoke-Grilled (with Aleppo Pepper, Mirin, and Cider Vinegar), 188, *189*
Coconut-Crusted Tiki, 186, *187*
internal temperature guide, xxvii
shopping for, 177
potato(es):
internal temperature guide, xxvii, 58
oven roasting to finish cooking smoked potatoes Dad Hack, 117
Perfect Grilled Potatoes, xxii, 58, *59,* 142, *143,* 169
Shrimp Niçoise, Grilled (with Fresh Tarragon Vinaigrette), 92, *93*
Tacos, Smoked Potato (with Smoked Tomatillo Salsa, Cotija, and Crunchy Red Cabbage), xi, *116,* 117–18
two-zone fire Dad Hack for, 59, 142
propane and natural gas, xvi
proteins:
grilled as an accent to improve a dish, xii, 81
obsession with over fiber and importance of fiber, xxviii, 123
See also specific proteins

Q
Queen's Raw Bar & Grill, 195
Quinoa with Grilled Halloumi and Charred Fennel, Mediterranean, 100, *101*

R
radicchio:
Chicken Caesar with Garlic Bread Croutons, Spicy Grilled, *84,* 85–6
Chicken Tricolore with Charred Pepperoncini Vinaigrette, Grilled, 88, *89*
radishes:
Hermosillo-Style Carne Asada, 158, 163, 165
Rancho Gordo beans, 75
recipes:
cooking for and feeding family, importance of nutrition and emotions in, xxviii–xxix
quality and seasonality of ingredients, xxviii–xxix
signifiers for wood and/or charcoal, xxviii
reverse-sear technique, xi, 172–3

rice:
"Kebab Plate" Rice (with Charred Tomato, Shallot, and Green Chile), xii, 68, 76, *77*, 129, 203
Mabo-Stuffed Mushrooms with Yaki-Onigiri, xxv, 102, *103*
Poblanos with Cilantro-Lime Tahini, Stuffed, *104*, 105
Pork Belly Bossam, BBQ, 190–1, *190*
Shrimp Stock Rice Dad Hack, Bonus, *202*, 203
Veggie Burritos, Grilled ("Christmas-Style," with Red & Green Salsas), *106*, 107
rice cooker, xxviii
rice noodles:
Brisket Noodle Bowl, Nước Chấm, 170, *171*
rosemary:
Pork Secret (Secreto with Rosemary, Garlic, Chile de Árbol, and Tangerine Zest), 180, *181*
Pork Tenderloin, "Pretend It's the '90s" Honey-Balsamic (with Grilled Red Onion and Arugula), *184*, 185
Sausage and Lentils with Grilled Leeks, *182*, 183
Turkey Burgers, The Juiciest (with Goat Cheese, Pickled Peppers, and Sprouts), *18*, 19

S
salads:
Big Salads, 78–95
Chicken Caesar with Garlic Bread Croutons, Spicy Grilled, *84*, 85–6
Chicken Tricolore with Charred Pepperoncini Vinaigrette, Grilled, 88, *89*
Citrus and Fennel Salad (Grilled and Raw, with Avocado), *54*, 55
dry-grilling vegetables for, 81
grilled vegetables and proteins to add to, xii, 81
Peanut-Miso Steak and Soba Salad (with a Crunchy, Shredded Vegetable Rainbow), *90*, 91
Sausage and Peppers Pasta Salad, *94*, 95
Shrimp Niçoise, Grilled (with Fresh Tarragon Vinaigrette), 92, *93*
Southwest Veggie Chop (with Charred Scallion Green Goddess), 82–3, *82*
salsas:
Bandera, Salsa (pico de gallo), 158, 161, *162*, 165, 211
Chiltepin, Salsa, 158, 161, 165, 211
Habanero, Salsa, 158, 163, 165, 211
Hatch Chile Pico de Gallo, 152, *152*, 153
Macha, Salsa, *62*, 63
Ranchera, Salsa, xii, *106*, 107, *108*, 109, 110, *111*
Tatemada, 158, 164, 165, 211
Veggie Burritos, Grilled ("Christmas-Style," with Red & Green Salsas), *106*, 107
Verde, Salsa, xii, *106*, 107, *108*, 109, 110, *111*
sandwiches, 4–35
Caprese Sandwich, Smoky Grilled, 24, *25*
Chicken Teriyaki Sandwiches with Jalapeño-Cabbage Slaw, 16, *17*
Pork Chop Sandwiches with Grilled Pineapple and Chili Crisp Mayo, 32, *33*
Steak Sandwich 2.0, Nostalgia (with Chimichurri Mayo and Tomato-Onion Salad), xxi, *10*, 11
Tofu Bánh Mì with Lemongrass BBQ Sauce, 22–3, *23*
Veggie Wraps, Better Grilled (with Avocado Hummus, Sprouts, and Feta), 26, *27*
See also burgers; hot dogs; pitas
Santa Maria and Santa Maria Tri-Tip, 152–3
Santa Maria–style grills, xv
sauces:
Apple-Horseradish Sauce, 152, *152*, 153
Chimichurri Mayo, xxi, 11
Cocktail Sauce, Ari Kolender's, 196, *197*
Curry Ketchup, 21
Dill Yogurt, 21
Ginger Sauce, Keisuke's, *130*, 131
Lemongrass BBQ Sauce, Tofu Bánh Mì with, 22–3, *23*
Miso-Mustard BBQ Sauce, 190–1, *190*
Mustard Sauce, *130*, 131
Parsley Pesto, 58, 206, *207*
Special Sauce, 8
Tzatziki, 30–1, *30*
sauerkraut:
Beer Brats (with Grilled Onions, Sauerkraut, and Spicy Brown Mustard), *34*, 35
sausage(s), 7
Beer Brats (with Grilled Onions, Sauerkraut, and Spicy Brown Mustard), *34*, 35
Sausage and Lentils with Grilled Leeks, *182*, 183
Sausage and Peppers Pasta Salad, *94*, 95
Smoke-Grill a Sausage, How to, 36, *37*
sausage stands (Würstelstands), 36
scallion(s):
Southwest Veggie Chop (with Charred Scallion Green Goddess), 82–3, *82*
Spring Onions, Grilled, 158, *159*, *162*, 163–4, 165
Scherer, Josh, xxviii
seafood and fish, 192–212
Clams with Cocktail Butter, Grilled, 196, *197*
Cod, Smoke-Grilled Miso Black, 212, *213*
Fish Fillet, Crispy-Skinned (with Parsley Pesto), 206, *207*
Fish Steak, Quick-Grilled (with Lemon and Herbs), 204, *205*
Fish Tacos with Chile Crunch, Grilled, 208, *209*
Fish Tacos with Maggi Onions, Whole Grilled, *210*, 211
Grilldas (or Grilled Squid Gildas), *200*, 201
internal temperature guide, xxvii
mayo use when grilling, xxi, 195
odor from cooking fish, xi, 195
Oysters with Miso-Ginger Calabrian Chili Butter, Grilled, 198, *199*
shopping for, 195, 204
steaky fillet examples, 204
Za'atar-Blackened Mahi-Mahi Pitas, *28*, 29
See also shrimp
sesame seeds:
Salsa Macha, *62*, 63
shallot(s):
Chicken Thighs, Shallot-Dijon, 50, *138*, 139
"Kebab Plate" Rice (with Charred Tomato, Shallot, and Green Chile), xii, 68, 76, *77*, 129, 203
Mansion Butter, Smoke-Grilled Bone-In Rib Eye with, 172–3, *172*
Sausage and Peppers Pasta Salad, *94*, 95
sheet pans, xxii
shrimp:
Dad Hack Bonus Shrimp Stock Rice, *202*, 203
Garlic-Butter Sriracha Shrimp, Grilled, *202*, 203
Niçoise, Grilled Shrimp (with Fresh Tarragon Vinaigrette), 92, *93*
Ode to a Benihana Birthday Party, *130*, 131
Silverton, Nancy, 73
skewers, xxii
smoke alarms, xi
smoke-grilling:
Cod, Smoke-Grilled Miso Black, 212, *213*
concept of and flavor from, xi
how to, *xxv*, xxv, *xxvi*
Pork Belly Bossam, BBQ, 190–1, *190*
Potato Tacos, Smoked (with Smoked Tomatillo Salsa, Cotija, and Crunchy Red Cabbage), xi, *116*, 117–18
Rib Eye with Mansion Butter, Smoke-Grilled Bone-In, xi, 172–3, *172*
Sausage, How to Smoke-Grill a, 36, *37*
Weekend Project Grilling and, xi
smokers and pellet smokers, xv, xix
snacks, *See* appetizers and snacks
snap peas:
Shrimp Niçoise, Grilled (with Fresh Tarragon Vinaigrette), 92, *93*
soba noodles:
Peanut-Miso Steak and Soba Salad (with a Crunchy, Shredded Vegetable Rainbow), *90*, 91
soup, 99
Broccoli-Cheddar Split Pea Soup, Blackened, xii, *114*, 115
sour cream:
Avocado Tostadas with Chipotle-Lime Crema, Grilled, 70, *71*
Souvlaki Pitas, 30–1, *30*
soy sauce and tamari:
Bok Choy, Grilled and Glazed Baby (with Tamari Vinaigrette), 52, *53*, 212
Brussels Sprouts, Charred (with Soy and Balsamic), 50, *51*
Chicken "Gyoza" Eggplant, xxv, 132, *133*
Chicken Teriyaki Sandwiches with Jalapeño-Cabbage Slaw, 16, *17*

Garlic-Butter Sriracha Shrimp, Grilled, *202,* 203
Ginger Sauce, Keisuke's, *130,* 131
Jalapeño and Onion Soy Sauce Pickles, 190–1, *190*
Maggi Onions, 161, 165, *210,* 211
Mushrooms, Buttered Soy Sauce (in a Foil Pouch with Lemon and Fresh Thyme), 66, *67,* 212
Skirt Steak, Soy and Citrus (with Chile de Árbol, Ginger, and Garlic), 149, *168,* 169
Spaghetti Squash with Charred Cherry Tomato Sauce, Grilled, 112, *113*
spatula and tongs, xxi
Split Pea Soup, Blackened Broccoli-Cheddar, xii, *114,* 115
sprouts:
Turkey Burgers, The Juiciest (with Goat Cheese, Pickled Peppers, and Sprouts), *18,* 19
Veggie Wraps, Better Grilled (with Avocado Hummus, Sprouts, and Feta), 26
squash, summer:
Southwest Veggie Chop (with Charred Scallion Green Goddess), 82–3, *82*
See also zucchini
squash, winter:
Kabocha Macha (Grilled Kabocha Squash with Salsa Macha and Lime), *62,* 63
Southwest Veggie Chop (with Charred Scallion Green Goddess), 82–3, *82*
Spaghetti Squash with Charred Cherry Tomato Sauce, Grilled, 112, *113*
Squid Gildas, Grilled, *200,* 201
Sriracha Shrimp, Grilled Garlic-Butter, *202,* 203
Stacey, Tad, 12
Steak Cookoff Association, xv
steak(s):
Hermosillo-Style Carne Asada, xvi, 149, 154–65, *154, 156, 157, 159, 162*
Peanut-Miso Steak and Soba Salad (with a Crunchy, Shredded Vegetable Rainbow), *90,* 91
reverse-sear technique, xi, 172–3
Rib Eye with Mansion Butter, Smoke-Grilled Bone-In, xi, 172–3, *172*
shopping for, 149
Skirt Steak, Soy and Citrus (with Chile de Árbol, Ginger, and Garlic), 149, *168,* 169
Steak Sandwich 2.0, Nostalgia (with Chimichurri Mayo and Tomato-Onion Salad), xxi, *10,* 11
Taverna Steak, 63, 149, 150, *151*
Steaks del Herradero, 155
Syhabout, James, 170

T
tacos:
Fish Tacos with Chile Crunch, Grilled, 208, *209*
Fish Tacos with Maggi Onions, Whole Grilled, *210,* 211
Potato Tacos, Smoked (with Smoked Tomatillo Salsa, Cotija, and Crunchy Red Cabbage), xi, *116,* 117–18
Tacos de Armando, 155
Tacos del Chava, 155
Tacos El Chato, 155
Tacos Jaas taqueria, 158
tahini:
Baba Ghanoush, 68, *69,* 129
Cauliflower with Tahini-Yogurt Sauce, Charred, *56,* 57, 129
Poblanos with Cilantro-Lime Tahini, Stuffed, *104,* 105
tamari, *See* soy sauce and tamari
tangerine:
Pork Secret (Secreto with Rosemary, Garlic, Chile de Árbol, and Tangerine Zest), 180, *181*
Tatemada, 158, 164, 165, 211
Taverna Steak, 63, 149, 150, *151*
temperatures:
grill temperatures, xxii, xxvii
hand test, xxii
internal temperature guide, xxvii, 123
thermometer, infrared, xxii
thermometer, instant-read, xxii, 58, *59*
toast test, *xxiii*
tofu:
Mabo-Stuffed Mushrooms with Yaki-Onigiri, xxv, 102, *103*
Tofu Bánh Mì with Lemongrass BBQ Sauce, 22–3, *23*
tomatillos:
Potato Tacos, Smoked (with Smoked Tomatillo Salsa, Cotija, and Crunchy Red Cabbage), xi, *116,* 117–18
Salsa Verde, xii, *106,* 107, *108,* 109, 110, *111*
tomato(es):
Artichokes alla Garlic Knots, Grilled, *48,* 49
Caprese Sandwich, Smoky Grilled, 24, *25*
cherry tomatoes substitution Dad Hack, 100
Hatch Chile Pico de Gallo, 152, *152,* 153
"Kebab Plate" Rice (with Charred Tomato, Shallot, and Green Chile), xii, 68, 76, *77,* 129, 203
Poblanos with Cilantro-Lime Tahini, Stuffed, *104,* 105
Quinoa with Grilled Halloumi and Charred Fennel, Mediterranean, 100, *101*
Salsa Bandera (pico de gallo), 158, 161, *162,* 165, 211
Salsa Chiltepin, 158, 161, 165, 211
Salsa Habanero, 158, 163, 165, 211
Salsa Ranchera, xii, *106,* 107, *108,* 109, 110, *111*
Salsa Verde, xii, *106,* 107, *108,* 109, 110, *111*
Spaghetti Squash with Charred Cherry Tomato Sauce, Grilled, 112, *113*
Steak Sandwich 2.0, Nostalgia (with Chimichurri Mayo and Tomato-Onion Salad), xxi, *10,* 11
Tatemada, 158, 164, 165, 211
tongs and spatula, xxi
tools, *xx,* xx–xxii
tortilla(s):
Avocado Tostadas with Chipotle-Lime Crema, Grilled, 70, *71*
Fish Tacos with Chile Crunch, Grilled, 208, *209*
Fish Tacos with Maggi Onions, Whole Grilled, *210,* 211
Hermosillo-Style Carne Asada, 155, 156, 158, *162,* 165
Huevos Divorciados, *108,* 109
Potato Tacos, Smoked (with Smoked Tomatillo Salsa, Cotija, and Crunchy Red Cabbage), xi, *116,* 117–18
sealing wraps Dad Hack, 26
Veggie Burritos, Grilled ("Christmas-Style," with Red & Green Salsas), *106,* 107
Veggie Wraps, Better Grilled (with Avocado Hummus, Sprouts, and Feta), 26, *27*
Traeger pellet smokers, xv
turkey:
Turkey Breast, Smoke-Grilled (for Cold Cuts), 123, 140, *141*
Turkey Burgers, The Juiciest (with Goat Cheese, Pickled Peppers, and Sprouts), *18,* 19
two-zone fires, xiv, xxv, *xxvi*
Avocado Tostadas with Chipotle-Lime Crema, Grilled, 70, *71*
Baby Backs, Smoke-Grilled (with Aleppo Pepper, Mirin, and Cider Vinegar), 188, *189*
Brussels Sprouts, Charred (with Soy and Balsamic), 50, *51*
Caprese Sandwich, Smoky Grilled, 24, *25*
Chicken Caesar with Garlic Bread Croutons, Spicy Grilled, *84,* 85–6
Chicken "Gyoza" Eggplant, xxv, 132, *133*
Chicken Thighs, Shallot-Dijon, 50, *138,* 139
Cod, Smoke-Grilled Miso Black, 212, *213*
Dad Hack for potatoes, 59, 142
Drumsticks with Spicy Honey, Pickle-Brined, *136,* 137
Mabo-Stuffed Mushrooms with Yaki-Onigiri, xxv, 102, *103*
Pollo a la Brasa with Ají Verde, Smoke-Grilled, 142–4, *143*
Pork Belly Bossam, BBQ, 190–1, *190*
Pork Chop with Grilled Lemon, Buttermilk-Brined, 178, *179*
Pork Ribs, Coconut-Crusted Tiki, 186, *187*
Pork Secret (Secreto with Rosemary, Garlic, Chile de Árbol, and Tangerine Zest), 180, *181*
Potatoes, Perfect Grilled, xxii, 58, *59,* 142, *143,* 169
Potato Tacos, Smoked (with Smoked Tomatillo Salsa, Cotija, and Crunchy Red Cabbage), xi, *116,* 117–18
Rib Eye with Mansion Butter, Smoke-Grilled Bone-In, xi, 172–3, *172*
Sausage and Peppers Pasta Salad, *94,* 95

two-zone fires *(continued)*
Smoke-Grill a Sausage, How to, 36, *37*
Spaghetti Squash with Charred Cherry Tomato Sauce, Grilled, 112, *113*
Tofu Bánh Mì with Lemongrass BBQ Sauce, 22–3, *23*
Tri-Tip Two Ways, California, 149, 152–3, *152*
Turkey Breast, Smoke-Grilled (for Cold Cuts), 123, 140, *141*
Wings, Ginger-Buffalo, 134, *135*

V
vegetables and veggie sides, 38–76
Artichokes alla Garlic Knots, Grilled, *48,* 49
Asparagus with Wilted White Cheddar, Grilled, *46,* 47, 139, 150
Avocado Tostadas with Chipotle-Lime Crema, Grilled, 70, *71*
Baba Ghanoush, 68, *69,* 129
Beans, Mezcal Charro (with Charred Peppers and Onions), xii, *74,* 75, 152, 178
Bok Choy, Grilled and Glazed Baby (with Tamari Vinaigrette), 52, *53,* 212
Broccolini with Preserved Lemon, 42, *43,* 178, 212
Brussels Sprouts, Charred (with Soy and Balsamic), 50, *51*
Cauliflower with Tahini-Yogurt Sauce, Charred, *56,* 57, 129
Citrus and Fennel Salad (Grilled and Raw, with Avocado), *54,* 55
Corn, Miso-Butter, *64,* 65
dry-grilling, 81
grilled vegetables as an accent to improve a dish, xii, 41, 81
grill pan Dad Hack, 131
Jimmy Nardellos with Red Yuzu Vinaigrette, 60, *61,* 180, 212
Kabocha Macha (Grilled Kabocha Squash with Salsa Macha and Lime), *62,* 63
Mushrooms, Buttered Soy Sauce (in a Foil Pouch with Lemon and Fresh Thyme), 66, *67,* 212
Potatoes, Perfect Grilled, xxii, 58, *59,* 142, *143,* 169
Rice, "Kebab Plate" (with Charred Tomato, Shallot, and Green Chile), xii, 68, 76, *77,* 129, 203
shopping for, 41
Veggie Wraps, Better Grilled (with Avocado Hummus, Sprouts, and Feta), 26, *27*
Zucchini Spears and Balsamic, Mint, and Garlic, 44, *45*
vegetarian mains, 96–118
Broccoli-Cheddar Split Pea Soup, Blackened, xii, *114,* 115
Huevos Divorciados, *108,* 109
Mabo-Stuffed Mushrooms with Yaki-Onigiri, xxv, 102, *103*
Poblanos with Cilantro-Lime Tahini, Stuffed, *104,* 105
Potato Tacos, Smoked (with Smoked Tomatillo Salsa, Cotija, and Crunchy Red Cabbage), xi, *116,* 117–18
Quinoa with Grilled Halloumi and Charred Fennel, Mediterranean, 100, *101*
Spaghetti Squash with Charred Cherry Tomato Sauce, Grilled, 112, *113*
Veggie Burritos, Grilled ("Christmas-Style," with Red & Green Salsas), *106,* 107
Vienna, Austria, 36
Vienna Beef frankfurters, 12, 15
vinaigrettes:
Bok Choy, Grilled and Glazed Baby (with Tamari Vinaigrette), 52, *53,* 212
Jimmy Nardellos with Red Yuzu Vinaigrette, 60, *61,* 180, 212
Oregano Vinaigrette, Fresh, 100
Tarragon Vinaigrette, Fresh, 92, *93*

W
Weber grill, xiv
weekend project grilling, xi
Wolfinger, Eric, 170
"wood and charcoal only" recipes, xxviii
Baby Backs, Smoke-Grilled (with Aleppo Pepper, Mirin, and Cider Vinegar), 188, *189*
Cod, Smoke-Grilled Miso Black, 212, *213*
Hermosillo-Style Carne Asada, xvi, 149, 154–65, *154, 156, 157, 159, 162*
Pollo a la Brasa with Ají Verde, Smoke-Grilled, 142–4, *143*
Pork Belly Bossam, BBQ, 190–1, *190*
Potato Tacos, Smoked (with Smoked Tomatillo Salsa, Cotija, and Crunchy Red Cabbage), xi, *116,* 117–18
Rib Eye with Mansion Butter, Smoke-Grilled Bone-In, xi, 172–3, *172*
Turkey Breast, Smoke-Grilled (for Cold Cuts), 123, 140, *141*
wood chunks:
charcoal and wood together, xvi, xix
types of and choosing which to use, *xvii, xviii,* xix
Würstelstands (sausage stands), 36

Y
yogurt:
Cauliflower with Tahini-Yogurt Sauce, Charred, *56,* 57, 129
Dill Yogurt, 21
Shish Tawook, xxii, 68, 123, *128,* 129
Tzatziki, 30–1, *30*
yuzu koshō, red:
Jimmy Nardellos with Red Yuzu Vinaigrette, 60, *61,* 180, 212

Z
Za'atar-Blackened Mahi-Mahi Pitas, *28,* 29
zucchini:
Costata Romanesco zucchini, 44
Ode to a Benihana Birthday Party, *130,* 131
Southwest Veggie Chop (with Charred Scallion Green Goddess), 82–3, *82*
Veggie Burritos, Grilled ("Christmas-Style," with Red & Green Salsas), *106,* 107
Veggie Wraps, Better Grilled (with Avocado Hummus, Sprouts, and Feta), 26, *27*
Zucchini Spears and Balsamic, Mint, and Garlic, 44, *45*